Life History Research

Life History Research
Epistemology, Methodology and Representation

Rubby Dhunpath
University of KwaZulu-Natal, South Africa

Michael Samuel
University of KwaZulu-Natal, South Africa

SENSE PUBLISHERS
ROTTERDAM/BOSTAN/TAIPEI

A C.I.P. record for this book is available from the Library of Congress.

ISBN 978-90-8790-856-0 (paperback)
ISBN 978-90-8790-857-7 (hardback)
ISBN 978-90-8790-858-4 (e-book)

Published by: Sense Publishers,
P.O. Box 21858, 3001 AW
Rotterdam, The Netherlands
http://www.sensepublishers.com

Printed on acid-free paper

TABLE OF CONTENTS

RUBBY DHUNPATH AND MICHAEL SAMUEL

INTRODUCTION

It is no coincidence that a book of this sort emerges out of the era of intense redefinitions of selves within post-apartheid South Africa, 15 years after the first democratic elections in 1994. In anticipation of another wave of changes in the political and socio-economic landscapes expected to be ushered in by the 2009 elections, the book reflects on opportunities to author our own lives in the wake of political liberations, in the optimism of new policy terrains which were aimed at fertilising our expressions of our freedoms and justices, and redefining our roles as researchers and academics. The book demonstrates that such redefinitions are enabled and constrained by the dominant hallmarks of (educational) academic research. It yields key conceptual interconnected issues which have always been part of the research enterprise: issues of epistemology, methodology and representation. The book makes explicit how these explorations unfolded and intersected within the unique socio-historical, political and cultural context of South Africa, but does not confine itself to a narcissistic preoccupation with this context. The contributors to this book explore the need to speak within and against themselves in developing new theoretical insights into the phenomena they chart: a responsibility that researchers worldwide must embrace. This is especially relevant within a hegemony of knowledge production by the economically powerful, and the privileged academic researcher.

This book draws on the collaborative culture of research that emerged amongst a group of doctoral students and researchers within the former University of Durban-Westville in South Africa, now merged within the University of KwaZulu-Natal. As students and supervisors, we found ourselves to be valuable resources (challenges?) to each other as we engaged with common (often troubling) concerns about our research contexts, spanning multiple disciplines: the professional education of teachers; the disciplinary dilemma of health practitioners; the troubled world of non-governmental organisations embattled by the econometric splurge; of researchers challenging social justice considerations; of researchers scripting the lives of teachers; and of researchers prefiguring and orchestrating our under-standings of the HIV and AIDS epidemic in South Africa.

The authors of the chapters of this book have all moved beyond their original contexts both geographically and structurally: the authors now assume the role of academics in Australia, as scholars in the United States of America, as readers of the surrounding war-conscious tyranny and the relatively benign world of the United Arab Emirates, as policymakers within the politicised bureaucracy and the national Ministry of Education, as deputy vice chancellors, and deans of higher education institutions, as managers of new curricula for teacher education and educational research, as leaders of departments forging new conceptions of health sciences research and professional education, as researchers of macro systemic issues within national studies. Our new vantages have given us telescopes and sometimes microscopes to look forwards and backwards on our doctoral studies, aiming to reflect on what contributions we are making and have made to academic research.

We were all grappling with how the lives and views of our research participants featured in our research reports. We were inspired by the possibility of experimenting with novel ways of re-presenting our reports – how we, as researchers, re-told the lives of our participants. This resulted simultaneously in questions about what constituted the data? Whose data is it? What are the ethical boundaries being traversed as the researcher and researched negotiated understanding of themselves, their roles and their agendas? Whose report is it? For whom? For what purpose?

Many of the researchers in this book chose to use a life history approach in producing data aimed at capturing at a deep level, the insights into their contexts through the lived experiences of their participants. Complexification of the research context, an understanding that provides thick, enriched awareness rather than reductionism, was accepted as a necessary value of such research.

Much has been written about life history research in recent times. It has been paraded as a counterculture to the traditional research canon, and celebrated as a genre that promotes methodological pluralism. However, as life history researchers we have an obligation to transcend spurious claims about the perceived merits of the methodology and extend the debates around how the genre simultaneously problematises and responds to the competing challenges of **Epistemology, Methodology and Representation** (the title of our book).

In conceiving of each of our chapters from an **epistemological** perspective, we focused on how our individual work has transgressed or expanded traditional boundaries of epistemology and ontology; of how the work has satisfied the rigours of thesis production and contributed to changing conceptions of knowledge, what knowledge gets produced and how knowledge is produced when we make particular methodological choices.

Since any **methodological** orientation is invariably selective, and the researcher is always involved and implicated in the production of data, we focus on what selections we made in our projects, what governed these choices, what benefits/deficits those choices yielded, and what the implications of our research are for those meta-narratives that have established the regimes of truth, legitimacy, and veracity in research.

Knowledge production is inextricably linked to **representation.** In the process of articulating our findings, each of us made particular representational choices, sometimes transgressing conventional approaches. We explore why we made these choices and how the choices influenced the kinds of knowledge generated. We provide theoretical justifications for these transgressions and reflect on how the experience of representation helped disrupt our essentialist notions of research production and for whom the research is produced.

When challenging established canons, we expose ourselves to intellectual culpability, which compounds our ethical vulnerability. This book highlights the ethical demands that accompany the complex set of interpersonal and power relations between researcher and researched. We record our dilemmas in dealing with issues of authorial legitimacy; how we came to terms with concerns such as validity and reliability, identity, truth, structure and agency, emotionality and neutrality and the influence of competing voices in research production.

WHAT TO EXPECT FROM THIS BOOK

The early era of the new democratic government in South Africa was characterised by a colossal undertaking to attempt to provide a "healing of the nation" through the establishment of the now famous Truth and Reconciliation Commission (TRC) 1998). In this commission, public hearings were set up throughout the land to gather the stories and experiences of those who had suffered either as perpetrators or as victims of injustices during the apartheid regime. These injustices extended not only to stories of physical violence (meted out by the prisons and police), but also to revelations of economic fraud, social crimes, political compassion and conviction, and exposés of the devious machinations that entrapped South African citizens who campaigned to liberate its society from oppression. People from all sectors of society, soldiers and sportsmen, priests and criminals, teachers and students were encouraged to testify.

These TRC stories were beamed daily via live broadcasts into the living rooms of homes with TVs, into mud huts over radio, into small town halls of rural villages, into the print media nationally and internationally. The nation stared in horror at the brutality and intensity of those who once stood on opposite sides of the political spectrum, but now were asking for forgiveness and reconciliation from each other. The prize for such revelation was amnesty from the legal courts. More recently, a TRC for academics has been proposed!

It is within this climate that we need to ask what **kinds of truth we as researchers are attempting to produce**. This question steered the doctoral studies of each of the authors of this book. Our researches became an exploration not only of the phenomena we chose to study, but also an endeavour to understand the mission and goals of researchers in a rapidly evolving society, attempting to dislodge the grips of constraint imposed by racist, sexist, classist and paradigmatic methodologies and epistemologies.

The TRC identifies four kinds of truth in their summative report released at about the time when we as researchers began our inquiry:
- Forensic truth
- Personal truth
- Dialogical truth
- Restorative truth

1. Forensic Truth: was referred to as a truth that could be treated as "objective facts"/"scientific truths" which could be validated through "empirical processes". This was sometimes referred to as "legal truth".

Within the tradition of life history research this kind of truth-making is referred to as capturing **"lives as lived".** Life historians would argue that documenting this "legal truth" is not their intention. As life historians we are concerned with more that simply whether a particular recalled event "actually happened". We are more than our legal identity.

2. ***Personal Truth****: was referred to as a truth based on the lived experiences of the individuals reporting events. It pointed to a "narrative truth" which understood that it could be infused with the hallmarks of nostalgia and public memory. It was seen as a kind of truth that drew on the constructed nature of meaning-making which allowed individuals to assemble personal images of their victims and perpetrators.*

   Within the tradition of life history research this kind of truth has dominated since it captures **"lives as experienced"**. It provides the qualitative interpretation individuals make of their lived circumstances and events. It shows how individuals make meaning of their lives. Its interpretivist and phenomenological roots are evident.

3. ***Dialogical Truth****: referred to a "social truth" that drew on the way in which public understandings of groups and individuals ("insiders and outsiders") were fuelled through the reporting within the public domain, in public rallies (oral discourse), in the spoken and written media (radio, newspapers, magazines, public notices).*

   Within the tradition of life history research, this kind of truth deconstructs the telling of lifestories within the data production moments. It captures the fragility and power of **"lives as told"** with all its potential and limitations.

4. ***Healing Truth****: this truth was seen as being driven by the agenda of restoring dignity amongst both the tellers and the listeners. Its agenda was to privilege the act of telling as having possibilities for reconciliation between the victims and perpetrators. It had an agenda to build new relations between not only the participants involved but also the wider public who were exposed to the stories.*

   This kind of truth-making is relatively under-explored within the tradition of life history research. Its roots are embedded in a campaign to understand the **"lives as capable of being reconstructed"**. It seeks for means to move beyond the structural (political/social/cultural/economic) constraints imposed on individuals and instead celebrates the power of agency.

"Narrative research methodology" therefore became not just a methodology for researchers in the ivory towers of academia working within an interpretivist, constructivist frame *(telling stories of lives)*, but a public enterprise with a national agenda *(telling stories as an act of realising the national agenda of justice for all)*[1].

For us as researchers the choice of the methodology is not co-incidental. We wanted to tell the lived experiences of the research participants we worked with. Their stories had been silenced as irrelevant and unavailable for theorising. But our methodologies of data production became intricately bound with the agenda of reconstructing previous relationships, negotiating expectations and responsibilities about ethical choices, about a wider social justice project. Hence, our methodological processes themselves had to promote democracy. Life history research provided a means to tell the muddy story with all its triumphs and pitfalls. The research process (and its thesis product) became concerned not only with the relationship between the researcher and the researched, the research participants and her social interactors, but also a catalyst for the broader society and the audience for whom the research was intended. Each of us was committed to the belief that doctoral studies cannot be only about credentialing by writing for an external examiner.

Our own identities were also being recast in the process: who we are cannot be denied or edited out of the research process. We are raced, classed, gendered, historical beings with positions of difference on a variety of levels: political, religious, social, cultural, linguistic, etc. As researchers we are individuals with diminished or enhanced power which has been entrenched through our positionalities within society. Nevertheless, our positionalities are not a solidified set of "psychological traits". We simultaneously hold multiple identities which react in dialogue with the forces around and within us. We construct our identities in the act of the research processes as we negotiate our relationship with the participants with whom we work, including our audience who co-constructs us.

The terrain of life history research that we present spans beyond simply telling the life history of individuals (e.g. the lives of people who stutter). The methodology has been transported to provide an analysis of the career lives of teachers during their training, and within the different stages of their careers. The methodology has extended to examine the experiences of professional education of individuals within the higher education curriculum (in different professions outside teacher education). The methodology has been extended to look not only at the lives of people, but also the "institutional lives" of organisations, providing an alternative glimpse of how an evaluation of organisations might be conducted.

This book is not another celebration of life history as a counterculture, another "victory narrative within the redemptive culture of the social sciences" (Cary, 1999, 2). There are too many of those around. The book hopes to be a deeply critical contribution to disrupt notions around epistemological authority, voice and power and how these are mediated by the delicate relations of the researcher and researched. We want to problematise and complicate the assumptions that frame this genre with a view to highlighting the potential hazards of the method while demonstrating its potentiality in shaping our conceptions of Ethics, Methodology and Representation.

The book is organised in a broad clustering of chapters, and could be read in collective units. However as a reader, a fluid inter-reading across different chapter clusters is to be encouraged as common and divergent insights into our research context could be said to emerge.

Chapter One, Two, Three and Four constitute the first of the chapter clusters. They focus broadly on the life history research approach from a conceptual point of view, focusing on the role of the researcher. **Chapter One** by Michael Samuel represents one of the early doctoral studies using a life history approach at the University of KwaZulu-Natal. The chapter defines the nature of life history research showing why it is more than simply the telling of tales about individuals' lives. It aims to explore, analyse and interpret the gaps and silences, biases and exaggerations of the tellers of the tales; it is produced within particular discourse settings which in themselves shape the telling. The research approach is framed with the overall intention of developing new theoretical insights beyond a simplistic reductionist explanation of "the truth"; it uncovers the complexity of knowing, and the complexity of the process of illuminating understandings of the world of "alive human beings". The world which comes to be represented in the "stories of the research participants" is infused with the spaces which they inhabit, percolated through their interpreting and re-interpreting their real and imagined experiences. Life history research becomes as much about the researcher as the researched, about the experienced worlds of the past and of the future, about the confined and confining world, and the world of possibility.

This chapter draws from an in-depth research study tracing the experiences of student teachers that are in the process of developing their professional competence as teachers of the English language. It uses a life history approach to collect data about their various stages of developing competence in the English language over different periods in their lives: within their homes, families, schools, university education, and within their school-based teaching practice courses. The study uses various creative data collection methods in an attempt to move beyond the verbal interview to include students' construction of their own autobiographies, as well as graphic and video representations of their experiences. It is located within the research tradition of "teacher thinking research" and shows how a grounded theory approach was used to develop a model for understanding teacher development. The force field model of teacher development highlights the complexity and depth needed to understand the process of teachers developing their professional identities.

The chapter focuses on what we learn about curriculum design of teacher education programmes from a life history research approach. It provides an exemplar of how choices of methodology in research influence the nature of the knowledge that is produced in the study. It foregrounds throughout the methodological descriptions the kinds of ethical considerations that are negotiated between the research and the research participants. Attention to these ethical considerations results in the production of a particular way of knowing the problem being explored, namely the process of becoming a teacher: coherent, contradictory and complementary challenges co-exist as (novice) teachers negotiate their identity.

Michael Samuel is now the Dean of the Faculty of Education at the University of KwaZulu-Natal. He has served on the Ministerial Committee on Teacher Education which was instrumental in introducing the new national policy framework for teacher education.

Lives and their histories are very complex by nature. It stands to reason that multilayered life history data demands an equally complex analysis process. In **Chapter Two**, Harsha Kathard explores the issues and processes in generating a first level analysis of life history data. The chapter reports on a study which sought to illuminate the processes of self-identity formations of people who stutter using a narrative life history methodology. The points of discussion include:

- The obligations of the researcher using a narrative methodology with people who have been traditionally constructed as having communication disorders
- The possibilities and pitfalls of creating new knowledge within a Bakthinian frame
- The problematic nature of crafting and representing and analysing personal truths.

The discussion is supported with case examples drawn from the research study and concludes with a critical commentary about the nature of knowledge generated in the context of life history research.

Harsha Kathard is now Head of Department at the University of Cape Town's School of Rehabilitation and Health Sciences. Her challenge of operating within the dominant empiricist and positivist paradigm of the medical profession continues in her work.

Chapter Three, by Mershen Pillay, demonstrates the privilege that researchers occupy both methodologically and theoretically. This he locates within an understanding of the situatedness of academic researchers within the broader social systems. He writes as a minority with a responsibility to read the world of others in the context of conventions which command capitulations to dominant theoretical "greats". Other lay readers of the world are arguably constrained by other normative conventions. His text is itself a resistance to such capitulations in the manner in which he shows how as authors (and linguists) we have the privilege to read and write the world in more authentic (creative) (and epistemologically rich) ways. His study draws on a wide range of resources including from inside and outside formal academe, developing a case for juxta-, inter-, intra-, and trans-disciplinary ways of knowing; from inspirational fictional literature; and from the confidence of heightened self-reflexivity (which is representative of its variety of sources) recontextualised as data for empirical imaginative elaboration. He argues,

> Blessed with this rare chance to do virtuous and noble things, we allow participants to, for example, unconventionally – but [common] sensibly – tell stories of their lives. We make them our own heroes (Ourselves, we place as morally superior to our Bunsen burner brothers in the labs). However, as I tap into my bleeding heart, strum a liberal tune, and dance in the lush sense of a person lucky to facilitate such privilege, I must remind myself of a truism: With any research, it is the researcher's voice that is always more privileged (more free?). In as much as we focus research participants' liberations, we also need to re-focus research onto ourselves: How do we deal with our liberation, our privilege in – what is – our research? Theoretically? Methodologically?

His chapter makes a strong case for understanding the biological apronstrings which enable our unique epistemologies. This argument is evocatively developed in theorising his own bio-epistemology as an identical-twin; his coining of "I-visibility" which celebrates the confidence in one's epistemologising; his encouragement to be more aware of the multiple resources for theory building that emerge from within, between and outside of (empirical) data production; his demonstration of using one's biological and social and cultural selves in one's intellectual practices. Nevertheless, his chapter makes the case for a *de-liberation*: the process which could help us re-understand our own intent, morality, and faithfulness to (less empirical, and perhaps) more critical ways of knowing.

The second part of the chapter deals with the way in which these above theoretical considerations were drawn into the research design of his study. He refers to this as the "process-product" considerations which make explicit the sources for interpreting and analysing "the data", for producing new data from empirical data collected, from imagined data. His chapter develops a model for theorising these levels of analysis and interpretation. The chapter makes explicit the use of "critical conversations" as a data production strategy defining it as theoretically different from interviews and discussions. He shows how these 'methodological issues' are deeply connected to the kind of epistemology that he intended to produce in his doctoral study.

One wonders whether the author's current location in the middle of the United Arab Emirates, dislocated from his South African roots, yet connected to a globalising discourse of "othering" fuels these present reflections on his doctoral studies.

Chapter Four[2], by Renuka Vithal explores the notion of the necessary coherence that should be developed between the methodological approach used and the theoretical intentions of the research process. If democratic development is the expressed intention of the research study, then it behoves the researcher to understand how this democratic principle infuses into the ways in which we produce the data for the research study. The study looks at how such a principle of democratic participation should become one of the hallmarks of validity when evaluating the quality of a research project. The author develops the notion of "democratic participatory validity" to become a means of integrating the theoretical, methodological, ethical and epistemological considerations when designing and reporting on research. The study draws from the exploration of how the world of practice speaks back to the world of theory-making drawing from a study of mathematics student teachers in an initial teacher education programme engaging with a political, social, cultural approach to their classroom pedagogy.

Renuka Vithal is now Deputy Vice Chancellor of the newly merged University of KwaZulu-Natal, which brings together the worlds of the former University of Durban-Westville and the University of Natal: two apartheid-constructed higher education institutions. Is a new democratic space being forged as competing conceptions of research are drawn together in this merger?

Chapters Five and Six (the second cluster of chapters) tend to concentrate on the construction and representation of the "research report", showing how this influences methodological and ethical choices. Underlying these choices is nevertheless a consideration of what kind of knowledge is being produced in the research processes. (Of course, the role of the researcher and the researched in the production of the report is again picked up in this cluster.)

Written at the time of overseeing the doctoral studies of many of the authors of this book, **Chapter Five**[3], by Michael Samuel, explores the landscape of research production within the academic terrain, suggesting how the constraints of representation promote particular one-dimensional ways of knowing. The chapter encourages researchers to explore new ways of representing research products, not simply as an ornamental feature to enhance readability of the research product, but as a means of exploring new epistemological possibilities. The paper nevertheless points to the limitations of exploring these alternative forms of representation within the world of research production and the conceptions of "research rigour" that characterise the academic/research production "business". Many of the researchers of this book have had to make these decisions in terms of how their research study reports were represented. Notably, many of the external examiners of their work commented favourably on the freshness of the representations of their reports, deeming that the representational choices made were fundamental to the kind of epistemology they were exploring.

Chapter Six, by Ruth Beecham, now located within a rural Australian university setting (Charles Sturt University), explores the notion of trust in the development of narrative knowledge creation. While she accepts that motivational pluralism (Sober and Wilson, 1998) governs the initial thrust of the narrative research project, she also believes that trust-in-the-truth-of-the-word-of-the-other is the primary moral condition for its success as a research method. She examines the idea of trust as an ethical condition for a research approach, linking this to three groups of danger. Firstly, she outlines the dangers within trustful speaker/hearer/ listener collusion and how trust itself can establish "insider-outsider", "us-and-them" polemics within and between the three-way narrative research relationship. Secondly, she talks about the dangers inherent in a non-trusting research relationship; in particular the status of words that are spoken, heard, interpreted – and later denied. And thirdly, she discusses those dangers that arise from trusting in the linguistic skills of the researcher who simultaneously mediates and creates the conditions for narrative truth-making. The first of these dangers concerns the ability of skilled fictive wordsmanship to both market and manipulate emotional response; while the second concerns the potential exclusivity of a research approach that is so dependent on skills of writing-as-fiction (and particularly English language writing-as-fiction) in order to promote its claims of knowledge creation. Because of the significant issue raised by these points, the final part of the chapter links the practice of narrative research to an additional danger within the method: of trusting-in-the-notion-of-equity.

Daisy Pillay, the author of **Chapter Seven**, is a creative painter trained in the visual arts and a teacher educator at the University of KwaZulu-Natal. In her doctoral studies she spread her empirical wings, exploring how some teachers remained passionate and committed to the enterprise of teaching, in a general environment of declining morale and increasing disillusionment. She explores how teachers' lives are constructed in the dialectical relationship between their unique personal experiences and the broader social political terrain of reconstruction of South Africa. She draws on her knowledge of cubism as a movement in art to develop a heuristic device to understand the multiple layers of complexity that could be analysed to interpret the lives of these "successful teachers". Her study explores how a cubist-narrative of teachers could be told with different imagined audiences in mind and how the audience and their intentions also help shape the construction of narratives. She shows how the choice of authorial presence of the researcher in the narratives could yield different insights into the data within a narrative research tradition. The narratives, constructed in first and third persons, allow different spaces for different interpretations. This approach resonates with her desire to represent the lives of teachers in a way that permits multiple interpretations, no one version being more privileged than another. The sources of influence for professional development of teachers are thereby advanced and this no doubt influences the way she now designs her professional development courses for teachers, at both school and university level.

Chapters Eight, Nine and Ten (the third cluster of chapters) consider how data is used methodologically in the research process: firstly, as an exemplar of alternative forms of representation of "research reports"; secondly, as a political tool and, thirdly, beyond the scope of individual life history research boundaries into organisational identity research.

Chapter Eight draws on the metaphor of the research process as a joining together of many instruments within an orchestra. It provides an exemplar of the kinds of alternative forms of representation that could characterise research reporting. The chapter is presented in the form of a drama script involving three actors: the researcher and two of the research participants. It aims to capture the interactive questioning and probing that epitomises the research process and shows that the participants are simultaneously negotiating several different layers of meaning-making as they make sense of the world of becoming teachers of the English language. The chapter provides the data set of the research study, which is described in the opening chapter of this book, providing the reader with a practical representation of how visual and verbal (written) data could be organised in the reporting of research. The immediacy of the narrative itself is created by attempting to represent as closely as possible to the told story of the research participants, including the uniqueness of the dialect of English the three participants use to ask and tell of their involvement in the research process.

Chapter Nine extends the problematic nature of what constitutes data in research. While the study does not use a life history approach, it is still deeply concerned with the same considerations of ethics, representation and epistemology that plagues research into HIV and AIDS. In this chapter, Labby Ramrathan focuses on the context that shapes research agendas. It attempts to frame, profile and interrogate the context for particular research agendas. In this respect it argues that the construction of research agendas at macro-level, whilst motivated by worthy epistemological considerations (such as a knowledge of the prevalence of HIV and AIDS within the society), can and is manipulated by political interests. The interest to direct resources towards HIV and AIDS interventions drives researchers to choose particular data production methods to fuel their agendas. Research on HIV and AIDS is used as a medium to explore the notion of "data as agency". By interrogating HIV and AIDS researchers' responses to the data they produce within a critical discourse analysis framework, they expose their positionality. Critical discourse analysis allows one to explore how researchers use and read data against a defined context that exposes their biases and agendas.

Labby Ramrathan at the time of the writing of this chapter was the Director of the School of Educational Studies at the University of KwaZulu-Natal, and became part of a large national team of researchers investigating through a direct epidemiological testing the prevalence of HIV and AIDS amongst teachers. He is presently the Dean's Assistant in the Faculty of Education at the University of KwaZulu-Natal.

Chapter Ten extends the use of the life history approach to the field of "evaluation research", showing how an organisational ethnography can be used to understand organisational behaviour. However, using the approach is necessarily complicated by considerations around methodology, representation and ethics in the process of constructing new knowledge.

During the latter part of the last century, empirical research has been characterised by an expansive proliferation of alternative paradigms, each claiming its space as a legitimate research genre in relation to the enfranchised positivist canon. The acceptance and popularisation of feminist methods and methodologies have encouraged researchers to resist speculative definitions and binary logic and to privilege narrative theorising. However, to date, the practice of narrative research has been largely confined to exploring individual identity as a window to other epistemological and ontological concerns. While its popularity in ethnographic studies as a tool for documenting the lives of marginals and subalterns, as well as communities and societies, is on the increase, the use of this approach in the study of organisations has only recently gained in popularity.

This chapter explores the value of appropriating the foundational principles of Empowerment and Illuminative Evaluation (which have their roots in an anthropological conception of organisations and institutions) as a tool to excavate organisational identity and behaviour. It interrogates the value of an organisational ethnography and its capacity to satisfy the intellectual curiosity of the researcher, while simultaneously providing illuminative insights for members of the organisation to revisit their praxis.

Engaging in an organisational ethnography enables a neo-institutional challenge to the structuralist-functionalist conceptions of organisational theorists such as Weber and Durkheim who view organisations as having a tangible material existence rather than being founded on an "ontology of becoming". In a mode of critical self-reflexivity, Rubby Dhunpath revisits the methodological wisdom of engaging in an institutional biography, providing insights into his journey as a researcher, highlighting critical episodes, as he appropriated a non-conventional approach to document the institutional memory of a non-governmental organisation (NGO). He touches on some of his insights and learnings, while putting up for scrutiny what for him were some of the unresolved theoretical and methodological dilemmas that served to disrupt his essentialist notions of narrative research. In particular he challenges the practice of member-checking as a necessary but potentially constraining exercise in narrative research.

Rubby Dhunpath, at the time of writing this chapter, was a Rockefeller post-doctoral Fellow at the University of Illinois' Centre for International Studies. His experience and position as Senior Research Specialist within the Human Sciences

Research Council in South Africa has trajected him into expanding the usually individual micro-level potential that life history methodology offers, and he argues now more forcibly for a hybridity of research approaches and the potential of life history approaches to expand into broader macro-level studies. He is presently the Director in the University Teaching and Learning Office at the University of KwaZulu-Natal.

THE ORIGINS OF THIS BOOK

This book has its roots within a community of researchers associated with the School of Education Studies at the former University of Durban-Westville, now known as the University of KwaZulu-Natal after its merger in 2005 with the former University of Natal.

The project was conceived as a post-doctoral activity to disseminate graduates' completed research, many of which were recommended for publication by the examiners. In mid 2004, 10 graduates and their supervisors participated in an authorship development workshop hosted by the Faculty of education to generate a book on innovative research methodologies.

During the authorship development workshop, the central idea of the book was conceptualized as falling broadly within the genre of life history research. Each of the authors' central thematic focus was extensively interrogated over two days, after which authors went on to develop their chapters which were collated into the 1st draft manuscript by the editors.

Over the following months, these chapters were reviewed by the doctoral supervisors, and refined by the authors leading to the 2nd draft. In 2005, the chapters were presented as papers at the first international conference on Qualitative Enquiry, held at the University of Illinois, Urbana Champaign. Having received valuable comment and critique from renowned scholars attending the conference, authors then developed their chapters further, leading to the 3rd draft. In 2006, this draft was circulated amongst the ten authors for interrogation and reworking, culminating in the 4th draft.

The 4th draft was sent to Prof Patti Lather of Ohio State University and Prof Norman Denzin of the University of Illinois who offered further critique and comment on the manuscript with suggestions for revisions. In 2007, the amended 5th draft was submitted to Claudia Mitchell of the University of KwaZulu-Natal who offered additional comment and recommendations. The 6th draft was then submitted to Dr Betty Govinden, for final comment, leading to the final draft which was accepted in 2008 for publication by Sense Publishers. Sense Publishers then subjected the book to its own rigorous editorial processes until completion.

[1] Many outsiders still marvel today at the "miracle" that post-apartheid South Africa demonstrates in the lack of overt racism and tolerance that many reveal in the agenda to move forward beyond our painful histories. Can this be attributed to the TRC? Or are we just a forgiving nation? A stubborn horse to subjugate? This of course does not mean that all vestiges of injustice have been removed.

[2] This chapter is based on and draws from two earlier sources: Vithal, R. (2003) In search of a pedagogy of conflict and dialogue for mathematics education. Drodrecht: Kluwer Academic Publishers; and Vithal, R. & Valero, P. (2003) Researching mathematics education in situations of social and political conflict. In A. J. Bishop, M. A. Clements, C. Keitel, J. Kilpatrick, & F. K. S. Leung (Eds.), *Second international handbook of mathematics education*. Dordrecht: Kluwer Academic Publishers.

[3] This article was first published in *Perspectives in Education*: Volume 18, Number 2 (1999).

REFERENCES

Arnason, H. H. (1969). *A history of modern art: Painting. Sculpture. Architecture*. London: Thames and Hudson.

Cary, L. J. (1999). Unexpected stories: Life history and the limits of representation. *Qualitative Enquiry*, 5(3), 411–427.

Sober, E., & Wilson, D. (1998). *Unto others: The evolution and psychology of unselfish behaviour*. Cambridge, MA: Harvard University Press.

Truth and Reconciliation Commission of South Africa. (1998) *Truth and reconciliation commission report of South Africa* (Vol. 1). Johannesburg: Juta & Company, Ltd..

The photograph on the cover page is an adaptation of the painting of Pablo Picasso, *'Les Demoiselles d'Avignon'* (Arnason 1986, 154).

PART ONE: CONCEPTUALISING LIFE HISTORY RESEARCH
EPISTEMOLOGICALLY

MICHAEL SAMUEL

1. ON BECOMING A TEACHER: LIFE HISTORY RESEARCH AND THE FORCE-FIELD MODEL OF TEACHER DEVELOPMENT

Any attempt at describing or evaluating the complex human social condition is prone to distortions, omissions, reductions and elaborations. All we hope to achieve in understanding the human condition is likely to be limited, little more than a glimpse through the window of research. Stories are one means by which human beings attempt to make sense of that complex human condition: to create some order out of the chaos of competing and contradictory experiences; to bring into dialogue the world of the real and the world of the imagination; to stand Janus-headed, looking backwards and forwards into past life experiences and anticipating the future.

MacIntyre (see Gough, 1998) argues for the critical role of narratives in practical reasoning and ethical thinking, suggesting that

> …we can only answer questions about what we should do if we can answer prior questions about the story or stories that we are caught up in, including the cultural myths and mythologies that we help to perpetuate.

Notably, telling stories about one's life is a process – not of documenting the truth of what exactly happened. Instead, the act of telling the story is a process of recording how the teller of the tale presently sees her position in relation to the subject/topic being discussed. Stories about one's lives therefore encapsulate the past, the future and the present. The story that is produced in the telling (the verbal or written text) also encodes the kind of authorial relationship that the teller wishes to establish in relation to the subject matter being discussed. The composer of the story chooses to frame herself as an assertive, ambiguous or passive believer in the explanations, interpretations and memories she offers. She creatively and constantly chooses (unconsciously or not) appropriate positionalities in relation to what she is telling. These positionalities vary in relation to the strength of her belief and confidence in the different aspects of what she professes. Her telling is a constant internal dialogue with herself.

The teller of the tale also creatively chooses the kind of relationship she shares with the listeners of the tale. The teller decides how she wishes to be seen. In this sense, the listeners/audience co-construct the tale and the telling. The ensuing narrative text represents that lived moment of the composer fictively, actively and creatively engaging with choices about how to represent the relationship between

R. Dhunpath and M. Samuel (eds.), Life History Research: Epistemology, Methodology and Representation, 3–17

herself as composer and the audience whom she has conjured up as the prime listeners of her tale, balancing the memories and interpretations of her experiences.

Whilst it might seem that the writer/composer of the tale is in supreme control, her telling of the tale is framed within the specific conventions of how tales are told, read and listened to in the cultural context. She is thus at the mercy of the social conventions of telling stories. Of course, she may choose to flout these conventions, but she does so as a constant foil/counterpoint to the existing convention, and she runs the risk of making the immediate accessibility of the text more difficult for the conservative reader. It may also be argued that the text that is produced is capable of being interpreted in a myriad of ways. The strength and weakness of language (verbal or written) is that it only has "potential for meaning". Listeners are therefore free to interpret what they will from the rendition of the story.

Given the promises and perils of life history research, it emerges as an approach responding to the stories that people habitually tell in everyday life. The life history researcher attempts to structure the process of the telling of stories to yield rich, in-depth details about the specific life experiences, memories and inter-pretations that the individuals produce. She aims to analyse and interpret these "told" memories, experiences and recollections of individuals in a systematic and ordered fashion, allowing other readers to decide on how credible, authentic and trustworthy the stories appear in relation to their (readers') own life world. Connelly and Clandinin (1990, p. 2) argue that education therefore is the construction and reconstruction of personal and social stories since teachers and learners all live "storied lives" which are ways of making sense of the world in which they live.

However, unlike the storyteller habitually constructing her stories, the life history researcher chooses to demarcate the realm of what is to be investigated, what realm of one's life is being researched. The researcher chooses to identify some specific dimensions of social reality that she wishes to illuminate. For example, the life history researcher may choose to focus on one's family experiences, one's career trajectory, one's sexual relations. The storyteller provides the ingredients for understanding more **in-depth and in interconnected ways** how the researcher's specified domain is reinforced, subverted, challenged in relation to other realms of the person's lives. What emerges in the life history approach thus is a relating of the complexity of the human condition, a representation of the fullness of life against the backdrop of some underlying interpretative or critical frame-work. As a representation of life, it is never the fullness itself but merely one glimpse in through the window into that fullness. That fullness, too, is never completely static, but evolving and dialoguing with itself. To some, a complete fullness cannot exist.

This creative process between the life history researcher and her research subject weaving an interconnective net to hold all the representations of fullnesses, stands in strong contrast to the processes of traditional researchers whose goals are to attempt to establish the veracity of certain truths. Life history research does not aim to test out a pre-formulated hypothesis. Instead, the life history researcher is

4

one who encourages herself to be surprised by her data, to be thrown off track from her original thoughts, to veer into territory that she did not anticipate, to find data that is contradictory. The life history researcher aims to develop an understanding or illumination of the specific realm under scrutiny in its complexity rather than in its reductionist abstraction; she does not expect to provide an explanation of the truth regarding that realm. The interpretative and critical framework is often offered as multi-dimensional illuminations of the phenomenon being investigated. The life history researcher's goal is to be generative of alternative ways of seeing, knowing, understanding and interpreting life experiences. To research is to look again with new eyes.

RE-SEARCHING STUDENTS TEACHERS IN SOUTH AFRICA

This chapter reflects on a study that attempts to understand the process of becoming a teacher of the English language. The study was conducted with a group of my student teachers within a teacher education programme at the University of KwaZulu-Natal, South Africa. It attempted to document the life experiences of student teachers over different periods of their lives as they journeyed through apartheid schooling into tertiary education and back into the classroom as novice teachers of the English language. Of the 82 potential students from the Special Method English course, which I taught, I purposefully selected nine students who typified the diversity of learners encountering English language teaching and learning in post-apartheid South Africa. Their ability to articulate lucidly their reflections was also a criterion in their selection.

My intention was to get students to look back on their own English language teaching and learning in their homes, families, communities, primary and secondary schooling. Whilst this reflected some more distant recollections and memories, the research design enabled me to probe more deeply into how they experienced learning English during their undergraduate years at the university. Having registered to become teachers of the English language in a Postgraduate Diploma, they were asked to document (tell their tale) their reflections on becoming teachers. The storytelling process included an attempt to bring into dialogue their own past experiences (home, families, schools), their present experiences (undergraduate education, student teacher programme) and their future (teaching as a professional career). The process of telling the story for each of the students encapsulated an overt and conscious process of documenting and representing during a one-year period their emerging views about English language teaching and learning. This approach is located within the tradition of "teacher thinking research" (Kennedy, 1991; Freeman, 1996). Here, the emphasis was not exclusively on what the teachers' actions were, but more importantly on how the student teachers made sense of their own and others' actions in the educational process.

DATA COLLECTION APPROACH

The aim of this paper is to document the rigorous process of data collection that was undertaken during the process of gathering insights into the life experiences of these student teachers. The intention of such a description is to suggest that life history research should not be seen simply as a vainglorious glamorising of the research subject's own individual life experiencing (see Reddy, 2000 for an explanation of what life history is not). The process of data collection attempted to develop as in-depth a way of knowing the life experiences of the research subject as is possible within the genre of telling stories.

My Positioning

In setting up the research process, I was consciously aware of my own privileged position in the research process. I could not escape my simultaneous roles as their teacher educator, a life history researcher and also a member of the faculty's management structures. As the researcher, I was fuelled by the exigencies of timeframes for data collection and deadlines for reporting on the study. My interest in their experiences was for the purpose of better understanding how English language teaching and learning could be improved, and the public renditions of their life histories in the research process became a way of fulfilling my role in preparing them to become teachers. My agenda and research questions filtered into their prescribed assignments for the course. As a manager of the university curriculum development process, the insights I gained from students allowed me to infuse a more sensitive awareness of how our student teachers were interpreting the curriculum that was being designed for them. I became aware of their own limited involvement in what and how they were being taught. This alerted me to how I was influencing the managerial decisions I was making as I attempted to develop quality control over the curriculum.

I was also aware of my own "disadvantage" in the position I adopted. I was not a novice English language student teacher, although I once was. My own more experienced status predisposed me to ask particular questions, looking at the classroom in specific ways. These ways did not necessarily coincide with what excites or troubles a novice student teacher. It was clear that in developing the life histories of my research participants, I would have to allow my self to be dislodged, to allow the students to feel comfortable with producing and revealing their own joys, desires, hopes and fears.

Negotiating Entry

Negotiating my entry into the worlds of the student teachers meant that I had to be quite explicit in mapping out the details of what my study was about and what the possible options for participation were. However, telling them about confidentiality and authenticity without showing tangibly how I wanted to hear their voices is insufficient. My data collection process had to disclose explicitly the "stance" that I wished to frame, i.e. what kind of relationship I anticipated in relation to my research (Freeman, 1996). I was interested in participants seeing themselves as the directors of their stories rather than pandering to the expectations of what I as researcher wanted to hear. I wanted them to realise that my own role in challenging and contesting their worldviews about teaching and learning English was also a part of my role as teacher educator. I wanted them to know that I saw them as active critics of the course and my own actions as teacher educator or researcher. The space within which the data was to be produced was guaranteed to be a cauldron of competing fiery voices, where both the researcher and the research participants felt confident to fuel the fire with their own opinions because we were all complicit in generating the data.

DATA GENERATING STRATEGIES

Who am I?

The first exercise focused on getting the students to be able to choose a means of representing who they are to the rest of the class. The exercise was designed over two weeks: the first week involved preparation and planning, and the second a report back to a plenary session. Surprisingly, it became evident that the students were only vaguely familiar with others in their class cohort. The groups were characteristically resistant to the exercise, expecting that the teacher education programme will be "demonstration lessons on how to teach". The class was set the task of pairing off with a person unfamiliar to them: using the racial, gender, cultural and geographic categories as the first demarcations of "difference". Identifying the differences/similarities proved interesting as students began to realise more similarities between their experiences/backgrounds than they initially expected. This was especially so across the race groups. Students were then asked to collaboratively develop and administer an interview schedule to construct a biographic text of their English learning and teaching experiences.

Another group of students was asked to work on designing a biographical form to capture the diversity of the whole class (82 students) and to present a written report a week later on the responses to the designed biographical questionnaire. This came to be recorded in a strongly quantitative representation. Another group was asked to enact an oral discourse of a critical incident in their schooling. The class was also asked to identify whom they considered to represent the "diversity" of the students in their class. After many debates, five students were selected. I then chose to interview these students about their expectations of being a teacher of English in a multicultural society. My own interview with these students was semi-structured. In the interview, I also focused on the students' expectations of the Special Method course. In the report back session, I was surprised by the level of openness and enthusiasm that students revealed in this early stage of the course.

In preparing for the report back session in the second week, the class and I began to negotiate the sensitivity of public disclosure of their biographies. We talked about the risky business drawing on Melnick's (1997) and Harris and Furlong's (1997) comments on the use of biographical work in the classroom.

We talked about the highly personal nature of the data – that data once revealed is public information; that individuals might be offended by the comments that classmates make about their worldviews; that the teacher cannot guarantee that insensitive remarks would be passed by student colleagues; that the researcher cannot protect the individual tellers of their stories from the consequences of what their revelations present. For example, if the storyteller reveals a criminal history, then the teacher educator/researcher cannot protect him/her from the social consequences of attitudes and inter-relationships that colleagues might show towards him/her. The need for a climate of co-operation and confidentiality was thus stressed.

Whilst this climate of trust is one that evolves over time, the sharing of their experiences proved to be a kind of restorative healing process, as I became aware that students wanted someone to hear their stories of pain, suffering, or triumph over the apartheid system. The mere fact that someone was listening to them proved to have the effect of making the other colleagues in the class more respectful of the teller. I am convinced that these early sessions helped create the climate of **critical open discursive spaces** between myself and the research participants, since the session proved to be one which allowed individuals to ask probing and critical questions. For many, the exposure to the lifeworld outside their own "tiny cocooned world" was a good educative experience. Above all, it created a feeling that the Special Method class was a community, more respectful of each other in their similarities and differences.

AUTOBIOGRAPHY

Having written a reflective biography of another individual, students were then tasked with documenting their own autobiographical account of their experiences of learning English within the contexts of their homes, families, communities and schools. The detailed assignment handout urged students to include in their written report reflections on their prior experiences and beliefs about English language teaching and learning, a critical analysis of these beliefs, and experiences and an explanation of how these experiences might influence them to become the kind of teacher of English that they would like to be.

The assignment requested students to include memories and impressions of former teachers and themselves as learners. The critical analysis aimed at tapping their current level of understanding of how individuals learn languages. They were asked to identify roles and practices that they would like to reject based on these reflections.

The assignment proved difficult for those students who had little experience of autobiographical writing. Many students, despite them having completed an undergraduate degree in English literature, had a poor (less developed) repertoire of reading experiences outside of their prescribed textbooks. Exemplars of written autobiographies of student teachers reflecting on their schooling experiences (e.g. Karen Johnson: Pennsylvanian University) proved to be useful in boosting their confidence.

As students progressed with the assignment, I became aware of the need to develop more sophisticated writing skills to "concisely and crisply" document their narratives. I was fairly satisfied with the detail of information (propositional content) yielded from each of the students in relation to the quality of their English language teaching experiences, but perhaps less pleased about their relatively under-developed writing skills. I became aware of the need for an alternative form of representation beyond the written words. I had in the early forms of data gathering relied exclusively on the oral mode (cf. "Who am I?" sessions described above). It was then that I introduced the collage.

Collages

My own interest in the use of visual collages inspired me to think of getting students to develop a collection/assemblage of different material/texts, objects of different styles codes, mediums to reflect their life experiences with English language learning and teaching. The development of the collage was to serve as the cover page of their autobiography. I provided an initial introduction to the medium of collage-making, which also serves also as a design tool for organising and developing curriculum units. The collage allowed students the opportunity to collect photographs or draw/assemble visual representations of themselves at different stages of their lives: at home, in the community, in primary and secondary school. A visual feast of A5 collage renditions accompanied the final hand-in of the autobiographies.

It is evident that in this approach to life history, I was consciously allowing the author to choose the best form of representing him or herself. Nevertheless, the visual texts do not necessarily speak for themselves, and needed to be mediated to me, the life history researcher. With the collage as a stimulus, I asked students to reflect on why they had chosen to represent their life experiences through the particular images on the collage. In fact, their collages themselves became the interview schedule, probing for more clarity about the choice of size, shape, position of the images, etc. These interviews with students about their experiences of English language teaching and learning sometimes spanned over two-and-a-half hours.

Reflective Journals

Drawing on the work of Schon (1987), Elliot (1985), Carr and Kemmis (1986), the Faculty of Education designed a teacher development programme which consciously encourages teachers to self-reflect on their own development as professionals. This reflection is not confined to a mere psychological interpretivist reflection on the successes and failures of one's development as a professional but also explores how one's own role as a professional contributes to the development of social justice within the contexts in which one operates.

As part of the research project the students were asked to reflect on their past and present experiences during the Special Method course. This allowed them the opportunity to record their changing/evolving sense of the theoretical and practical input that they were receiving during their teacher training. As a teacher education tool the reflective journal was a means of consolidating what was being learnt. It was also a useful tool to gain insight into what sense teachers were making of the experiences of the courses (my own interest as researcher). These reflective journals were periodically "marked" by the faculty during the on-campus component of the course. However, during the field-based Teaching Practice session where students were placed in schools, the formal expectation was that the student had to keep a daily record of his/her involvement in the school. These journals provided an invaluable source of data for my research.

Student Assignments

During the School-based Teaching Practice sessions the student were set the assignment of investigating the "lived language policy at the school". In the absence of a formal written language policy in most schools at the time, the students were expected to document a detailed description of how different languages were taught, learnt, experienced, reinforced or challenged at their schools. The students were grouped in teams of four to five and were assigned different dimensions of establishing the status quo regarding language usage. This data, it was believed, would assist students to understand the specific localised problems regarding language teaching and learning. Students were encouraged to locate official documents, interview teachers of different grades, as well as talk to different learners across racial and linguistic heritages. A formal written report of their involvement in understanding the lived language policy at the school also constituted part of the data for the study: revealing how students interpreted what constituted the challenges facing language teaching and learning at a systemic level within the school as an institution.

The students were also asked to develop a planned intervention in terms of addressing an identified problem of English language teaching and learning. The students were set the task of engaging in an action research project. They worked in collaborative teams with mentor teachers, lecturers and student teachers. The students were asked to record in their daily reflective journals their reflections on the success of these efforts. At the end of the project the student were expected to assemble a portfolio of all the interventions they had engaged in, in the form of a packaged Curriculum Unit. Besides developing the students' ability to design materials, it also provided the school with a useful set of materials. In addition, the curriculum packages served as data for me to interpret how student teachers experienced and understood English language teaching and learning.

CLASSROOM TEACHING: OBSERVATIONS, REFLECTIONS AND EVALUATIONS

During the School-based Teaching Practice (SBTP), I was also involved in supervising the student teachers whose life histories I was documenting. I took the opportunity of working with these nine students in their schools. This entailed detailed interviews as we discussed their lesson preparation, their action research projects and their reflective journal comments. It also included visits to the classrooms to observe the student teachers teaching. Some of these lessons were videotaped and played back for collaborative viewing between the research subject and myself. In this second viewing of the videotape immediately after the lesson was taught, the student was asked to pause the videotape to comment on any aspect of the lesson that s/he considered appropriate for reflection. This second interview involving stimulated recall was also recorded, providing rich data about the relationship between the teacher and the classroom world. In the stimulus recall interview the focus was on getting students to provide a rationale for their actions and/or the reactions of the learners in the classroom. In this way, I was able to probe deeply into the numerous contemporaneous concerns that the novice teachers were dealing with during their teaching.

During the course of SBTP, students were encouraged to sit in on each other's lessons, producing a set of written reports for their peers. At the end of SBTP the student team members were asked to write detailed peer review evaluations. Students were also tasked with writing self-evaluations. These evaluations were added to the assigned mark awarded for the SBTP session.

After School -Based Teaching Practice: Summative evaluations

As a form of consolidating or confirming the kind of growth experiences that the students had undergone, I designed a focus group interview which was conducted at the end of the course just prior to the final examinations. The purpose of the interview was to get the students to look with hindsight at all the kinds of activities that they had engaged in during the course and comment on their usefulness in shaping them as teachers of English. Present in the room were all the artefacts that they had produced during the course of the year, including artefacts from an excursion that they had organised. These included lesson preparation books, action research reports, evaluation reports, charts produced, etc. The interview was video-recorded. Another summative assessment/record of their growth was the final year examination script that each student produced.

DATA GATHERING

The purpose of this detailed account of how data was gathered is to demonstrate that the methods attempt to go beyond simply extracting an individual's life history record using exclusively verbal interview data. The range of methods used to generate life history data is rich and varied. The data itself exists in many different modes: verbal data, visual data and written data. The data itself is written at and about various stages of the individual's life and therefore contains a developmental feel over the one-year data gathering process. The audience for the production of the data in each of the cases varies slightly. The producer of the data (the story teller) is placed in many different positions of telling in many different research contexts: in the lecture classroom; in the researcher's office; in the audio recording room; in the art classroom; in the school classroom, reflecting after one's teaching at school; in the examination room, reflecting on a range of aspects related to becoming a teacher.

I would like to acknowledge that in the gathering of this data, I as researcher am very much part of the data that is produced. My role as teacher educator further compounds this since many of the discussions about English language teaching and learning were a consequence of the stimulus that I myself may have inspired or referred students to. This is the nature of teacher education and this is what I was researching: how do student teachers make sense of the input from their lecturers? Do they value them? Feign respect for them? Use them or discard them?

I consider that the process of generating the data was collaborative, but shaped by my own agenda. The student teachers were assigned tasks, which involved them engaging with their theoretical and practical understandings of being a teacher. It may be argued that the research participants saw my detailed probing as an extended form of teacher preparation which encouraged them to be more highly reflective and critical of their own engagement with the teaching process. Their willingness to participate was clearly evidence of this.

DATA ANALYSIS

I believe that the data analysis process for this study began from the very start of the project. I believe that the research participants were always aware that I was attempting to verbalise and make sense of their actions and thoughts. This is evident in the tape recording of our discussions where I constantly probed deeper to help the students and myself understand what it is that they were explaining. The process of data collection involved my having to "enter and re-enter the field". Over time, the process of data collection became more refined and sophisticated. As the study unfolded, new methodologies for data collection were designed. This process of constant refinement of the data collection strategy constituted the first stages of data analysis. The approach that was used may be regarded as an "iterative" rather than a "linear" data **gathering process** (Freeman, 1996).

Another consideration about data analysis is when and how the **categories** for the analysis emerge. In an "a priori analysis" the categories are determined in advance of the data collection and the analysis proceeds in relation to the pre-specified categories. This approach is akin to the hypothesis testing kind of research evident in most empirical studies. On the opposite end of the continuum of data analysis is the approach which allows the categories of analysis to emerge from the data with minimal *a priori* expectation: The grounded theory approach is akin to research aiming at generating hypotheses as the outcome of research. Two in-between analytical categorisation processes could be envisaged: a "negotiated analysis" and a "guided analysis". The first entails the categories and analysis being developed by the researcher with the input of the research participants, and the second involves developing categories in an *a priori* way, but subsequent analysis guides the categories to be modified through interaction with the data.

In my study, the approach adopted tended to be located toward the end of the continuum related to a grounded theory approach of analysis (see Figure 1 below). Nevertheless, I believe that my own perhaps unarticulated theory of teacher development could have served as some form of *a priori* categories that guided the analysis. My approach relied almost exclusively on privileging my own interpretation of the data, since the student teachers had already left university by the time I engaged in the final stages of data analysis. Although access to students was difficult, I was able to get them to look at the represented stories that I had constructed to document an analysis of their lives. I do therefore believe that my own data analytical stance hovered along the continuum below.

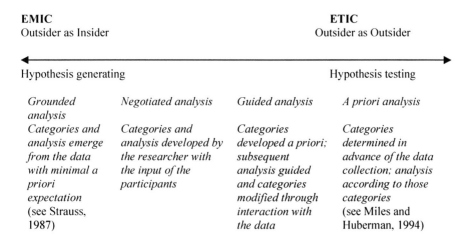

Figure 1. Data analysis and interpretation (Freeman, 1996, p. 372) Adapted

THE FORCE FIELD MODEL OF TEACHER DEVELOPMENT

Whilst it is not the intention of this chapter to reveal a detailed analysis of the data yielded, it is necessary to summarise briefly the findings of the research. This will inform the discussion concerning the use value of the life history research approach, especially in two spheres: in the sphere of curriculum development; in the sphere of policymaking.

The findings of the study postulated that student teachers find themselves pushed and pulled by various competing, contradictory and complimentary forces as they try to negotiate their identities as professional teachers in post-apartheid South Africa. It is argued that a stable or fixed identity is not possible (nor desirable) in a multicultural, polyglot society. The student teachers' own rich biographies of experiences of English language teaching and learning developed during their formative years in their homes and communities predispose them to approaching the formal learning of English with hesitation. For some, the expectation is that English will yield the passport to better life opportunities;

nevertheless, they simultaneously and contradictorily anticipate the subversion of their own linguistic heritages in their homes.[1] Schooling represents the transition to the loss of this dimension of their home identity. The specific racial, biographical and class positions of different individuals each yield unique interpretations of what it is to learn English which is related to how consonant the cultural world of the home and the school are. Some interpreted English (and schooling) as the deliberate escape out of their everyday lifeworld outside school. Some individuals choose their linguistic suicide willingly because of the economic prosperity it is professed to yield. Others revisit the abandonment to the forces of the colonising influence of English in their worlds. This questioning, however, is more an activity of hindsight.

These biographical forces are nevertheless mediated further in relation to the quality of institutional forces that were presented into the lifeworld of the individual. The quality of teaching and learning of English is interpreted by the research participants as strongly dependent on their school teacher's own conception of what language learning is and how it ought to occur. Different school teachers' often unexpressed theoretical understandings of language acquisition and learning filter into their classrooms. Often, second language classrooms in African schools were characterised by repetitive and behaviourist interpretations of language learning accompanied by several reported cases of physical punishment and rewards systems to drive learning English. Most learners reported poor experiences of learning to communicate the language, which ironically motivated them to choose language teaching as a career.

As learners entered the tertiary education world, they experienced the teaching of English as the study of English literature which in many respects they found not directly related to their own goals of improving the quality of the poorly developed language competence. Their exposure to alternative theories and practices of English language teaching and learning in the teacher education programme is regarded as only remotely connected to their own schooling experiences. They remain ambiguously sceptical of the potential of alternative approaches, yet convinced that they are the new generation of English language teachers who potentially could make a difference.

The experiences of school-based teaching practice destabilise again the student teachers' conceptions of becoming a teacher. They are exposed to the world of schooling again through the lens of the new theories they have been exposed to and through the lens of a largely disillusioned teaching force which is having to cope with the demands of enacting and interpreting a new curriculum (Curriculum 2005). Resident teachers are sceptical of "new fangled theories and approaches" and attempt to co-opt teachers into their routines and rituals of teaching and learning languages.

All of these forces compete for attention as the teacher attempts to negotiate his/her identity. The novice teacher is thus pushed or pulled into adopting certain value systems or practices. The dynamism of being different, true to what one believes, is chosen by only those few who are able to resist the temptation to "flow with the stream". Even in choosing to flow with the stream, the internal dialogue of what one "could be" as opposed to what one "chooses to be" persists in the novice teacher of language. As novice teachers progress during the course of their training, they become more circumspect of the theoretical world of academe, choosing instead the pragmatics of what works best in the situated specific classrooms they teach. They do not necessarily abandon the "crutch" of theories debated and discussed in their university lecture halls, but come to develop their own interpretations of what may be called a "personal working theory". This personal working theory is reliant on their teaching practice sessions having presented sufficient opportunities for contestation, challenge and debate.

REPORTING THE RESEARCH STUDENT

What appears in the descriptive of the Force Field model above seems commonplace. This is because in the choice of the representation of this summary, it is necessary to generalise, create abstractions and gloss over the nuances and subtleties of meanings. Hence, it is important that one considers specifically how life history research is to be reported. (Issues of representation are explored in Samuel, 1999.) In my study, I chose to represent the telling of the tale in the form of narrative stories about the lives of particular individual student teachers. In the first two stories, I represent the story in first person narrative to evoke a sense of immediacy of the teller. I also chose in doing so to reflect as closely as possible the unique dialectical variation of language usage of the particular participants. Therefore, I chose to remain close to the direct transcript records in the telling of the story. In the remaining seven stories I resorted to a third person narrative which allowed me the opportunity to critically comment as omniscient narrator on the plot of the story as it unfolded in the lives of the different individuals.

As can be seen from the above brief description, the representation of the text of the storied life history is important. The presence or distance of the storytellers and the life history researcher can be creatively manipulated through the choice of the quality of the text displayed as the outcome of the research process. The degree of interactivity that the writer of the life history intends with his/her potential audience is also enhanced through the use of different modes of data, and having generated valuable visual data, this was included in the presentation of the students' represented life history.

WHAT CAN WE LEARN FOR LIFE HISTORY RESEARCH?

My view is that life history research is unlikely to have any direct one-to-one influence on the research context/academic worldview unless the life history report/story is ingested through a slow process of diffusion into the consciousness of the users. Too often, curriculum developers and policymakers are anxious to be directed with some degree of certainty into action as the consequence of having been presented the research's "hard facts". Users of research often want to be inspired with some concrete action to follow the presentation of "the report". Unfortunately, the aim of life history research is not to provide such certainty. Life history research presents an opportunity to its users to be able to think and look at the world for its blurry bits, its complexities and complications. The world is not capable of being reduced into simplicities. The writers of life histories should hope only to have presented fresh illuminations of the phenomenon being investigated.

Stories are meant to be told to allow readers to be able to see others and themselves in new ways. What those new ways will be are not always controllable by the author of the story. Nevertheless, the telling of the story in a particular sequence, in a particular form, with particular representation, is more likely to conjure up particular kinds of responses. The life history approach, therefore, is only useful in that it can provide another lens to interpret the complexity of the world in which we live.

The storytelling process is thus a process of understanding the myths and mythologies that our life experiences have harvested. It is an opportunity to challenge those myths, to make decisions about which dimensions of the myths we wish to endure, eradicate and/or alter. However, it is unlikely that one researcher's descriptive and evaluative account of the life experiences of teachers is likely to fundamentally open up the box of mythologies. It is by drawing comparisons across several different storytellers that the mythologies can come to be examined. The authors of the stories should be diverse in their origin and outlook, so that various vantages on our mythologies are illuminated. The decision of what use to make of all these repeated contestations, confirmations and consolidations of the mythologies is thus the role of the policymaker.

On a smaller scale it is likely that the life history approach could help the curriculum designer as has been the case in my study. In the study located in the realm of understanding student teachers' experiences of a curriculum (English language teaching and learning), I have, together with the students, come to understand more deeply the decision-making process which impinges on the development of an identity for novice student teachers. I am now much more acutely aware of the many pushes and pulls impacting on the student teachers as they negotiate their identity. I am more aware of the ability of student teachers (all teachers perhaps) to strategically mimic a chosen preferred identity in relation to specific audiences, contexts and purposes. I am aware that teachers need to be supported to be confident to share their somewhat schizophrenic responsibilities to many masters: the department of education, the school management, the parent body, the pupils and their own personal working theory of teaching. I am aware now more of the deep internal dialogue that teachers need to be able to engage in as they refine their personal working theories. I am aware that teacher education programmes need to be designed in such a way that does not simply involve the replacement of old orthodoxies with new fashions. I am aware as a teacher educator that teachers are deeply rational professionals negotiating simultaneously several competing forces which pull or push them in different directions. The naïve idealism that I once had of "altering teaching practices" in English language teaching and learning is now more tempered with an understanding of the specific dynamics of the rich and challenging world that teachers negotiate everyday in their actions in localised contexts. Nevertheless, I am now more certain of how I present my own voice into that world to be seen and heard as another of the competing possible influences in the lives of teachers. Such insights are the benefits of a life history research study of the kind that I have described. Other readers would have to choose what inspires them after listening attentively to what the stories have to offer them.

NOTES

[1] It should be noted that the students who were involved in the study were both first and second language speakers of English and were largely from the so-called "Indian" and "African" race group.

REFERENCES

Carr, W., & Kemmis, S. (1986). *Becoming critical*. London: Falmer Press.
Connelly, F. M., & Clandinin, D. J. (1990). Stories of experience and narrative inquiry. *Educational Researcher, 19*(5), 2–14.
Elliot, J. (1985). Educational action research. In J. Nisbet & S. Nisbet (Eds.) *Research policy and practice*. World Year Book of Education.
Freeman, D. (1996). The "unstudied problem": Research on teacher learning in language teaching. In D. Freeman & J. Richards (Eds.), *Teacher learning in language teaching*. Cambridge: Cambridge University Press.
Freeman, D., & Richards, J. (Eds.). (1996). *Teacher learning in language teaching*. Cambridge: Cambridge University Press.
Gough, N. (1998). Narrative and educational inquiry. In J. Mousley, N. Gough, M. Robinson, & D. Colquhoun (Eds.), *Horizons, images and experiences: The research stories collection*. Geelong: Deakin University.
Harris, B., & Furlong, L.D. (1997, March). *Using autobiography to teach teachers: A resource for teacher educators*. Paper presented at American Educational Research Association (AERA) annual meeting, Chicago, Illinois.
Kennedy, M. (1991). *An agenda for research on teacher learning*. National Center for Research on Teacher Learning Special Report.
MacIntyre, A. (1984). *After virtue*. Notre Dame, IN: University of Notre Dame Press.
Melnick, C. (1997, March). *Autobiography: Discovering self in a teacher education program*. Paper presented at American Educational Research Association (AERA) annual meeting, Chicago, Illinois.
Miles, M., & Huberman, A. M. (1994). *Qualitative data analysis* (2nd ed.). Thousand Oaks, CA: Sage.
Reddy, V. (2000). *Lifehistories of black South African scientists: Academic success in an unequal society*. D.Education Thesis. Durban: University of KwaZulu-Natal.
Samuel, M. (1998). *Words, lives and music: On becoming a teacher of English*. D.Education Thesis. Durban: University of KwaZulu-Natal.
Samuel, M. (1999). Exploring voice in educational research. *Perspectives in Education, 18*(2).
Schon, D. (1987). *Educating the reflective practitioner*. San Franscisco: Jossey Bass.
Strauss, A. (1987). *Qualitative analysis for social scientists*. New York: Cambridge University Press.

HARSHA KATHARD

2. PERSONAL TRUTH MAKING: A CAUTIOUS CELEBRATION

In this chapter I draw attention to the researcher's responsibilities and ethical dilemmas in the life history research process by reflecting on a study of self-identity formations of People Who Stutter. I begin with a rationale for appropriating life history research into the Speech-Language Pathology profession (henceforth referred to as "the profession") as a means of challenging and expanding the dominant canon of research practice within the profession and signalling alternative ways of knowing. While maintaining a celebratory agenda, I argue for researchers to be vigilant of their ethical responsibilities, particularly their non-innocence in the research enterprise. I raise issues that troubled me during the research, alluding to my attempts at resolving them. However, my intention is not to offer resolutions but rather to invite debate around three critical issues:

- The obligations of the researcher using a narrative methodology with people who have been traditionally constructed as having communication disorders
- The possibilities and pitfalls of creating new knowledge within a Bakthinian frame
- The problematic nature of crafting, representing and analysing personal truths.

CELEBRATING LIFE HISTORY RESEARCH: WORKING AGAINST THE GRAIN?

Life history research is interested in exploring personal truths. The need to engage with personal truths is well known in many disciplinary fields such as education, sociology and psychology (Cole & Knowles, 2001). However, when life history methodology is newly appropriated into a profession, the onus is on the researcher to clarify issues about the relevance of the methodology and the kind of knowledge it has the potential to generate. My study (Kathard, 2003) explored self-identity formations of People Who Stutter (PWS) using a life history methodology. The participants' life experiences of stuttering, a communication impairment affecting speech fluency, were explored with seven adult participants through a process of prolonged engagement. First, let me provide a rationale for engaging with the methodology.

The impetus for my inquiry arose from my dissatisfaction around the dearth of knowledge around the personal, experiential dimensions of stuttering in formalised

R. Dhunpath and M. Samuel (eds.), Life History Research: Epistemology, Methodology and Representation, 19–37

research. This knowledge gap can be explained by critiquing the profession's historical location. The profession of Speech-Language Pathology was established in the 1920s and over time constructed its identity as *scientific* by developing an alliance with Medicine and Linguistics, appropriating their *methods of science*. As a consequence, the majority of research on stuttering has been generated within a positivist frame as it simultaneously excluded the personal dimensions associated with the discipline. Such reductionist knowledge is problematic in a discipline that offers personal interventions involving real people and complex lives. Silverman (2001, p. 4) explains:

> The Method of Science with all its assumptions about reality from a human perspective including the need for objectivity of the so-called observer, linearity of experience and the uses of inferential and descriptive statistical analyses to interpret observations simply can not, at this point in space-time, generate information completely useful to modify behaviours of multitasking, complexly functioning human beings. Personal, more than impersonal, knowledge is required.

The positivist science combined with the influence of the medical model has resulted in negative stereotyping of PWS by speech-language therapists. As a consequence of their professional knowledge base, therapists' negative attitudes are strong and resistant to change (Snyder, 2001). Restrictive professional knowledge has constrained clinical interventions because it has typically promoted symptom reduction (be more fluent) with intention to fix the deficit without sufficient attention to issues of people living with stuttering in their complex life-worlds. I argue that People Who Stutter have been studied as objects and subjects, and have been constructed as subaltern. However, when clinicians who have recognised the limitations of traditional knowledge are interested in the disorder rather than the person living with it, they have shifted their practices towards narratively-based therapeutic methodologies (DiLollo, Manning, & Neimeyer, 2002). When our interventions demand engagement with personal, outside-of-a-deficit frame dimensions, it seems logical and important to create a different knowledge. In seeking new understandings, I was instinctively inspired by life history methodology. It had potential to produce a fundamentally different knowledge by admitting the personal and engaging a discourse of possibility.

As a first step, however, let us consider who is "subaltern". According to Spivak (1988), it is not just a sophisticated word for oppressed, Other, or for someone who is not getting a piece of the pie. It refers to people whose voices have been sectioned out of the capitalist bourgeois narrative, or – in post-colonial terms – everything that has limited access to cultural imperialism is subaltern. Given the dominant research tradition and its courtship with the larger colonial narrative, Pillay (2003) described the profession's use of a research science as "curiously coincidental" to the project of colonialism, a period within which its research was birthed and thrived. He cogently argued that both empirical, positivist research and empire are aimed at dominating, which includes creating knowledge about Other's lives. Continuing this train of thought, I argue that PWS have been constituted as subaltern – created as "Other" in the research domain as they have been constructed as voiceless objects of study. Their active participation in research processes cannot be described as equitable.

NARRATIVE METHODOLOGY AND THE RESEARCHERS' OBLIGATIONS

What are the obligations of the researcher engaging with participants who have been constructed as subaltern? What was my obligation? The question raised by Spivak, "Can the subaltern speak?" is fitting here. Can the subaltern speak? Yes. The people on the margins (poor, black, women, children, disabled) and PWS, can speak and have spoken, outside of the research domain. They have stories to tell (St. Louis, 2001) but the mechanisms for acknowledging their voices do not exist in the dominant research tradition. PWS can speak and do speak. They speak *with a stutter*. Some may have great difficulty with the "fluency" of speech but are able to communicate. The problem is that they have had *limited ear* within the research arena. There has been little listening and dialogue to develop communication and meaning and knowledge of the worlds of PWS. Engaging in the dialogue does not mean that the researcher speaks for the participants or offers participants a voice. Spivak (1988) is adamant that no researcher who works in the interests of her participants speaks on behalf of them or gives them voice. I concur with this view. However, it raised critical questions about my positionality as researcher: Was I an activist trying to produce different knowledge? A leftist liberal? Was I was giving voice, giving ear or perhaps taking voice?

In the midst of such a quandary, Spivak's (1988) advice is useful again. She suggests that the researcher should recognise that his/her privilege is also a kind of insularity that cuts off privilege from certain kinds of other knowledge. One should therefore strive to recognise these limitations and overcome them, not as a magnanimous gesture of inclusion, but to allow new knowledges to emerge. The way to do this is to work critically through one's own beliefs, prejudices and assumptions to understand how they arose and became naturalised. At a practical level, it meant interrogating who I was, who I am, where my own knowledge base comes from, what my concerns are and how they have impacted on the research process. In this way, the researcher undergoes an obligatory process of self-discovery (Plummer, 2001), as he/she interrogates himself/herself as the instrument of enquiry. The process of self-discovery was no easy path for me and I share some examples of how I began to understand myself as complex, multifaceted, contradictory.

OBLIGATORY SELF-DISCOVERY

Professional Baggage...

In confronting my professional baggage, I was terrified of committing symbolic violence (Bourdieu, 1999) by becoming unconsciously dominant during the research process by the very words I chose and issues I emphasised. My frame of reference had been shaped historically by the medical model and there remained the constant threat that it would continue to be the dominant frame, channelling me to do exactly the opposite of what I intended: I could recreate the professional story and become oppressive in the very knowledge I produced. I had blindspots of which I was unaware, and therefore engaged fellow researchers to review how the interview was unfolding by listening to the audiotape and critique of transcripts, how I was enhancing and limiting the interview. For example, there was critique about the words I chose, the issues I expanded on, and the issues I left unattended. This was a challenge to my mindset – it was not about interview techniques. I was made aware that I probed aspects because I wanted to know more about a particular issue which was not important to the participant. For example, I asked about therapy experience in detail when it was raised only as a minor issue in the life of the participant. I learned that it was the participant's story I had to value it as it was.

Living on the Margins

At another level, I also understood myself as an individual who could identify with the life experiences of PWS who have traditionally been constructed as being on the margins. My sense of being on the margins came from different sources. My life experience has been shaped by some degree of "voicelessness" growing up as a diasporic Indian female in a segregated apartheid South Africa. My sense of inferiority in a world aspiring to be White and West cannot be sectioned out of my existence. Added to this dynamic was my professionalisation which could be described as a cultural kidnapping through which I uncritically imbibed the practices of a profession. As a professional, I felt a "voicelessness" and an uneasy tension. I was a ventriloquist practicing the rituals of a different culture. Therefore, being on the margins was a part of my experience. Through these experiences I came to understand that there was a different story to be told, contrary to the authoritative, public story.

Privilege

However, I have also lived in a world of relative privilege as an English-speaking, university-educated, fair-skinned, middle-class professional accustomed to good food, restaurants, holidays and nice cars. I was introduced to the world of books almost before I was born and above all I possess "researchers' privilege" – which carries a power and authority of its own in an unequal world that is knowledge-driven.

NEGOTIATING COMMUNICATION: PITFALLS AND POSSIBLITIES

How can you get someone who has a communication disorder to share a story? (Ask Stephen Hawkins, Bauby, Sue Gilpin, Chris Ireland, People Who Stutter, deaf people). This is a question I have frequently been asked. Was it possible that I would further threaten the participant by inviting him to be part of a process that privileges (verbal) communication as a means of meaning-making? It almost seemed an anomaly – a contradiction – trying to understand stories of people who have communication problems. Will the end of understanding personal truth be realised? The data was being produced narratively with people who repeat words, struggle, have blocks. While Samuel in Chapter One has pointed to the multiple and innovative ways in which data can be produced in a life history study, I want to attend to the narrative interview because it stands as the primary method of data in a life history study (Plummer, 2001).

I reiterate. People with impairments can and do communicate stories. People who stutter can tell stories and do tell stories. As a clinician, I have heard many stories from PWS in various settings. Creating meaningful communication is the first and fundamental step in restoring humanity, something we have not been successful in doing in the speech and language research arena because we have foregrounded the deficits of our "objects" of enquiry, highlighting what they cannot do (Kathard, 2001). What does it mean to create a context for meaningful communication?

The potentially disruptive influences of the stutter at the communicative interface were real for me. How would this disruption influence the quality of data being produced? What if the participant had difficulty speaking or I listening? What would I do in the moments of the long blocks and struggles and silences? Was there a story in the silences? There are great variations in the communicative styles of PWS. Therefore, it seemed important to negotiate with participants in an open and honest manner how communication could be enhanced, encouraging me to take an exploratory-learning stance in the research process. I discussed with participants how communication between us could be enhanced: What helped me, what helped them, what did not help. Participants offered different suggestions, each inventing guidelines to enhance communication. Our suggestions were not uniform or generalisable but could be described as specific to each interaction. Some suggestions included:

Don't stare at me when I stutter
Where do I look?
Don't complete the sentence for me
I will wait till you are done
Help me by filling a word in, if necessary
Write down a word if it gets too difficult
Ask for repetition or clarification
We will stop when we are tired

The challenge was to listen past the stutter – with the stutter – to the story. Given my background as a speech therapist socialised into the habit of counting and analysing the stutter, I soon realised the fruitlessness of the exercise. It did not help me to listen to the story. I had to engage with the meaning of the communication, listen carefully, and stay with the story. When I did not understand,

I asked for help. I paraphrased, asked for clarification, and used the available interview techniques (Rubin & Rubin, 2005) to maximise the communication. It took practice but gradually I was able to shift emphasis from the stutter to listen to the story.

However, I have only problematised one dimension of communication, that of fluency and stuttering. Communication is far more complex than mere fluency of words. People in general have wide-ranging communicative styles and strategies. My own style is fairly formal, perhaps too clinical and sanitised with no expletives or vulgarities compared to my colleague who cannot refrain from sexualised, lewd talk as part of his flavourful, communicative style. Is it possible that I, as researcher, could further alienate participants through my own idiosyncratic communicative style, "otherising" them? These dilemmas remain unresolved.

While the technicalities of communication can be attended to, the context of personal truth-telling relies on the creation of a trusting and honest interpersonal environment. If the participant doubts the researcher, it is unlikely that truths will be told. It is unsurprising that biographical researchers aspire to being sensitive, ethical, honest and sincere. However, always lurking in my mind was a more sinister issue. There is a different context that forces truth, another extreme. What of torture? It is well known that the powerful agents of wars, the Rumsfelds of the world, torture prisoners to extract truths. Ethically, researchers are obliged to do no harm. However, the very process of storytelling can be akin to torture, although masked by the congeniality of the process. I often felt that there were difficult spaces I disrupted, generating pain by going back to moments of terror. I felt like an intruder, somewhat impure and uncomfortable about how I probed their personal lives. While I had arranged for additional help and counselling, my concern was about the personal costs incurred by participants for telling truths. While storytelling in the research process can have a therapeutic effect, it also has potential to be destructive, and this cannot and should not be ignored by researchers who pronounce their practices to be ethical.

However, enhancing communication means that we also admit the many innovative strategies to share the personal story. Samuel, in Chapter One, describes multiple strategies such as the use of collages, visual data and journals and diaries. I add to this bouquet drama, poetry and mime. One participant in my study was a dramatist. On occasion, he would tell his story through drama. He would act out scenes he experienced in a classroom and through this presented what it was like to be publicly "outed" as disabled. He explained through miming what it meant to be silent, how he prayed to ancestors. He broke out into poetry and song where appropriate. Another participant told of his experiences about public speaking and then brought in a video-recording of the event to help tell his story. Participants communicate in ways in which they feel comfortable. My strategy was to invite communication in multiple ways, each encouraging a unique communicative style.

With these issues weighing heavily, I consider the issues of the interview as an interpretive act.

INTER-VIEWING

The intention of the interview is not just to hear participants' words, but to interpret meaning (verbal and non-verbal) to understand life stories. In this respect, active interviewing is an interpretative act. To enhance the sensitivity of this interpretive act, three suggestions made by Anderson and Jack (1991) and Frank (2000) were particularly useful in listening to the "bigger story". Firstly, it was necessary to listen to the participant's *moral* language. When participants said, "I feel embarrassed, I feel like a failure, I work against the odds," they were introducing a moral element into the discourse. These moral self-evaluative comments in turn provided an opportunity for me to explore the relationships between self-concept and cultural norms and general expectations of how society expects one to behave (Anderson & Jack, 1991). Listening to moral imperatives of what constitutes "good" and "bad" in context, and the choices participants make in their life worlds, allows the space to honour their individuality. As a researcher I felt that it was important to preserve and foster this freedom because it allowed me to understand how participants came to value, devalue and construct their experiences through their own stories.

Secondly, it was necessary to interpret the participant's meta-statements. These are the places where the participant stops and reflects on what was said. I became sensitive to the participant's analysis of the discrepancy between what should be done and what they did, or between what they thought was correct and what was society's expectation. I gained insights into how participants can struggle with dominant frames of reference that construct them as people with pathology and their challenge or submissions to them. These conversations created the space for participants to construct and share their own frames to construct their identities rather than be restricted by public validation frameworks.

Thirdly, it was important to listen to the logic of the narrative with the intention of noting themes, internal consistencies and contradictions. For example, those who said they were living successfully with stuttering told stories that showed how they reached this point. However, I was also aware that because there were dominant and competing discourses, contradictions in the story were not a bad thing. Contradictions did not lead me to doubt participants but rather offered opportunities to explore the nature of such contradictions. This allowed me the opportunity to appreciate the difficult and complex spaces participants lived in and the choices they made. In this way the intersections between personal and social became more visible to me. The stories were not neat, coherent narratives and required that I probe various aspects with the intention of establishing coherence by linking different parts of our conversation.

While I attended to these issues, there seemed to be a far more critical shift in listening to the story – letting myself into the meaning-making process. Despite my great affinity for life history methodology, I still carried the baggage of the "objective" research scientist – the challenge was to engage with the process rather than remain an anonymous outsider.

Letting Myself in – Emotive Knowing

Feminist methodologies (Anderson & Jack, 1991; Fine, 1998; Josselson, 1995) promoting empathetic meaning-making was useful in the research process. I use two constructs, "sensing" and "connecting", to explain how I approached the *refined nature of the interpretative process*. Sensing is an interpretative practice that does not stop at listening but involves sensitivity to a combination of all sensory input. This might be regarded as an intuitive, extrasensory stance to interpreting conversations. My task was not just to listen to what participants were saying, but to be attentive to what they were not saying and, more importantly, to decipher what all of this meant. The tone of voice, emotions, silences, gestures, body language and words are all instructive, as sensing becomes a core aspect of the interpretative process. As I actively constructed meaning with participants, I fed the "sense", the "intuitive-emotive-knowing" back into the research conversation for further discussion. Connecting with my participants during the process was crucial to obtain deeper insights into their stories. But to do this I first had to confront my own positionality. How was I doing this? On what basis? Did I want to negotiate this interaction on the basis of the theory that was floating in my head? Which theory – social theory which was beginning to inform my practice or speech pathology theory which defined the professional domain I was practicing in? I could not pretend to be a-theoretical. I felt I needed to use all of my resources to "connect" with the participant's experience.

There was no simple way to resolve these dilemmas that continued to influence the interpretation process. I attempted to connect with their experience through my own multiple subjectivities. If I was intending an inter-subjective understanding, then I had to "let myself in". If I expected participants to engage with my interpretation of their stories, it was important to shift away from being an objective outsider/spectator to one where I could stand "with" participants to foster an empathetic relationship. A useful strategy to "connect" was using a strategy of "imagining from multiple positions" (Josselson, 1995). As a researcher, I could occupy a variety of positions including female, mother, daughter, wife, university student and advocate, not just the singular position as clinical practitioner or educator. Peshkin (1988, 2001) recommends using a well-informed subjectivity to reveal the multiple personas of the researcher. My different subjectivities enabled me to admit a range of interests and beliefs as I engaged with my participants. In a similar fashion, the multiple subjectivities of participants also find space creating the personal story as a rich weave of multiplicity.

Fine (1998) described this relational stance as "Working-in-Hyphens". She suggested that when working with participants we are always in multiple and improvised relationships in an effort to *improve the quality of data*. Working-in-hyphens means:

> ...creating occasions for researchers and informants to discuss what is, and what is not, 'happening between', within the negotiated relations of whose story is being told, why, with what interpretation, and whose story is being shadowed, why, for whom and with what consequence.

It is through this recognition of the interplay of the various parts that a story can be written and the researcher is in a position to "imagine the real" (Josselson, 1995, p. 42). Josselson (1995) is emphatic that we listen to all dimensions of the very personal, moral and social to do justice to the "whole" person in a way which embraces the essential message of a hermeneutic research stance, in which "to be human is to mean".

CREATING NEW TRUTHS? LEARNING FROM BAKHTIN

The research emerging from the speech and pathology discipline has cast PWS with a passive, deficit discourse of suffering. The challenge for me, as a researcher, was to create a conversation outside of this frame, to create alternative conversations and self-identities. I draw on the work of Bakhtin (1981, 1984, p. 287) who has theorised the potential for discovery through dialogue:

> I cannot manage without another, I cannot become myself without another; I must find myself in another by finding another in myself.

Bakhtin asserts that stories, as a means of accessing subjective experience, are never "just there" and "ready-made", but are constructed via dialogic processes through which the researcher and participant create meaning. The construction is therefore *inter-subjective*. Against this background, it was plausible to assume that the researcher and participant co-create and shape the identities of each other in a fluid way. The dialogic process insists on mutual inter-subjectivity created moment-by-moment in a non-systematic, fluid way within a climate that is necessarily *non-judgemental and open to possibilities* for exploration, unconstrained by hierarchies. He presents communicating as key to the process of human becoming, of self-identity creation: "To *be* means to *communicate*" (1984, p. 287). Human utterances are always in relation and open to possibility. Such interaction goes beyond give-and-take, story-listening and storytelling, to a mutual interaction in which the speaker, utterance and hearer are in unfixed relations to each other. Bakhtin (1984) also emphasises that because communication/interactive possibilities occur at many levels, a good story need not include words. The "languaging" of experience must go beyond words to include the paralinguistic communication that creates meaning.

Of great relevance is Bakhtin's description of the dialogic relationship which is mutually-educative, and while it assists with discovery, it also *activates potentials – for researcher and participant*. Because nothing in the interaction remains fixed, unchallenged, or is without reconsideration, there is always a space for creating new potential and possibility. It has the potential to create *new selves*.

> An independent, active, responsible discourse is *the* fundamental indicator of an ethical, legal and political human being Bakhtin (1981, p. 349).

As a researcher schooled within a research tradition that emphasised prediction and control, I found creating open-ended dialogues difficult initially. I had to become an explorer and learner and not a director. I had to negotiate new possibilities and embrace uncertainty. The story often ran in directions that were never anticipated, creating new understandings, sometimes beyond my scope and experience as researcher. I began to flounder because I did not understand the story – some participants had well-developed philosophical viewpoints which I could not connect with. As an example, let me allude to one participant's discourse on spirituality: I became a learner and asked participants to educate me about their lives, points of view and philosophies. I was mindful that researchers are people with restricted knowledge in limited domains. I knew I had potential to misinterpret personal truths. My strategy to let the story run, embrace uncertainty and willingness to be educated proved useful. It uncovered some of my blindspots and allowed me to see new identities (my own and that of the participants). I read new texts, watched TV programmes, read stories, biographies, and indulged in self-analysis and analysed conversations around me to enhance self-discovery as a precondition for the discovery of my participants.

RE-PRESENTING PERSONAL TRUTHS

The task of representing personal truths is challenging, requiring sensitive and delicate balances. In representing the data, the rich production of stories as biographies of each participant was constructed as an iterative process and formed the first level of analysis. The data analysis process was multi-layered, dynamic and iterative. Given the complexity of the data, I chose narrative analysis (Polkinghorne, 1995) as the first level of analysis. The choice of narrative analysis and story as a representation device requires the researcher to address many issues (Reddy, 2000) about the purpose of the story, theoretical location, textual representation and language, truth-value, the intended audience, voice, selections, style and artistic devices in constructing the story. A discussion of these issues follows. This process was a novel one for me and the part of the project I found both interesting and destabilising.

The purpose of the story, a biography, is to illuminate individual experiences of stuttering in their lifeworld by understanding how they form their identities and negotiate stuttering over time. The research story was therefore constructed with intent to answer the critical questions. As such, it is analytic-descriptive in nature because it addresses critical questions whilst providing the descriptive details of each participant in context. The research stories were structured chronologically to explain a particular endpoint in each biography. The connections with the research story were not necessarily linear but combinations and accumulations of events, responses and actions that explain a particular end. The product was reflective of a temporal ordering in which each part is given meaning via its reciprocal relationship with other parts, before and after, and to the whole. The plot functions to compose events into a story (Polkinghorne, 1995) by:
- delimiting the temporal range which marks the beginning and end of the story;
- providing criteria for the selection of events/issues to be included;
- providing temporal ordering and unfolding of events leading to a conclusion and;
- clarifying the meaning events have as contributors to the story.

In producing the narrative, the researcher therefore draws on her *theoretical influences* to make sense of responses and actions. The process required extensive engagement with the interview data and was influenced by the theoretical stances of the researcher. The research story, while resisting any specific theoretical location, had elements of varied influences: Foucault (power), Bauman (sociology), Spivak (postcolonial), Roy (activist), Dr. Phil (psychology). The story had a life history orientation with social, personal and temporal lenses actively appropriated in the construction. It was also theoretically slanted to reveal the intersections between the *personal and sociological dimensions* of experience in illuminating the issues of stuttering in society. I had an interest in an *active* story about living with stuttering with an *ethical* obligation to illuminate what participants thought was important to them and explaining why they chose to act in particular ways.

An immediate concern in writing a research story is the question of *truth-value* when translating data into the research story. I was interested in the personal truths of participants. However, these truths about the individual's experience are manufactured within the context of the dialogic interview. Some narrative researchers therefore see their roles as similar to artists who reconstruct a situation to convey something about it (Lawrence-Lightfoot & Hoffman-Davis, 1997). Other researchers contest the issue or refer to truth-value by using terms such as believability (Lawrence-Lightfoot & Hoffman-Davis, 1997), credibility and validity (Polkinghorne, 1995; 2007), or fidelity (Blumfield-Jones, 1995). In what remains a debatable issue, I considered the plausibility of the plot and the issue of coherence in the story as two ways to reflect on truth-value. Firstly, the plot is constructed after the researcher has been immersed in the data and it is the *explanatory potential* of the plot I considered to be a means of gauging truth-value. Secondly, I was guided strongly by the fidelity of the plot with regard to what the experience was like for the teller of the tale, that is, as experience in the context of a particular life, showing (a degree) of faithfulness to the teller.

Another challenge is the responsibility of weaving the personal story against a complex set of *social issues* (Goodson, 1995). It is here that the issue of truth and fidelity becomes more complex because the researcher has the unenviable task of locating a personal narrative within a social context and while doing so, runs the risk of losing the original teller's perspective. The task of bringing together both the individual story and social context is the challenge of writing an interpretive story (Goodson, 1995). In all research stories there was a deliberate effort (on my part) to locate participants within their contexts. I did this by gaining insights into the nature of contexts during the interviews and assembling them as a plausible plot. I highlighted the time period in which the story unfolded, the place/s in which participants spent much of their time and the significant sociopolitical events, social discourses, value systems, and participants' interpretation of how these influenced them at a personal level. Although participants included the social context in their stories, they did not necessarily do so in an overt, interpretive or political manner. For example, they might have talked about how women were treated but did not necessarily interpret these issues in the same (political) way I did. This created an uneasy tension because of competing or one-sided interpretations. The resolutions were difficult, thus throwing into doubt the credibility of the representation which I address later.

The *coherence* of a story is an important consideration, especially for life history researchers who have the task to bring together a coherent story spread through time (Mishler, 1999; Plummer, 2001). The traditional notion of a coherent story as a single, neat, unfolding trajectory in which the actor acts consistently, has been challenged within poststructural theory. I agree with Mishler (1999) that the interpretation of coherence in a research story should be revised to admit multiplicities and non-linearity. It is this story which is more likely to be coherent within social and personal realities that are changing. A complicated coherence? Mishler explains that traditional notions of coherence have been challenged in text-centred linguistic domains by linguists, as they have moved beyond the structural features of discourse analysis. The researcher must have an "intuitive" understanding in reviewing different parts of the text, to create coherence from a seeming randomness. However, coherence cannot be limited to linguistic forms and meaning but that it should be understood within a broader context of social and cultural meanings evident in discourse. My interpretation of Mishler's (1999) stance is that "coherence" should bring together disparate, multiple, shifting, contradictory and seemingly random elements of a story to create a "complicated" or "fractured" coherence within a social frame. This stance overlaps with Blumfeld-Jones' (1995) understanding of fidelity. The story should be coherent within an approximate of the "complex" lifelikeness establishing not truth but verisimilitude, the appearance of being true.

Stories are written using *language as medium* which offers opportunities for representation but which can be simultaneously constraining. The issues of textual representation have been debated in the domain of postmodern research (Abma, 2002; Lather, 1991; Rhodes, 2000). Lather (1991) uses Derrida's deconstructive theory and explains that language cannot claim to "mirror reality". The inner life of an individual is filtered through the glaze of language, signs and processes of signification. We are born into a world where language is available and we appropriate such language to construct meaning. Therefore, language in itself is not neutral but is a social vehicle for creating particular realities. The language used by participants was an important consideration in story construction because participants have a particular set of discourses available to them by virtue of living in a particular social world. The stories therefore do not mirror lives but create realities. Thus, in engaging with data, it was important to attend to the language the participant uses to get an impression of how the story links to the social world and make decisions about the language she uses to construct the research story.

However, language can also be constraining because it may not be able to adequately address some dimensions of human emotion such as suffering, which resists "knowing". In the research contexts, participants say: "I don't know how to explain this" or, "Words fail," which are indications that language is also constraining. Frank (2001) argues that "knowing" is a positivist phenomenon and challenges the possibility that we will "know" the personal story. Instead, he takes a hermeneutic stance and suggests that researchers should seek to show understandings.

The research story is *interpretive* in that it is not just a verbatim recording of words but rather a documentation of the meaning created through our multi-faceted conversations. The "languaging" of the story includes an interpretation of textual and non-textual cues in meaning-making. In the first version of the stories I wrote in the first-person, I did not attend sufficiently to the participant's exact words and style. Participants tended to agree with the interpretation but were somewhat confused about the voice; it was their story but not as they would speak it or write it. I rewrote their stories relying closely on their words and style of speaking but keeping the interpretative element. In this way it sounded like them, speaking in their style and words. I was guided by Fairclough's (1989) critical discourse analysis framework as a means of heightening my awareness of "how" participants speak, thereby integrating a presentational analysis with a representational analysis.

One of the key issues in writing narratives is about which *voice* it is to be written in. The options include first-person, and third-person narrator, with the researcher as the writer and the participant the storyteller. I explored two voices (first and third person) for the purposes of representation and discovered that they both have value and limitations. My initial draft during the pilot phase was written in the third-person, supported by direct quotes from the participant. I found this voice useful because the researcher's voice is obvious as he/she analyses the story (Samuel, 1998). However, with the analytical story, the impact of the participant's voice is lost. I then experimented with writing the story in the first-person account that accommodated the descriptive and analytical elements. This voice seemed more "authentic" because the participant's words and style could be represented, making the research story more life-like. With this choice, however, the analytic voice of the researcher can be muted. However, I felt that the research story should remain close to the voice of the participant, especially because I had an interest in issues of self-identity formation in this study. It also seemed easier to read the story about self-identity formations when narrated in the first person.

The stories were then written by considering what was said: the content and how it was said, thereby combining presentational and representational elements. In the interview, participants talked about many things and it was necessary to select events and issues for inclusion in the research story. These selections were informed by what participants emphasised during the interviews. However, to construct the research story, I re-read each transcript many times over and carefully reviewed and revised the selections with the intention of responding to the critical questions. In this regard I actively selected aspects of the interview to create a research story with a plausible and coherent plot with the intention of answering the critical questions. Essentially, I was the storywriter.

A story is meant to be interesting and should engage the reader. What of artistic techniques? I felt that artistic techniques would help to illuminate the personal truth-value of a story. Blumfeld-Jones (1995) suggests that artistic representations can enhance the fidelity of the research story. I was enthused by the creative and artistic suggestion made by Barone (1997) and the motivations provided by Richardson (1992) and Denzin (2000). They argued for interesting ways in which researchers can stage texts to provide interpretation and provoke discussion. I felt the "giddiness" Barone (2001) talks about when researchers are released from methodological straightjackets. I wanted the stories to be alive in the interests of enhancing scholastic potential (Abma, 2002) and therefore used common literary devices such as similes, metaphors, hyperbole, rhetorical questions, repetition, irony and understatement, purposely writing in the present tense.

Barone (2001) extended this interest in advocating the use of *fictional* techniques based on Maxine Greene's persuasive stance on how imaginative literature can serve us well in understanding our lives. He argued that if all stories, including research stories, are fashioned by human beings, then they are all, to differing extents, fictional. He coined the word *factional* to blur the boundaries between fiction and fact. While the empirical story, the "inside" story, provides the "fidelity" requirement, or an honest version of the participant's experience, there is the external story which can be fictional in that it contains a mixture of real and unreal (imagined) events. This is possible because stories are active creations between participants. There are often incomplete scenes that the listener "fills in by imagining" or makes sense of, based on her own experience. Could it have happened like this? When such dialogue is invented it is *critical* that it is done with the intention of serving a legitimate research purpose. The text should serve the end of generating conversation as good stories should invest in ambiguity and should not conclude.

Stimulated by Barone's suggestions, I experimented with *fictional techniques* only at points where I felt that their use would enhance the significance of what was being said. For example, if a participant placed repeated emphasis on or spoke emotionally about some issue to convey its sense of importance, then fictional techniques were used to amplify the meaning. For example, techniques used included: re-creations of scenes, making them "full-blooded" through the use of imagery and choosing words which helped to convey the emotionality and ladenness of meaning. At some points there were nuanced elements in the story, or 'throwaway' comments that shaped the story in a significant way. These were also illuminated through the use of fictional techniques by recreating scenes in the story to offer clarity. However, I did not retain the fictional elements when participants felt such techniques did not enhance the meaning of the story or indicated that they were uncomfortable with them. In one instance, the participant insisted that the fictional and interpretive story was a better representation of her story than she could "say in her own words". She therefore felt that her story should be retained using fiction techniques where necessary. Other participants differed.

Against the backdrop of fiction, the issue of *credibility* surfaces. Although the researcher is the writer/author and the participant is the storyteller, the data is jointly constructed between two unique individuals. Therefore, it is sensible and fair to suggest that the participant should also contribute to establishing the credibility of the research story. Participants were invited to review the research story and to influence it so that it was faithful to the meaning generated in the interview process and offered analytic commentary. My sense of panic unfolded as I handed the stories over to participants. It was then that I realised the risks and dangers of writing another's life. I did not know how participants would respond. I was anxious about whether I had understood and represented their experiences in a faithful and sensible way. Writing the story of another is a difficult political process. The contestation about personal truth unravelled when participants provided feedback. By this point, they were not reserved in their commentary and my role in influencing their stories was again challenged. Their comments raised the following issues:

- Some participants felt that telling their story and reading their stories were very different processes. Reading their lives was not a simple process because a whole life experience was summarised in few pages. As a consequence, the interpretative account was a "harder and sharper" account. One participant explained that reading the story was like "going back to the scene of the accident". There was nothing that was untrue but it was vivid and sometimes "difficult to look at". He suggested that some "sharp edges" be revised.
- The use of fictional techniques and other literary devices were received differently. Two participants described it as dramatic but making their story more "real" than less "real". However, they also drew attention to the fact that it did not sound like their voices in some parts, while in other parts it was very close to how the experience unfolded. Five participants suggested that the interpretive story was a close, intuitive account. They recommended that the artistic techniques should be retained because it enhanced the meaning of their stories.
- The review process afforded the opportunity to extend the interview process to generate a more sharpened analytical interview, which produced additional data. I was able to revisit key issues and clarify aspects that needed further discussion. It also provided an opportunity for collaborative participation because participants were actively shaping the story and contributing to analysis and credibility.
- One participant requested that some words be removed although he had used them in the interview. He felt that the written story was more formal than the spoken word. He also queried my deliberate foregrounding of his race and socio-economic status. I explained that the stories were intertextual and required grounding in a social context. Therefore, issues of race and class had to become apparent in the story. After our discussion, he understood the intention and in recognising the importance, began to elaborate further, providing very useful additional information about the particular time period. Another participant requested that an incident involving his "failing" be removed, because it "spoiled" his story. However, when I explained that it was one of the incidents that shaped his life story, he agreed to leave it in since that this was a research story.

These discussions revealed that the writing process is not an innocent one. It was an occasion for me to reflect on the power of (MY) written word and how dangerous constructing research stories can be. On receiving feedback from participants, I rewrote the stories using a significant proportion of actual spoken words and specific styles of speaking of the participants, attending to their comments and critique. Thereafter, I asked participants to comment on the revised version of the stories. However, despite these attempts, the contestations remained because personal truths are interpretations. It is unlikely that even with the most democratic process there will be complete consensual understanding. Therefore, as researcher, I declared the nature of the disputes between us so that they remain visible to the reader. Despite every intention to understand stories, I could never have claimed to stand in their shoes. I do not think that is possible. My intention was to get as close as possible to understanding their experiences.

I invited participants into the process of data analysis. While participants were generally comfortable with reading their stories (first level analysis), and offered general suggestions, they did not see it as their role to offer an in-depth analysis. Some participants were adamant about being constructed as "more that just PWS" and requested that I carry this idea into analysis. The (theoretical) analysis seemed to be an exercise which (un)comfortably sat within the realm of academics. While it is true that the participant always sits on your shoulder, the analysis at the theoretical/abstract second and third levels is the (dangerous) work of the researcher.

What have I done with the personal truths? Have I been true to my ethical and moral obligations in purporting to create new knowledge? I have constantly questioned: What is the nature of the knowledge I have produced? To what extent has it also created subalternity? Has the knowledge produced further sub-ordination? Who would judge this? Is this beautiful knowledge (ala Lather) dangerous knowledge, troubling knowledge, disrupting knowledge (and if so, who does it disrupt?). Having reached the end of the theorising process, my concern was about how to position myself – as expert? One who knows the story better than the participant who lives with it? Will I (re)create myself as expert professional who claims to know the inside story better than anyone else because she has a set of theoretical constructs to explain it? Is it possible I will have greater humility because I know the limits of my knowing? Is there authority on personal truth making?

These epistemological concerns are crucial because as knowledge workers we occupy potentially powerful positions in a knowledge-driven society. We have the power to transmute private knowledge into public knowledge domain. It could become official, contested, rejected, or marginal. Nevertheless, it remains in the public arena for debate. It is therefore my hope that such knowledge is always open to critique and interpretation in the interests of engendering further knowledge.

CONCLUSION

In this chapter I have illuminated the researcher's dilemmas and ethical responsibilities in the life history research process. Firstly, I have raised the concerns that the researcher must attend to when appropriating life history methodology into a disciplinary field rooted in positivism. Whilst I have deliberated on the issues of "communication impairment or disorder" in a specific way, the importance of engendering good communication as a basis for life history research is clearly apparent. Among the many obligations the researcher has, I have given particular consideration to understanding issues of subalternity, obligatory self-discovery and empathetic communication. Secondly, I have presented the potential and pitfalls inherent in the processes of discovering new knowledge through dialogue within a Bakhtinian philosophy. This philosophy has foregrounded the importance of open-ended dialogue which challenges the researcher to embrace the uncertain nature of the dialogic process. Lastly, I have considered the complex task of representing personal truths and generating analyses. I have highlighted the importance of attending to the multiplicity of issues of voice, style, ethics, credibility, truth value which underpin the processes of representation and analysis of the research story. I have endeavoured to present the truth-making process as political and non-innocent and signal a case for critical reflexivity of the researcher, explored further by Pillay in the next chapter.

While I have raised the issues and potential hazards in arguing for a cautious celebration of life history research, I want to clarify my stance around the need to produce different knowledges in the profession. My sense is that metho-dological risk-taking in producing new knowledge differently is worthwhile. We cannot afford not to proceed safely with tired and questionable factual certainties when we are charged with an obligation to create relevant practices in a complex, political and rapidly changing social world. Our research practice, through the knowledges we produce and methodologies we adopt, must aid this endeavour. Life history is one such methodology but there are many others. As we expand our methodological toolbox in innovative, risky but reflexive ways, I am convinced that our discipline will mature and we will create accountable practices we desperately desire.

REFERENCES

Abma, T. A. (2002). Emerging narrative forms of knowledge representation in health sciences. Two texts in the postmodern contex. *Qualitative Health Research, 12*(1), 5–27.

Anderson, K., & Jack, D. C. (1991). Learning to listen. Interview techniques and analyses. In S. B. Luck & D. Pataki (Eds.), *Women's words. The feminist practice of oral history.* New York: Rutledge.

Bakhtin, M. M. (1981). *The dialogical imagination.* Austin, TX: University of Texas Press.

Bakhtin, M. M. (1984). *Problems of Dostoyevsky's poetics.* Manchester: Manchester University Press.

Barone, T. E. (1997). Among the chosen: A collaborative educational (auto)biography. *Qualitative Inquiry, 3*(2), 222–236.

Barone, T. E. (2001). *Pragmatizing the imaginary: Using life narratives as fiction.* Annual meeting of the American Educational Research Association, Sec 44.28: The Educated Imagination: Fiction and Knowledge.

Bourdieu, P. (Ed.). (1999). *The weight of the world. Social suffering in contemporary society.* London: Polity Press.

Blumfeld-Jones, D. (1995). Fidelity as a criterion for practising and evaluating narrative inquiry. In J. A. Hatch & R. Wisniewski (Eds.), *Life history and narrative.* London: Falmer Press.

Cole, A. L., & Knowles, J. G. (2001). *Lives in context. The art of life history research.* Walnut Creek, CA: Rowman and Littlefield Publishers, Inc.

Denzin, N. K. (2000). Aesthetics and the practices of qualitative inquiry. *Qualitative Inquiry, 6*(2), 256–265.

DiLollo, A., Manning, W., & Neimeyer, R. (2002). A personal construct psychology view of relapse: Indications for a narrative component to stuttering treatment. *Journal of Fluency Disorders, 27*(1), 19–42.

Fairclough, N. (1989). *Language and power.* London: Longman.

Fine, M. (1998). Working the hyphens: Reinventing self and other in qualitative research. In N. K. Denzin & Y. S. Lincoln (Eds.), *The landscape of qualitative research. Theories and issues.* London: Sage Publications.

Frank, A. W. (2000). The standpoint of storyteller. *Qualitative Health Researcher, 10*(3), 354–365.

Frank, A. W. (2001). Can we research suffering. *Qualitative Health Researcher, 11*(3), 353–362.

Goodson, I. F. (1995). The story so far: Personal knowledge and the political. In J. A. Hatch & R. Wisniewski (Eds.), *Life history and narrative.* London: Falmer Press.

Josselson, R. (1995). Imagining the real: Empathy, narrative and the dialogic self. In R. Josselson & A. Lieblich (Eds.), *Interpreting experience. The narrative study of lives* (Vol. 3). London: Sage Publications.

Kathard, H. (2001). Sharing stories: Life history narratives in stuttering research. *International Journal of Language and Communication Disorder, 36*(Special Supplement), 52–57.

Kathard, H. (2003). *Life histories of people who stutter. On becoming someone.* Unpublished Doctoral Dissertation, University of KwaZulu-Natal, KwaZulu-Natal, South Africa.

Lawrence-Lightfoot, S., & Hoffman-Davis, J. (1997). *The art and science of portraiture.* San Francisco: Jossey-Bass.

Lather, P. (1991). *Getting smart. Feminist research and pedagogy with/in the postmodern.* New York: Routledge.

Mishler, E. G. (1999). *Storylines. Craftartists narratives of identity.* London: Harvard University Press.

Peshkin, A. (1988). In search of one of subjectivity - one's own. *Educational Researcher, 17*(1), 17–22.

Peshkin, A. (2001). Angles of vision: Enhancing perception in qualitative research. *Qualitative Inquiry, 7*(2), 238–253.

Pillay, M. (2003). *(Re) Positioning the powerful expert and the sick person: The case of communication pathology.* PhD thesis, University of KwaZulu-Natal, South Africa.

Plummer, K. (2001). *Documents of life. 2. An invitation to critical humanism.* London: Sage Publications.

Polkinghorne, D. E. (1995). Narrative configuration in qualitative analysis. In J. A. Hatch & R. Wisniewski (Eds.), *Life history and narrative.* London: Falmer Press.

Polkinghorne, D. E. (2007). Validity issues in qualitative research. *Qualitative Inquiry, 13,* 471–487.

Reddy, V. (2000). *Life histories of black South African scientists: Academic success in an unequal society.* Unpublished Doctoral Dissertation, University of KwaZulu-Natal, South Africa.

Rhodes, C. (2000). Ghostwriting research: Positioning the researcher in the interview text. *Qualitative Inquiry, 6*(4), 511–525.

Richardson, L. (1992). The consequences of poetic representation: Writing the other. Rewriting the self. In C. Ellis & M. G Flaherty (Eds.), *Investigating subjectivity. Research on lived experience.* London: Sage Publications.

Rubin, H. J., & Rubin, I. (2005). *Qualitative interviewing. The art of hearing data* (2nd ed.). Thousand Oaks, CA: Sage Publications.

Samuel, M. (1998). *Words, lives and music. On becoming a teacher of English.* Unpublished Doctoral Dissertation, University of KwaZulu-Natal, South Africa.

Shiffrin, D. (1996). Narrative as self-portrait: Sociolinguistic constructions of identity. *Language in Society, 25*(2), 167–203.

Silverman, E. (2001). *Consumer alert: Stuttering and gender research.* Paper presented at Fourth International Stuttering Awareness Day conference. Retrieved October 2001, from http://www.mnsu.edu/dept/comradis/isad4/papers/silverman2.html

Snyder, G. J. (2001). Exploratory research in the measurement and modification of attitudes toward stuttering. *Journal of Fluency Disorders, 26*(2), 149–160.

Spivak, G. C. (1988). Can the subaltern speak? In C. Nelson & L. Grossberg (Eds.), *Marxism and the interpretation of culture*. Chicago: University of Illinois Press.

St. Louis, K. O. (2001). *Living with stuttering. Stories, basic resources and hope*. Morgantown, WV: Populore Publishers.

MERSHEN PILLAY

3. RESEARCHERS ENGAGING THEIR PRIVILEGE: EPISTEMOLOGICAL AND METHODOLOGICAL DE-LIBERATIONS

In a world, where we live with our Derrida's, Foucault's, Habermas's, Bakhtin's, and Durkheim's (and where we die with our Bush's, Blair's & Bechtel's); what can I offer from my safe place of actually being alive? What can I say (as part of a small cadre of Researchers[1]) engaged & enraged with words like *epistemology*, *representation* and *ethics*?

WHAT DO I OFFER IN THIS CHAPTER?

Firstly, I take cognisance of, and draw into focus our privilege as Researchers. I situate the commonsense (versus the Academy's uncommonsense) acknowledgement that the Researcher's voice is privileged. Always.

Secondly, in acknowledging Researcher privilege, I push for explicit consideration of Researchers' voices in their researches. In this first section (the 'epistemological' part) of my chapter, I pore over ways in which we engage *privilege as Liberation*. Of how critically-oriented epistemologies enForce and reinForce the eMANcipation[2] of our intellect into our researches. In doing so, I highlight my dissatisfaction with how we douche the inclusion of intellect by excluding and/or minimising our intellect as a *biological* operation. In engaging this idea, I present *privilege by Deliberation* where I deliberate ways (methodological considerations) in which we may include our(biological⇔social⇔ cultural⇔political)selves via our researches. Finally, I re-consider the dubious nature of epistemologies that promote liberation. I state the case for Researchers to think about using their *privilege for de-Liberation*.

For now, I foreground the sagacity behind my focus on Researchers' privilege. Is such a focus necessary? Maybe not. For me, however, I am tired of reading about how Africans run faster[3] or are more corrupt[4] than non-Africans. I need to listen to more than the crude banality of CNN's newsreaders waxing lyrical about Democracies delivering democracy to decimated Muslim lives, or of the magnanimity of USAID to Africa [while concurrently bankrolling and/or arming despots' wars]. These things remind me that those prosaic (and privileged) amongst us have pusillanimous interests. That these interests dominate our print, electronic, and audio-visual media. That such knowledge actively keeps us stupid. And (unfortunately) such knowledge is used to form friends, enemies, lovers, and guardians. I join others in our world who say: "There's an alternative". South

R. Dhunpath and M. Samuel (eds.), Life History Research: Epistemology, Methodology and Representation, 39–65

Africans use the word *themba* for this expression. And as I refer to themba I am reminded that in the Nguni languages, themba is *also* used to mean hope (Alexander, 2001). So, what alternative, what hope do I offer here? I remind us of why we are called clever people. Of why we are special people. And (importantly) I argue for research that befits our Researcher status as powerful experts. Clever people. Special people. Powerful experts: These are the identity descriptors that I shall refer to in the rest of my paper – and more especially as I discuss how we may extend the way we engage...

...*PRIVILEGE AS LIBERATION*: EPISTEMOLOGICAL CONSIDERATIONS OF OURSELVES

I have referred to this process of *privilege as Liberation* relative to the notion of **I-visibility** (Pillay, 2003b). *I* and *the researcher* are words that plagued me throughout the writing of my postgraduate research dissertations. Could I, should I, say *I* when writing my report? To some, such a question borders on the ridiculous and is definitely within the realm of the sublime. Of course it is *I* that is *the researcher*! However, research writing conventions (like the use of 'the researcher') show our prejudices about not only how we must know, but also how we must (re)present this knowing. This not-new idea[5] has been mooted by social scientists who have argued for the inclusion of the self in the research process. Notably, Van Maanen's (1995) assertion that research *is* authorship, best captures this stream of thought. In synch with such assertions, I share thoughts about my growing realisation that what and how I write is solidly connected to what it means to be *me*.....in a *very* material way. And, here, I make just one, core epistemological point:

(RESEARCHER'S) THINKING (INTELLECT) HAS A BIOLOGICAL NUCLEUS.

Sounds simple, basic (sounds stale, even). Why then, am I asking for the <u>inclusion</u> of Researchers' biological selves in the research process? I have reviewed research trends where our *privilege as Liberation* is promoted – specifically – as liberation of the Researcher's voice into his/her own research. These methodological shifts have occurred in (especially) the social sciences[6], (increasingly in the) medical sciences[7], and (interestingly) within economics, information systems, and such-like[8]. Within these researches is recognition of knowing as a kind of *embodied* practice. While I realise that I have meshed a wide range of perspectives together, it is possible to offer the following comments:

Firstly, I argue that there is an *active* exclusion of the biological processes involved in generating intellectual activity. At this point, I must emphasise that I promote the inclusion (not the absolute foregrounding) of our biological selves in knowledge-making processes. In this way, I do *not* see current researches including the biological self as interpenetrating with our social, cultural, and political Researcher-selves as we engage our privilege as Liberation.

Secondly, however, even when these biological processes (or "the body") are acknowledged there appears to be a disconnection between intellectualism and biological processes. In many ways, Researchers appear far more comfortable locating "embodied" knowings within the domain of our research subjects[9]. It is significant that the same knowing of the usefulness of bodily processes in making knowledge is perhaps denied (lacking, minimised) for most Researchers *themselves*. Indeed, if we are to agree with perspectives that emphasise biological events (= "the body") as annexing historical events (see, e.g., Skultans, 1999), then we ought to explore how our *own* bodies – as Researchers – bear the signatures of our public histories, of how Researchers' subjectivities, bodily processes (emotions, mental associations and the like) have all influenced our knowings, our research stories. Insofar as stories go, one may argue against Barthes' (1977) point that the *ideas* stories contain ought to be devoid of the person, that narratives be divorced from the hysteria of human expression.

In seeking not to sanitise ideas (thinking, intellect, cognition) from the human experience of it, we may trace how intellect has been understood as biological via the work of, for example, Maturana and Varela (1980). In the 1980s they represented cognition as "the realisation of the living". Later on, authors such as Bruner (1986; 1990) have argued that a narrative mode of cognition is the way we articulate our world. He promoted such thinking over paradigmatic cognition as it occurs *vis-à-vis* scientific traditions. Indeed, Maturana and Varela (1992) have eloquently located biology (specifically genetics) as due to an interaction with nature: asserting that thinking, knowledge has a biological base. It is not only a set of knowns that can be isolated. Objectified. Understood as social. Displayed as cultural. Recently (and encouragingly) several Researchers are arguing for a stronger presence of their embodied processes via, for example, the promotion of methodologies like autoethnography and self-reflexivity. These methodologies represent a rising re-Cognition to consider our biological selves (for example, see Orland-Barak, 2002; Day, 2002; Hanarahan, 2003; Etherington, 2004; Ellis, 2004). But when I argue for the inclusion of our biological selves, what *exactly* does this mean? To answer this question, I share my....

...Personal-Professional Realisations

In explaining the inclusion of our biological selves as we engage our privilege as Liberation, I shall trace how my understanding of biology stems from two key sources/realisations, i.e. (1) my identity as an identical twin, and (2) my professional focus on people with communication disorders.

The two-twins: mergren & I. Friends and family in apartheid Indian/Coloured designated group-areas we grew up in (Sydenham, Overport, and Woodview/ Phoenix) sometimes referred to my brother, Mergren, and I as 'the two-twins': A dialectically and conceptually very appropriate description! Why so? Mergren and I had various responses to others' knowings of our knowings. As two people. Separately. And as twins. Together. (Or, as Mergren says, "It's OUR life"). When people meet us, inevitably there is the usual: *do-you-know-what-the-other-is-thinking* question or the *I can't believe how similar you are* judgment. (My mother had stories of people asking if we, as infants, coordinated biological processes like crying, hunger, flatulence and defecation). I/we learned, early on in life, to make the point that we were the "same person" inasmuch as we were not the same people. We developed ways of showing off our sameness: Saying the same things, completing sentences, communicating privately with non-verbal signs/symbols, similar senses of humour, similar laughs, amongst other things. However, we also show off our differences. People who know us know that we passionately defend our *different* perspectives – to the point of what appears to be sibling termination sessions ("It's over. I don't want to see you again!"), followed by us being fearfully in care of each other. This confuses people inasmuch as we realise that this *is* (the only way we know) how to interact. The point is: As identical twins, we know that *knowing* with, and from ourselves (separately, together), is very dependant on the *individual*. Even people who are (according to modern science) genetically (= biologically?) similar, have varying intellects. Had I *not* been a twin, I may have explored how other interesting factors have helped me realise the role of my biology in developing intellect – such as my sexual orientation or gender. Indeed, it may be argued that those who have referenced *something* about their biologies – like people of colour, feminists, gay/lesbians, or people with disabilities[10] – have all overtly referenced the notion of intellect as linked to their biologies. bell hooks (1989), a black, woman, and lesbian author/academic, has argued that the *personal* [read as the biological self, the body in this world] *is the political*: a perspective she has theorised from, and out of her biological/body's experiences of being a colour, a gender, a sexual orientation.

While foregrounding biological ways of knowing, one may extend this argument to include the recognition that peoples' biological-sexual selves provide a useful (currently under-valued) sex-text ([inter][dis]course?). I argue that within such sex-text we may position relationships of all kinds....especially that between the Researcher and her researched. Think about it for a little while. Could our sexual knowings – our sexual engagements, identities/orientations, rituals, and rights – illuminate what we *really* think-feel about relationships? Research ones included? Perhaps, Foucault would more than rhyme & resemble with what we do with our 'participants'. However, to fix on *one* (even an intersection) of biological would be to betray the point I am making, viz.: As twins Mergren and I learnt that our biologies (individually) *and* our interactive (social, cultural, political) development have produced same-different ways of knowing, of being. And what specifically might this mean?

Mergren and I, as same-different intellectual beings, learnt in biologically real terms to make way for thinkings in forms conscious and unconscious (dreams? tacit knowing? gut feelings?). Perhaps I am alluding to our cognitive-perceptual abilities. Such things may refer to our sensory processing abilities: the way our senses of vision, hearing, touch, smell, taste, balance, etc – all contribute to what and how we "know"; our ability to attend and focus, to process, store, and retrieve information. It could include our ability to engage logic and reasoning (either divergently/convergently) amongst other functions. Other biologically dependant aspects include the nature of our "synaptic connections", our perceptual (auditory? visual?) processing neurological capabilities – amongst other things. Additionally, hunches, intuitions, feelings: affective/emotive components are integrally involved in our knowledge-making. All of these things are what I mean when I talk of the biological aspect of knowings. And, of course, I am not drawing on anything new. The biological basis of thinking has long been established in fields such as the neurosciences, psychology, and linguistics, amongst many others. Perhaps what is "new" is that these biological phenomena are largely ignored by Researchers in our own researches.

Consider the following examples for how our-my ways of thinking influence my intellect as a Researcher: Mergren and I acknowledge thinkings that allow us to *just know something*. Intuitions. (Extra?) sensory perceptions. Feeling good/bad about the ideas we have. Engaging feelings – whatever they are – that drive us to have our say. Experiencing satisfaction from doing something about our worries. Connecting with others' thoughts. Making associations (fast ones, slow ones) between his/my, and others' ideas. Working out how we hear words/knowing thoughts before they have been said. *Knowing* when words are not said. Anticipating what thinking will happen next. Understanding our frustrations with practices. Knowing more than our language allows us to say. Saying more than we really know.... It is these things that – as Researchers – we must explore and exploit if we recognise our intellect as a biologically embedded practice. Later, I share how biological processes may be codified into practical research methodologies. For now, I digress toward how I discovered myself as biological via researching my professional subject: people with communication disorders.

Ears, tongues, brains and things: Their Biology. My Biology? As a speech-language therapy and audiology practitioner, I practice a profession focused on speech, language, voice, hearing, and other aspects of communication. Even with the recent focus on preventative practices, we really begin our work from the moment things go wrong: When stutterers begin to stutter. When the brain's language-hemispheres haemorrhage. When vocal chords become cancerous. When babies are born with palates that have holes in them. As a student, I was trained to respect the biological form of people as supreme to developing an understanding of their lives. I disagreed with this focus. Instead, I promoted that understanding communication disorders as mainly biological may be countered. Initially, focusing on Zulu beliefs and perceptions regarding communication and its "disorders", I emphasised that communication (speaking, hearing, etc.) while strongly referenced to biology, may be culturally re-situated (Pillay, 1992). Later, I expanded this idea, theorising and faulting the profession's reliance on an empirical science as enabling an inappropriate biological focus (see Pillay, 1997). More recently, I have argued that patients subjectified relative to a biological metaphor, should be recontextualised as more than *but* including the body, a form of ideological hyper-corporeality. Curiously, in recognising that patients occupied a social, cultural, political and biological "space", I also have come to see my creation as a

Researcher via similar spaces. What began as my rejection of biology (as I knew it), shifted toward recognition of the importance of biology in my intellectual development. So, in attempting to re-position patients' biological realities, I began to re-contextualise, and (paradoxically) not entirely reject this biological metaphor for *myself*. Allow me to explain this further.

When I began my doctoral research[11], I began with great empirical intentions. I intended to gather data via a variety of sources and methods. For example, I designed an analysis of professional texts and policies, discussion and observations with selected practitioners, amongst a range of strategies. As suggested by especially qualitative Researchers[12], I attempted to rigorously analyse data, once transcribed, by scanning, categorising, organising and codifying data (Eisner, 1998). I developed interpretations when I could *directly* link such interpretations to hard data (or evidence) that was collected. I attempted to always support my findings/statements with data obtained from interviews, documents, and/or actual observations. I tried several analytical techniques, ranging from factoring data to more abstract techniques like the use of metaphors (Miles & Huberman, 1984). But, somehow, none of these techniques satisfied me. Why? During my process of data collection and analysis, I began to identity factors in *relation* to my data for which I could not find direct evidence. I found myself restricting my *use* of data only within a causal, explanatory framework. I realised that I was uncomfortable with the methods I used.

Was this dissatisfaction a product of my own (latent/inherent) positivist bias? Or was I attempting *good* qualitative research, and hence experiencing *its* own latent/inherent biases, its empirical echoes[13], and problems with discovery? For example, I made connections, developed insights, and generally "got thinking" about issues from *across* data, and sometimes apparently unconnected to actual data obtained. Because I was unable to always find specific empirical support for these thoughts; I found myself moving from making ideas invisible to making *I* invisible. If I could not *explain* insights relative to data procured, if there was no evidence to directly substantiate my thoughts, I made these insights non-existent, invisible. And this made me question myself. Surely, that these insights existed implies that they must have come from *somewhere*. By relegating my insights to nothingness, I became acutely aware that (a) I was repressing what I regarded as valuable thoughts, and (b) I was not being true to the several, *real sources* of my insights: Me. Indeed, my worries with the use of *I* reflects a greater debate about how writing conventions and research methods honour a false duality between "the intellect" and our biological processes. Ideas are promoted as existing outside of who we are. By *who*, I not only refer to the autobiographical details of lives, but highlight our bodily processes relative to how we develop *intellect*. In other words I argue...

...in Defence of Intellect as Social, Cultural, Political AND Biological Practice. Our thinking is produced and reproduced by our biology inasmuch as it inter- actively occurs in other ways: Socially. Culturally. Politically. AND: Neurologically. Cognitively. Physiologically. Psychologically. Emotionally. Perceptually. Via

these latter known (and perhaps via other unknown) bodily processes, intellect is (re)produced. Of course, this is no Great Revelation: This not-new idea has been emphasised by cognitive psychologists, neuro-scientists, psycho-linguists and the like (e.g., Gesell, 1925; Searle, 1969; Luria, 1976; and Vygotsky, 1978, 1987). They have long been investigating and theorising the biological bases of human thinking processes. Perhaps what is *new* is that currently we engage our knowledge-making processes in ways that either minimise or ~~erase~~ the influence of such thinking/biological processes.

Even when we present our intellect as a set of statements that demonstrate our involvement as, for example, co-participants in the research process; we present ourselves in largely non-biological terms, referring mainly to cultural, social, gender, racial and other framings of *I* as knowledge producers. And we are well encouraged to do so. Consider how the type of I-visibility I refer to is epistemologically promoted. For example, think about how Researchers ascribing to, for example, (French) post-structuralism argue that subjective knowledges, human beings, are the products of social, cultural, political, gender, and historical influences. That the mind (intellect) is seen as something that can exist outside of the body. Others, too – like German anthropologists, humanists – have emphasised gazing at the subject as "the human subject *without* the human subject" (emphasis mine, Zimmerman, 2001, p. 406), a looking that goes beyond biological forms, into the social, cultural, political and related critical realities of our lives. Interestingly, while this is a very appealing position, consider what such perspectives do. Ultimately, they minimise the usefulness of individual, biological processes in the way intellect is presented in research. Perhaps (and I realise how contestable this is, but...) classical Cartesian dichotomies are *perpetuated* via such perspectives. That intellect can exist as without the body. Sans biology. As operating metaphysically. A bit like a *cyborg* or *humanoid* – just without both the fleshy *and* metal bits! Not even as a brain wired to a Researcher's Compaq in a futuristic Frankenstein lab. It may be argued that the transcending of such dichotomies of the mind/body, spirit/life, human/animal, and person/world are insufficient to situate ourselves as knowing, intentful individuals, (inter)actively relating to our (changing) selves and environments. In other words, our "**agency**" is a muchly-valued factor when we engage privilege for Liberation.

"Agency" (another not-new idea) is further explored for the relevance it has here: Agency, perhaps, is what (in the 1920s and 1930s) Russian psychologists, such as Vygotsky (1978, 1987) and Luria (1976)[14] have argued for – a cultural situatedness of cognition via an understanding of its social *and* biological origins. Recently, Researchers and theorists have paid vigorous attention to this aspect of psychology (for example, see Price-Williams, 1980). In the sub-disciplines of cognitive psychology, and of cognitive science, the move toward understanding *where* thinking occurs has resulted in the generation of many theoretical notions, such as situated cognition or distributed cognition[15]. Others – such as Finnish activity theorists (see Engestrom & Miettinen, 1999), have argued that our thinking[16] is performed in conditions of joint, collective activity.

So, via reflecting on my personal identity as a twin, and on people with communication disorders, I began to realise that the lives (of those researched and mine) *both* offered a vital theatrical space for biological *and* social-cultural-political interpenetrating ways of intellectual development. In engaging this form of I-visibility, I made a deliberate *representational* and *pragmatic* choice regarding the incorporation of myself in my study, one that was *not* about the use of focused, overtly autobiographical data, or even of a deep analysis of self-thinking processes. *I* was far more insidious. For, while I realised the importance of myself as data producer, data source, and data interpreter – amongst other roles – I remembered that the focus of my study was not on me. In engaging this, the **Insidious I**, I let myself into my research in guileful ways, perhaps as *all* Researchers do. The exception was that I overtly referred to the ways in which *I* influenced data collection, analysis and interpretation during the theorising of the study design, in the "methodology". I discuss these strategies, next.

In summary, including the self is a commonsensical thing to do. Liberated, we engage our privilege to free the body *with* our soul to develop our biological (and social, cultural) selves *as* intellectual practices. To make impractical thinkings possible in an impossibly practical world, I want to share my experience of how these ideas were harnessed into my research methodology:

PRIVILEGE WITH DELIBERATION

In this section, I discuss how I engaged *deliberations*, i.e. the process of coding theoretical ideas into practical strategies for the research process. Deliberations, a term I have constructed for this chapter, is really about how we Stop&Think about what to do as we engage the privileged "I" in our research. Here, I bind discussions to my experience of research. Here, I remember that as Researchers we cannot merely position ourselves as impassioned, immaterial, biologically invisible conduits whose intellectual province and skill (whose privilege) it is to "pass on the word". I argue that as we (unfashionably) engage the material privileges of our biologically (*and* culturally-socially-politically) situated thoughts, we must also explore how to practically share this engagement. Via this methodological angle, we need to make our thinking apparent to ourselves. Of course, the parallel responsibility we have within the current structure and demands of the Academy is to make this thinking apparent to others. This means being able to both theorise it AND practically review it. I share – broadly – my methodological strategies which I have theorised within the categories of:
– Process & product strategies
– Structure & style devices
    Both these categories were engaged in several ways. To begin:

Process and Product Strategies

Process and product refer to what traditionally is called "methodology" and "results". Indeed, I prefer to hyphenate [process-product] these research report sections because of how they are so intimately connected. So, what did I do to increase I-visibility within my research's process-product? I focus an idea set referred to as…

Reflexive-inspirational interpretation. Reflexive. Inspiration. And Interpretation. Big words. Big ideas. Let me thin(k) it out a bit: The strategy of Reflexive-Inspirational Interpretation is concerned with *self reflections*. It is also concerned with issues of *reflexivity*. However, in order to explain what is meant by Reflexive-Inspirational Interpretation I shall, initially, deliberate on **self-reflections**:

   In recording my reflections in a researcher's journal, I referred to Altricher, Posch and Somekh's (1993) framework of (i) theoretical notes, i.e., focused on developing a theoretical understanding of practice; (ii) personal emotive notes, i.e., notations regarding my feelings, attitudes, and other affective responses; (iii) methodological notes – regarding *how* my study was performed, and (iv) planning notes – for recording insights to develop recommendations, and/or the thesis within my study. Alvesson and Skoldberg (2000) give consideration, within their level of self-reflection, to the *linguistic* aspects of interpretation. Here, they focus on the limiting, ambiguous nature of language in expressing what may be known. For including the biological sense of *I* such a diary was invaluable. I recorded *everything*. I carried a pen and paper wherever I went. I had a notepad and pencil next to my bed. I scribbled on serviettes, made notes on the back of my hand. Committed idle conversations to memory. Stored letters to friends and family. Memorised events I had experienced. Recited what someone said. Recounted others' actions, even when it did not make sense at the time. Things that for No Apparent Reason (perhaps *especially* because it lacked Reason) seemed *critical* to record… But why was I so actively engaged with this process of recording everything? Largely, my self-reflective notes were driven by my (initial, and ongoing) confusion about what/how to understand my study design. I decided before I began that I was *not* going to engage some kind of merging of empirical and theoretical designs. During my research, I felt uncomfortable with representing what I did as constituting empirical and theoretical components. The closest to feeling comfortable with what I did may be located in the idea of **reflexivity**:

   Alvesson and Skoldberg (2000, p. 5) use reflexivity to describe a methodology that is

   …a particular, specified version of reflective research, involving reflection on several levels or directed at several themes…

In particular, they focus on interpretation, and – importantly – the political nature of qualitative research relative to empirically based notions of interpretation, of the Researcher's relationship to the *subject* within the process of interpretation. They present four levels of interpretation, represented below in **Figure 1**. These interpretational levels include the (i) empirical level, (ii) interpretation (=hermeneutic/interpretive) level, (iii) critical level, and (iv) self-critical/linguistic reflection level.

   In **Figure 1**, the vertical arrows to the left indicate interaction between the four levels of interpretation (i.e., between empirical, interpretation/hermeneutic, critical,

47

and self-critical/linguistic reflection). The long horizontal arrows refer to outcomes of these interpretive interactions, while the long vertical arrow in the middle represents a single, potential variant, i.e., one that *bypasses* the critical level, incorporating only the second and fourth levels (interpretive and self critical/ linguistic level). The two short arrows (A1 & A2) represent emphasis placed on either interpretive (A1), or self-critical and linguistic reflection (A2). In considering the various directions in which the Researcher may move between this *meta-theoretical* field, I opted for the following directions across these fields:

I engaged empirical data (like policy statements) within a hermeneutic analysis (e.g., discussion), then onto a critical analysis, and finally a level of self-analysis. At this point, I must define what I mean by self-analysis. In my study, I provided interpretations of service, research, and professional higher education by recognising that I was simultaneously engaged in all these forms of practice. Some may regard this form of research as participatory action research or even as participant observation[17]. However, I have focused on how these roles have been incorporated within a framework of **reflexive interpretation.** To explain:

While I moved *from* empirical *to* self-critical levels of interpretation, I think it is important to focus on another direction that I used – one that occurred in an *opposite* movement of interpretation. I engaged a movement **from "self-critical/linguistic" toward the empirical** level of interpretation. Here, I was inspired by the incoherent, asynchronous view of people, of social justice, democracy and such-like (as I know it). All of this may be viewed relative to Alvesson and Skoldberg's (2000) first level of interpretation regarding empirical data. In terms of empirical data, I produced three broad categories of data sources: visual, verbal and document(ed) data. Visual data include video-recorded observations and self portraits, while verbal data included group and individual discussions, and documented data refers to policies, articles, texts of various kinds, and research journal entries. All data were primarily used for the purposes of an empirical analysis in **direct** ways to serve as *evidence*, e.g., textual extracts, examples of actual practices, visual and verbal data extracts. This is a more traditional version of how empirical data is used. I also used empirical data in **indirect** ways to construct evidence.

There are several ways in which I used such data. In one way in which empirical data was used indirectly, the **empirical data was (re)constructed** via employing some level of imagination. Firstly, I (re)constructed a clinical encounter between a practitioner and a patient. This hypothetical encounter, labelled a vignette, was based on several sources, i.e., direct observations of actual practice, discussions held with practitioners, data from my research diary, and data derived from textual representations of practice, for example, text books, and practice reports.

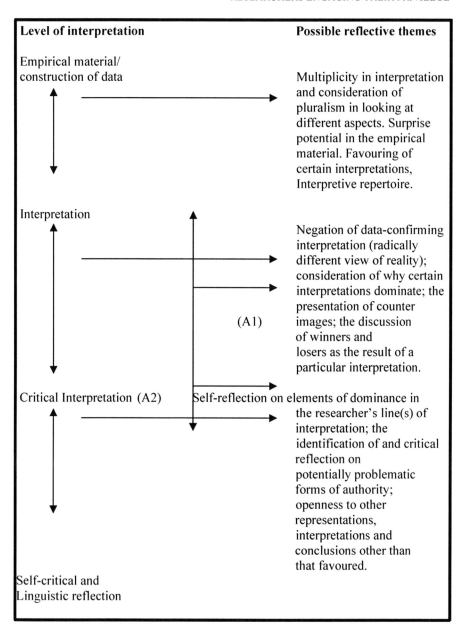

Figure 1. Interaction between different levels of interpretation (Adapted from Alvesson & Skoldberg, 2000, p. 255)

Each idea, each action described in the vignette may be referred to any and/or all of my data sources. For all intents and purposes this may have been an actual encounter. It was carefully re-constructed with reference to empirical data I had collected, but not in direct relation to any specific, actual/real event. However, it served the purpose of illustrating all of the theoretical themes that had been developed out of an initial qualitative analysis of my raw data. In a sense, I selected specific examples of data *backwards* relative to the recurrent themes that emerged from my analysis of all my data. Then, I re-stitched these specific examples into this cohesive vignette to narrate an example of practice. This is why I situate this use of empirical data as imaginatively (re)constructed from empirical evidence.

There are several issues raised when empirical data becomes (re)constructed. For example, how much is excluded and/or inserted in the (re)construction? What happens when fictional-type writing devices are used to represent a data? Does it lose *authenticity*? Indeed, even the issue of what constitutes data may be queried. While some of these (and other) issues shall and always will plague Researchers, because they centre on the choices we make to produce/represent data, they must be debated. Here, I want to focus on, as important, two factors: Firstly, it is vital that I have explicitly implicated myself as part of the (re)constructed data. I am the data, too. In using my own practice data (cf. details above), I can directly (empirically) substantiate such (re)constructions. And I can only do this once I make it explicit that I am part of my data sources *in empirical ways*. Locating myself as practitioner in the same activity that is represented lends an (empirically demanded?) authenticity that is not possible if (a) we are invisible in this process, and (b) we deliberately position ourselves as *outsiders* to our own data producing experience.

I am not arguing for the (mere?) deed of researching one's own practice, but that when we engage empirical data in indirect ways, it then becomes the Researcher's responsibility to be explicit about her location *inside* it. This is especially so when/if we are researching that which we practice, for example, teachers investigating *teaching* or health care workers investigating *caring*. Such direct location within one's research need not be autobiographical, narrative representations, but they could be, if appropriate. Or they could be (re)constructions of the sort I have described above. Importantly, that I am able to demonstrate how such (re)constructions are (indirectly) related to empirical data is very useful in achieving an I-visibility where the (biological?) *Researcher is data*. Empirically, authenticity may be substantiated in this process, especially when there is a rich cross-referencing, a triangulation to multiple data sources. Herein lies the problem with the use of such data. Empirical ways of representing data are notoriously dubious for the way in which truth is presented as singular, as definite, and as neutral. So while such empirical data producing strategies – within a frame of reflexivity – is useful, we need to think of other ways to produce/represent data. When I review my use of literary devices to increase I-visibility (see below), I do provide ways of addressing this concern. In the meantime, I wish to digress to how reflexivity – while useful as a strategy to show off I-visibility – was inadequate for *how much* I-visibility was possible in the thick mist of empirical, interpretive, critical, and self-critical/linguistic data.

In attempting to become *more* visible, I relied on the *inspirational interpretation* part of Reflexive-Inspiration Interpretation. Practically, there were two key strategies which I used to increase I-visibility. Both these strategies are enmeshed with reflexivity, but do focus more on what inspired me to engage knowing, interpreting in certain ways. These strategies include (1) Critical Conversations, and (2) Inspirations.

Before I describe what these strategies are, it is important to note that after a meta-analysis of data recorded in my research journal (see above), I realised that I was operating, thinking in several ways that were cloudy even to myself! However, this was not to say that I did not value these thoughts, just that I did not know either what to do with them, or if in fact they constituted *data*. What I became increasingly passionate about was that the *products* of my thinkings (which I considered valuable, *somehow*, to my research) needed to be included into my research report. Like other Ordinary People, I interpret the world in *less* academic/formal ways. Here, I am specifically referring to those wild associations that were made just before I fell asleep. To the dreams (nightmares?) of researching while I was asleep. To thoughts that niggled at me, as I read and re-read my data. To things that made me angry, that made me cry, that made me happy. To all sorts of hunches, feelings, sparks, and whispers. Things that I just knew, but couldn't really articulate: That I drew diagrams for, made analogies of, and had mind-pictures of. Ideas that begged for words to reify them. One of the ways in which I (naturally) reified these thoughts was via what I called….

….Critical conversations. Why *conversations* and not, for example, *interviews* or *discussions*? The key problem I have with the term interview is that it connotes Researcher/researched dualities, promotes uni-directional movement of knowledge (from "interviewee" to "interviewer"), and dishonestly portrays the interviewer as logical, sensible, ordered (with prepared questions, organised schedules and such-like) in control of the activity of interviewing[18]. Conversely, discussions frame dialogue in far too innocent ways to be trusted. The whole notion of *joint-meaning making*, or co-construction of knowledge seemed *too* constructed. Research discussions may be (are?) dangerously liberal acts, acts that – if left unanalysed – could mask an insidious manipulation of Others within what really is a power-imbalanced relationship. Consider that it was I who began an interest in my study. It was I who gathered research participants. It was I who assembled the texts, the discussions, and so on. The point I wish to make is that discussions falsely frame the level on which we organise (i.e. control) our studies. Of course, I am making an extreme point here, and am betraying the roles that people do assume within research discussion. I am just dissatisfied with what we claim discussions achieve. As power imbalances exist in all relationships, I did not wish to falsely portray *equality* inasmuch as I realised that inequality was not my goal. This methodological dilemma gave rise to what I referred to as Critical Conversations.

The aim of Critical Conversations is to facilitate an overt, obvious engagement of social, political, cultural and related forms of practice with, and importantly *through,* research participants. While this may be regarded (meta-theoretically) as thinking about thinking, it is a strategy that is relative to *Ubuntu* epistemology. Ubuntu, fashionably in use since its absorption into South African (education, social, and even health) policies, is how I conceived of, amongst other things, Critical Conversations. Specifically, that Ubuntu involves dialogue, that it facilitates an open system of being – by referencing experience, knowing, and truth relative to a pluralistic system (*a person is a person through other persons*) (Ramose, 2002), is what specifically appealed to me and my sense of knowledge making. Relative to Ubuntu, how might one develop critical knowings? Perhaps, a review of the core features of Critical Conversations may provide insight into how I interpreted the use of Ubuntu's axiom, i.e., *a person is a person through other persons*:

– The deliberate introduction of social, political and cultural interpretations of the subject in question.
– Overtly challenging our [researcher's/"researched's"] notions of gender, race, class and suchlike by asking questions like: What about the way you practice relative to "boys" and "girls"? What about our identities as, e.g., Black South Africans of Indian descent or as White people relative to Black African patients?
– Critiquing inertial moments – such as the lack of/slow incorporation of discourses about transformation, of critical science, of anti-racism, amongst other factors.
– Imagining (with practitioners) alternative forms of our practice relationship.
– Conceding defeat when solutions to "problems" seemed "impossible".
– Situating and re-situating practice relative to local, national, and global concerns, such as South Africa's Constitutional framing of "dignity" and "respect", the framing of eleven languages as "official", the World Health Organisation's classification of "disability", the World Trade Organisation's focus on the commodification of professions, etc.

Importantly, these strategies were not engaged from a point of higher morality, i.e., where I portrayed that I "knew it all". Critical Conversations were about joint knowledge making inasmuch as they were about creating uncomfortable feelings with questions of social, political and cultural relevance. The key purpose, then, was to use Critical Conversations to develop an *epistemological* and *ontological* positioning (and re-positioning) of the practitioner and patient *from* and *by* engaging 'critical' issues. In this way I-visibility was engaged, and – importantly – increased. Indeed, I would consider this as a form of *embodied* reflexivity because of my use of thinkings as described above (cf. my research diary) within this strategy of Critical Conversations. For me, the value of such data led me to decide where I ought to lay theoretical allegiance: Was it with *grand* theorists? Or with me and mine... To explain:

I referred to theorists (Grand ones?) such as Habermas, Foucault, Bourdieu, and Bakhtin without making them/their work central to what I had to say. I had some important epistemological reasons for this: Firstly, I did/still do not intend to sew together regurgitated texts and theories from philosophy, sociology, and the like, in order to present a "new" theoretical offering within my research. I decided that such a thing would only serve to deviate from my immediate focus, and would make space for an (unnecessary) critique of the Habermas's of this world, and/or my interpretations/presentation of his work. Secondly, and more importantly, I do not wish to lay allegiance to specific theorists' theories. This is because I have chosen to make explicit and/or implicit reference to *my* understandings of the notion of communication, as it has arisen from sociology and philosophy and related disciplines. In other words, I have made sense of several theories for the relevance that they may have within my research. Moreover, I was more interested in how *locally*, people such as I and others, made sense of our situation. This was the theorising that I was primarily interested in. So, for me it was…

….Sandhya (not Saussure). Harsha (not Hegel). Critical Conversations work well…with some people! If we think about them, Critical Conversations could be rude, raw, crude, and border on fine lines between vulgarity, ugliness, and feudalism! While I did engage many people in such conversations, they were really only possible (in the form described above) with those who knew[19] me very intimately outside of the research process. I specifically wish to highlight how they worked with two friends, colleagues, and doctoral student peers at the ex-University of Natal, i.e., Sandhya Chetty and Harsha Kathard.

While we all declared the need to *talk* about our work while enrolled for our Doctorates in Education, these Critical Conversations evolved naturally. So, even though Sandhya and Harsha had agreed to formally participate in this study, we had already been engaged in such Critical Conversations in informal ways. In this way, Critical Conversations have been an excellent Hermeneutic/Critical/Self-Critical activity for data production and interpretation. Because of the nature of our relationship, we were able to naturally engage Critical Conversations that were *very* critical in nature. These Conversations focused (directly and indirectly) on developing my critique of the practitioner-patient relationship, and my offering of my thesis referred to as the Relationship of Labouring Affinities [RoLA]. What was difficult to record were the Critical Conversations that Sandhya, Harsha and I engaged in the last year around my research. This was because they were not managed in an empirical manner. To explain:

Critical Conversations (with Harsha and Sandhya) usually involved individual and/or group Conversations where the stimulus for the conversations was either a draft chapter written for this study, and/or an idea, an academic paper, methodological issues, or Harsha and Sandhya's own research writings, academic papers, daily issues raised in practice within a higher education setting, and such like. Critical Conversations of this nature were audio-recorded and/or incorporated within self-reflection journal entries; they were equally valuable to the formal, scheduled Conversations. Informal Conversations occurred during work tea-breaks, inbetween lectures, during social events (like mealtimes), and inserted into social telephone calls, amongst other interactions. In whatever form, the point is that the data developed within Critical Conversations were *not* used in an empirical manner. Rather, they *inspired* my reflections in significant ways that helped me to theorise. As such, Critical Conversations functioned as *inspirational* sources to my interpretation, alongside other...

.....*Inspirations.* Returning to my use of **self-reflections**, i.e., data recorded in my research journal, I isolated several sources that inspired my notations. These include, amongst other things, critical theory, post-colonial theory and literatures, feminist and gender studies, and queer theory. To explain: critical theory has inspired the manner in which I have interpreted data. For example, I wrote eleven[20] separate analyses of the same event (i.e., the practitioner-patient relationship) ranging from the profession's positioning of this relationship, to an official policy framing of it. In other words, multiple interpretations [vis-à-vis critical epistemology] were provided. Specifically, critical theory inspired me to perform my initial analyses of power/dominance within the professional relationship we have with our patients. In referring this relationship to notions of, for example, Othering, and a positioning of this relationship as a *curious coincidence* of the Rich-White-Man (or class/race/gender) triumvirate, I have appropriated from post-colonial, feminist, and/or queer theory literature. An example of this inspiration is my use of Arundhati Roy's work to explain a concept developed regarding the transgression of social dualities. Additionally, I used specific analytical strategies – like Edward Said's critique of Joseph Conrad's *Heart of Darkness* as a way to read the practitioner-patient relationship. Indeed, many empirical, hermeneutic, critical, and self-critical/linguistic data sources have all collectively inspired me. For me, such inspiration serves as a core element that is enmeshed with Reflexivity.

In this way, I wish to extend Alvesson and Skoldberg's (2000) notion of reflexive interpretation to highlight my engagement with what I refer to as Reflexive-Inspirational Interpretation. Importantly, all levels of reflection (and this term is used to denote the *activity*) interact with one another to produce interpretations, which – according to Maranhao (1991) – occur as a result of the Researcher's (i) judgment, (ii) intuition, and (iii) ability to identify issues of ideological significance.

Crucially, the Researcher's consideration of (as best as possible) explicit dialogue with the research *subject* is incorporated. This dialogue promotes that the Researcher is "...not entrenched behind the research position, and with the reader" (Alvesson & Skoldberg, 2000, p. 248). What this point really alludes to is that by adhering to any one level of interpretation (e.g., self-critical and linguistic reflection) there is a danger of being *stuck* in this level, and – importantly – that explicit/overt reflexivity provides a way out of this situation. A further implication of this factor is that reflexivity permits attention to the interpretive, political, and *rhetorical* nature of empirical research (Alvesson & Skoldberg, 2000). As such, via reflexivity, I freed myself to develop a certain mulitvoicedness. To discuss how I represented my multivoicedness, I refer to both the structural arrangement of my chapters, and the stylistic literary devices used within my writing of the report.

Style and Structure Devices

I used (played with) language in ways that contained/transported my ideas as well as made the point themselves via the selected literary device/style. For example, I used brackets in several ways. I bracketed prefixes to words such as *(re)positions* or as in the phrase *Disorder, Order & (Re)Order* that allowed for dual readings of the same word/phrase. Brackets, along with hyphens and/or slashes, were used to represent my genuine, wider uncertainty with some of the ideas I wrote about. See the first line of this paragraph for an example of this strategy.

I created words (neologisms) when I found current words limiting in expressing my idea, or when I wished to signal an epistemological source or allegiance. For example, *Dis-Othering* was created out of Gayatri Spivak's (1985a) Othering as used within post-colonial theories. I used such epistemological allegiances to hint at bigger points – arguing within a whole chapter (e.g., Chapter Five) for how the Practitioner-patient Relationship is ideologically linked to Othering – where the seizure and control of the means of interpretation and communication is made possible via colonial processes, and the colonised Other is spoken for. In including the 'dis' prefix – I related profession's use of deficit theories, focused on *dis*order, to *dis*[21] people. Other neologisms include hyphenated words like *not-new, ideological-practical*, and qualified adaptations of word like moral into *moralism*. Capitalisations of words and phrases were also strategies used to highlight aphorisms such as *Rich-White-Men*; to reify other's or my ideas such as *Critical Realism, End-Beginnings, Poors*, and the *Condition of our World*; or to indicate established power relations – such as in *Practitioner-patient Relationship*. Additionally, capitalisations served to introduce the several, reframed idea-sets I offered within my dissertation, like *Clinical Moment, Forms of Practice, Biological Metaphor,* and suchlike.

I used exclamation marks to show emotive responses to issues. I broke sentences. Right in the middle of where Standard Writing Rules say we should not. And I started sentences with conjunctions like *And's, But's*. Even *Since's*. Sometime to symbolise continuity with ideas across idea-sets. Sometimes to draw attention to alternative perspectives. Sometimes to show (offensively?) that *the message* may be understood in another, equally acceptable, pragmatic manner. I also extracted....

...Headings...

...from sentences that ran from one paragraph, across a section heading, to the next paragraph – showing the linkages of thought between the text as a whole. This last point regarding style is important as my research was a site for the meeting of many voices: From those within the profession, the neurosciences, psychology, sociology, history, linguistics, education and so on. So, in reporting my data, I decided to use the way I organised my chapters (my report structure) to maximum benefit. I wanted my report's overall structure to serve as a statement in itself about what I was saying in my research: A kind of meta-analytical, epistemological point. In doing so, I had to consider several variables. I had to remember that I was writing a dissertation that was going be evaluated against traditional research dissertation criteria. That there was a Certain Order in which things had to appear in a dissertation. So, as a privileged Researcher, I realised that my freedom to make knowledge is bar-coded, marketed and mediated via political controls. Parastatal research foundations act as governing councils. Their soldiers serve in state-subsidised research committees. State-run data services tell us what we want (need?) to know. We write according to report writing rules, regulations. So, I wrote my report, not as a flag-waving patriot of democratic states world-wide but as a (privileged)(liberated) citizen in a knowledge-making empire. I wrote as someone who knew his place.

And in this location, I realised that to be appreciated by the Academy, I had to expose my theoretical framework, review my "methodology", deliver my "results & discussion", humbly and critically state my "limitations" and so on. So, I straddled my freedom to engage I-visibility AND my desire to actually obtain a degree certificate! However, in focusing on my need to be I-visible, I necessarily had to find a meaningful and acceptable way to represent my empirical data, and the many ideas/themes that I reflexively engaged across the multiple levels of interpretation (as reviewed above). In doing so, I strategised to knock (slightly) at the edges of our Academy's reason. I offended the Certain Order of reporting, and re-arranged the standard manner in which chapters are presented. This served several purposes. Let me explain what I mean by this by sharing an overview of my chapter. In Text Box 1, I provide a broad overview of the organisation of my report.

Chapter One: Beginnings, Ideas & Moments
Chapter Two: The Powerful Expert
Chapter Three: The Sick Person
Chapter Four: The Community Biographical Perspective
Chapter Five: The Community Biography: An Analysis Of Co-Incidences
Chapter Six: An Analysis of the Profession's Minor Positions
Chapter Seven: Ideas From 'Outside' The Profession: Policy
Chapter Eight: Moving Toward Critical Identities
Chapter Nine: Critical Ideological-Practical Positions
Chapter Ten: Re-Positioning the Powerful Expert & the Sick Person
Chapter Eleven: End-Beginnings: Is The Transformation Of The Practitioner-Patient Relationship Possible?
Chapter Twelve: Methodological Reflections
A Conversation with a Practitioner: Sandhya (An Epi-Pro-Logue)

Text Box 1. Content overview as a way to demonstrate the methodological use of chapter organisation

In Chapter One, I presented my core unit of analysis (the Practitioner-patient Relationship) which was then subjected to <u>eleven</u> (re)presentations (or *positionings*) across subsequent chapters. Notably, I did not look at my unit of analysis from the point of view of the patient. I deliberately chose not to write their story with, or for, them. Instead, I privileged my (the Practitioner-Educator-Researcher's) perspective across each chapter. How did I do this? Practically? In each chapter, I emphasised different "ways of seeing" (Berger, 1986) the relationship in question. For example, in Chapters Two and Three, I emphasised the biological focus predominantly promoted by my profession. In Chapters Four and Five, I looked at my subject within the political societies (apartheid and colonialism) in which they occurred. I also situated my analysis to minor/non-dominant practices from within the profession itself (Chapter Six). I leapt into the future and positioned my subject within South Africa's intended policy context, centring *democracy* as an imagined framework (Chapter Seven).

In Chapters Eight and Nine, I took my imaginings further by deeply exploring the essences of the notions contained within South Africa's intended policy statements regarding democracy. These core ideas were pulled together via a conceptual framework and, conclusively, offered as a final re-positioning of (Chapter Ten) a "transformed" Practitioner-patient Relationship. However, even this offering was thrown into disillusion by Chapter Eleven which questioned the nature of the transformed relationship's existence in a world focused on globalisation, privatisation, and burgeoning reference to fundamental identities. I ended the report with two things: My methodology (Chapter Twelve), and a practitioner's "narrative" (Chapter Thirteen). This last chapter really served multiple purposes, including being a "summary" of ideas contained within previous chapters, and as an alternate way of speaking/delivering those same ideas.

PRIVILEGE AS DE-LIBERATION

Why De-Liberation? As I stated in my introduction: Privilege is about Liberation. And, it is also about De-Liberation. What do I mean by this? The kind of Liberation I have argued for above – that which frees us to engage our bodily process of insight, intuition, our feelings, our associative thinkings, and so on – is good for the development of ourselves as Researchers. However, I would argue that while this is a good thing, we perpetuate our privileging in perhaps less tasteful ways. To explain:

There is a specific sense of how we (re)produce ourselves in our research. In some ways, we engage a form of *autopoiesis*, described above (cf. Maturana & Varela, 1980). I take this notion (perhaps not as Maturana & Varela wholly intended) to show what we do when Researchers engage privilege as Liberation. When we liberate ourselves, we become – simultaneously – the source (or "subject"), the medium, and object (the goal) within this act of being. And what's wrong with this? Why would this need De-Liberation? Swinging sideways a bit, let me say more about De-Liberation. As I see it, De-Liberation would imply an "undoing" of the Liberation. A removing of the extent to which we include ourselves in our researches. Strange, that in a chapter where I have argued for the stronger inclusion of ourselves, I should also argue for the undoing of ourselves.

In De-Liberation, I suggest that we must undermine our own authorship, our authoredness, our Authority. In some way, the maxim that "all freedom has its limits" may be absorbed into our research selves. What I am arguing for here is for

Self-Dissent
Self-Disobedience
Self-Disarray
Self-Disrespect...
.....Not quite self-flagellation.....

.....but a ying-yang inspired dose of disobeying one's own thinkings, own feelings RELATIVE to what "they" say....relative to even the cultural, social, and political Gods of our own Private Academy of Cool People. Of The Great Philosophers. The Great Minds. In a world where so many of our freedoms are actively taken away from us, perhaps all (and "the most") we will be left with is ourselves. If anything, as we re-interpret and re-work the world within its socialnesses, culturalnesses, politicalnesses – that is perhaps what we must never let the Academy do – is to take away our right to use our body-minds to reflexively interpret, to dialogue with others. That as Researchers, insurgency is a vital form of opposition, and that our biologies carry the "knowledge" and the "tools" to help us move onto Better Things.

We must be wary even if/when we recognise that we are of the same blood, that even as we fight the Good Fight, that as we play being Good Crusaders of Critical epistemologies, that it is so important to "feel" if something is wrong or right. And I may not always be able to say all/exactly *why* I feel it, but that I do feel that current researches are sometimes wrong is important for me to think-feel. In this way I keep a check on how I deal with possessing power as a Researcher. I am then able to deal with "thinking" as really a privileged activity. Is such a position paranoid? Neurotic? ....Perhaps. Necessary? I think so.

For 194 pages (most of my research report) I argued for a democratic form of the Practitioner-patient relationship. I favoured Freedom. Liberty. That is, of course, until I reached Chapter 11, where I argued for why democratic practice relationships *will* fail. I believe that as embodied, Liberated knowledge-makers within democratic relationships (in research and other forms of "relating") we may benefit from locating this form of knowing in a World Space. That re-positioning our embodied selves "in the world" may *oblige* us to consider ourselves – critically – as Researchers in relation to our theoretical and phenomenological influences. Here, I wish to focus on a rather broad influence. I argue that we really must re-look at the influence of dominant philosophies by which current notions of Liberty (or "democracy" and such like) are inspired (at least within the Academy).

Our Use of Critically-Oriented Philosophical Inspirations

As we reference critically-oriented philosophical inspirations we need to ask: *How have notions like Liberty been developed via such philosophies*? For me, Liberty as theorised by philosophers such as Habermas, Derrida, Bakhtin, and Foucault, has developed in strange ways: Indeed, these revered critical philosophers, bent on freedom, democracy, emancipation and so on must be managed *suspiciously*. Why do I say that? Well, let us consider just one of these influential theorists' perspectives on Liberty. For example, Jurgen Habermas, the founding father of the

Second Frankfurt School (Germany) has always promoted our conscious Liberation via the recognition of a knowing for emancipation. However, it is argued that, in doing so, he has ignored the influences of colonialism and slavery in his offerings of a thinking that emancipates. Actively so, perhaps. Even as recently as 2003, Habermas continued to turn his back on how these factors are inextricably related to European, American and British modernisation. On how, as he theorised his and his brothers' emancipation, such theories were far from being emancipatory for people's of the majority world (see, for example, his analysis of terrorism in the West: Borradori, 2003). We could interpret his agnosia as meaning that – philosophically speaking – Liberty is alright. For some. That Liberty *can* exist only in context of the maiming, killing and wiping out of Others. Their civilisations, cultures. Their ways of knowing. That – as Chomsky (2003) says – such ideals of justice and freedom are easily said by the lips, and far more difficult to defend or advance. That perhaps "...justice was an idea invented by the big crooks who run the world to keep the small people in their corners" (Okri, 1998). Indeed, a good practical exemplar of such philosophy in action may be the current Bush-does-Liberty-for-Iraq style Liberty......But: What have such things to do with us? As Liberated Researchers?

This notion of Liberty-For-Some must be analysed for how we engage people in, for example, the narratives of their lives. And of how we engage ourselves in our ethnographic researches. It must not be forgotten that such types of qualitative research has evolved from practices influenced by ideologies like racism, ethnocentrism, and colonial frameworks. That such ideas continue to be narrowly theorised by philosophers' works, theories which are widely referenced either by us, or by those who evaluate our work for our notions of Liberation. That current methods used within ethnographic researches (adapted, evolved) were the same methods used to essentialise, and reduce whole, complex cultures into labels like *Africans* and *Indians*. Perhaps, in using these methods now, we are marginalised by ourselves (and others). We "essentialise" ourselves as (complex)(fluid)(tentative) (post-structuralist)(on the Fringes)(outside the Mainstream)(and in other Cool Ways)... Perhaps, blinded by our own Liberty we fail to see how the portrayal of ourselves as Liberated Researchers, and this perpetuates newer dualities. That when "we" see ourselves different to "them" such dualisms serve to keep us falsely secure with our methods of Liberation.

So, as we create theories of Liberation with people with disabilities, we fail to see that there is a "thin dividing line between identification with one's research subjects and their exploitation" (Vernon, 1997). Interestingly, Finkelstein (a South African/British disability rights activist) said that he left the Academy because as universities become more market led (vs. market responsive)

...the relationship between academics and oppressed peoples will be parasitic... [2002a, p.16].

Similarly, as women liberate themselves, we fail to see how that one group of women is granted privileges that they obtain by actively supporting the oppression and exploitation of other groups of [black] women [insertion mine] hooks (1988: 329).

And as we engage Queer theory for social change (see, for example, Grace, Hill, Johnson & Lewis, 2004[22]), as we critique hetero-hegemony (Sedgewick, 1990), we fail to adequately see that such Liberation, for example, in Palestine (Habib, 2003) may be somewhat different than for those located in the gay ghettos of New York, London, or Paris. In some sense, perhaps such liberated Researchers are in the employ of ideologies and ideology-makers; they are like *native* spies[23]: Citizens of their research countries employed to spy on their ilk. Not quite the Kim of Rudyard Kipling's world. But native spies nevertheless…

Liberation epistemologies may not help us to see how we perpetuate the very things we seek to critique, to change. Indeed, perhaps narrative Researchers' (such as Clandinin & Connelly, 2000 and Munro, 1998) notions of how researched peoples' non-unitary subjectivity is channelled via their narratives may have relevance here for the *Researcher's* own appropriation of <u>*cultural*</u> narratives. That we, too, perversely represent ourselves through the narrative structures of our cultures as heroes, as de-colonising activists, as post-colonial theorists writing back to the Empire[24]. As Cool People. Marginalised, we encourage a false existence of ourselves as "outsiders" when, perhaps, we are "insiders" *too*.

We must attempt to understand by what Means & Memes[25] pedestrianised ideas of Liberty (like Habermas') have filtered into our research. Critically, when we engage Liberation ideologies we ought to trace such ideas to their ontological bases. Following Vidich and Lyman (1998), I argue that as I raise my I-visibility, I simultaneously must raise several questions around issues of **authenticity** and **positionality**. Even in studies intended to be sensitive to authorship and representational issues. We must engage our privilege in ways that allow us the freedom to not only theorise ourselves relative to our data but to locate our voices <u>within</u> the empire of knowledge-making[26]. That maybe "we were not free, merely licensed" (Morrison, 1970). So, even as Cool People smoking marijuana in the school toilets we must remember: We're still in the <u>School's</u> toilets….

IN ENDING THIS CHAPTER FOR *NOW* (BECAUSE NOTHING IS EVER CONCLUDED)…

….We must (insofar as is possible) recognise who, and where we are: Such things go toward ways in which we use our privilege to De-Liberate ourselves by not only authoritatively persuading readers that we are Liberated members of the Academy. As we rely on epistemologies critiqued as espousing Liberty-For-Some (But-Not-For-Others), we must seek Other inspirations, *too*. Perhaps, as we wave away the smoke clouds, and settle into the headiness of our marijuana highs, we need to listen to what fellow smokers in the school toilets are saying.

For me, Harsha and Sandhya were my inspirations, structured into my research (via Critical Conversations) from the toilets we found ourselves in. So, I developed meaning via our interactions, our thinkings. Resonating with the Ubuntu way, my being and knowing via others' voices has allowed me to weave myself as Researcher through their ideas, their cultural narratives. Similarly, I did attempt, in various direct and indirect ways (and with a consciousness that I was not using these voices *enough*[27]) to listen to others, too. That people, as (apparently) far removed from my immediate geographical space – such as the Inuit people – could be paralleled with our own lives as South Africans (Mandela, 1994). I searched for texts that did such things. For example, I deliberately sought inspiration from People like Franz Fanon, Steve Biko, Homi Bhabha, Jamaica Kincaid, Gayathri Spivak, Aime Cesaire, Tsitsi Dangarembga, Nadine Gordimer, Bessie Head, Hanif Kureishi, Dambudzo Marechera, Ezekiel Mphahlele, Ngugi Wa Thiong'o, Ben Okri, Arundhati Roy, Trinh T. Minh-ha, Zakes Mda, Vandana Shiva, and Edward Said. This list of people – fictional authors, academics, philosophers, theorists – write about Liberty as they see it.

Perhaps – and this is what appeals to me – their versions of Liberty are not necessarily one-sided. They make my *Litost*[28] fade. They speak from, with, and for an appealing non-provincialism and pluralism that may be lacking in mainstream, critical philosophies and theories. They acknowledge places[29] that we (all of us) occupy in the world. They represent the interests of the (muted?) *subaltern* (Spivak, 1985b) in Asia, the Middle East, Africa, and other parts of the world. Epistemologically, they map a world for us.....beyond even the wildest imaginations of our map-making man Mercator, who in limiting his cartographic dreams to the celestial and terrestrial world (Crane, 2002), left the project of epistemology maps to Others. So, in seeking to identify the limits of my own Liberation, I have recognised that no freedom is limitless, borderless, bounBarryess. The peoples from who I sought epistemological inspiration are my borders, my boundaries, my limits. It is *these* limits that I desire as I De-Liberate myself.

NOTES

[1] In economically developed countries, there are 10 researchers per 1 000 people as compared to less economically developed countries – where there are 10 per 10 000 people who are researchers. Importantly, 27% of the world's researchers are from less economically developed countries [see: United Nations Educational, Scientific and Cultural Organisation (UNESCO) Institute for Statistics, 2004].

[2] Textual representations like the use of capital letters are intended. I am hoping for these to assist in augmenting and providing alternative readings of the written work – similar to interpretations of when you see me, e.g., roll my eyes, wink, or use non-verbal signals to augment the 'hearing' of my spoken words.

[3] See Noakes, Harley, Bosch, Marino, St Clair Gibson, & Lambert (2004).

[4] See, for example, Peta (2005).

[5] ....as no idea is ever a new idea.....

[6] I have analysed this inclusion of researchers' voices via a wide variety of genres from narrative research, grounded theory, educational research to Queer qualitative research, and others. Examples of these texts are contained within this chapter's reference list.

[7] For example, see: Greenlagh (1999), Greenlagh & Hurwitz (1999).

[8] For example, see: Wagner (2002).

[9] And I do use this term advisedly.

[10] See, for example: Vernon (1997), Oliver (1992), Finkelstein (2002a), and Finkelstein (2002b).

11 This study was toward a doctorate in education and dealt with my professional focus, i.e. audiology and speech-language therapy (Pillay, 2003a).
12 See for example: Miles & Huberman (1984); Denzin & Lincoln (1994), and Flick (1998).
13 This term is after Winter (1989).
14 These references are later English translations of Vygotsky and Luria's works.
15 These terms refer to a theoretical turn in the field of cognitive science to understand learning as a cultural/contextual phenomenon. For example, see: Salomon (1993).
16 Activity theorists have made reference to Marx's (such as Marx & Engels, 1968) notion of labour and thinking/cognition where they, like Marx, argued that thinking (and subsequent labour/work) interacts with political ideologies.
17 In some ways this may be 'true' as I have made use of data collected via my 'research diary', amongst other strategies.
18 Of course, I am referring to *one* sense of interviewing, here.
19 Insofar as knowing another is possible...and here, I am alluding to knowing my thinking in ways that other friends, lovers, or my family may *not* know me.
20 Details of these chapters are provided below.
21 To *dis* is a common American slang used as such to refer to disrespectful behaviour. (*verb: dissing, past tense: dissed, root: dis*)
22 See for example: Grace (2004).
23 As described by Tzu over 2000 years ago (403-221BC). [see Tzu (c403-221BC/1998].
24 A reference to author Salman Rushdie's situating of post-colonial literatures. See: Ashcroft, Griffiths, & Tiffin (1989).
25 Memes refer to the smallest unit of an "idea" that exists, and that which may be traced to its origins, and analysed for how it has developed in society. See Heylighen (2001).
26 I do not wish to portray that, for example, narrative researchers *fail* to acknowledge this location, but that perhaps we pay less attention to the multivoiced context of our ponderings. See, for example, Elbaz-Luwisch, Moen & Gudmundsdottir (2002) who argue for greater multivoicedness via the use of a Bakhtinian perspective.
27 ....which is something that I would like to do more intensively (better) in my post-doctoral thinkings.
28 Although a complex, and difficult concept to translate from Czech, *Litost* refers to "a state of torment created by the sudden sight of one's own misery" (Kundera, 1978/1996).
29 And here, I mean this quite literally, geographically, politically. As Elbaz-Luwisch (2004) has argued that while the concept of place has been neglected in contemporary education, we still may need (in postmodern spaces) to examine what meanings come out of the places we inhabit.

REFERENCES

Alexander, A. (2001). The politics of identity in post-Apartheid South Africa. In J. Muller (Ed.), *Challenges of globalisation: South African debates with Manuel Castells.*
Altrichter, H., Posch, P., & Somekh, B. (1993). Teachers investigate their work: An introduction to the methods of action research. London: Routledge.
Alvesson, M., & Skoldberg, K. (2000). Reflexive methodology: New vistas for qualitative research. London: Sage.
Ashcroft, B., Griffiths, G., & Tiffin, H. (1989). *The empire writes back: Theory and practice in post-colonial literatures.* London: Routledge.
Barthes, R. (1977). Introduction to the structural analysis of narratives. In R. Barthes (Ed.), *Images-music-text.* London: Macmillan.
Berger, J. (1986). *Ways of seeing.* London: Penguin.
Borradori, G. (2003). *Philosophy in a time of terror: Dialogues with Jurgen Habermas and Jacque Derrida.* Chicago: University of Chicago Press.
Bruner, J. S. (1986). *Actual minds, possible worlds.* Cambridge: Harvard University Press.

Chomsky, N. (2003). *Hegemony or survival*. New York: Metropolitan Books.

Clandinin, D. J., & Connelly, F. M. (2000). *Narrative inquiry: Experience and story in qualitative research*. San Francisco: Jossey Bass.

Crane, N. (2002). *Mercator: The man who mapped the planet*. Great Britain: Phoenix.

Day, E. (2002). September, Me, My*Self and I: Personal and professional re-constructions in ethnographic research. *Forum Qualitative Sozialforschung/Forum Qualitative Research [On-line Journal]*, *3*(3). Retrieved June 18, 2004, from http://www.qualitative-research.net/fqs-eng.htm

Denzin, N., & Lincoln, Y. (Eds.). (1994). *Handbook of qualitative research*. Thousand Oaks, CA: Sage.

Eisner, E. (1998). *The enlightened eye: Qualitative Inquiry and the enhancement of education practice*. New Jersey, NJ: Prentice-Hall, Inc.

Elbaz-Luwisch, F., Moen, T., & Gudmundsdottir, S. (2002). The multivoicedness of classrooms: Bakhtin and narratives of teaching. In H. Heikekinen, R. Huttunen, & L. Syrjala (Eds.), *Biographical research and narrativity: Voices of teachers and philosophers*. University of Jyvaskyla SoPhi Press.

Elbaz-Luwisch, F. (2004). Immigrant teachers: Stories of self and place. *International Journal of Qualitative Studies in Education*, *17*(3), 387–414.

Ellis, C. (2004). *The ethnographic I: A methodological novel about ethnography*. New York: Rowman & Littlefield.

Engestrom, Y., & Miettinen, R. (1999). Introduction. In Y. Engestrom, R. Miettinen, & R. Punamaki (Eds.), *Perspectives on activity theory*. Cambridge: Cambridge University Press.

Etherington, K. (2004). *Becoming a reflexive researcher – Using ourselves in research*. London: Jessica Kingsley Publishers.

Finkelstein, V. (2002a). *A personal journey into disability politics*. Paper presented at Leeds University Centre for Disability Studies, Leeds, England.

Finkelstein, V. (2002b). *Whose history???* Keynote address, Disability History Week, Birmingham, England.

Flick, U. (1998). *An introduction to qualitative research*. London: Sage.

Gesell, A. (1925). *The mental growth of the pre-school child: A psychological outline of normal development from birth to the sixth year, including a system of developmental diagnosis*. New York: Macmillan.

Grace, P. A., Hill, J. P., Johnson, W. C., & Lewis, B. J. (2004). In other words: Queer voices/dissident subjectivities impelling social change. *International Journal of Qualitative Studies in Education*, *17*(3), 301–324.

Greenlagh, T. (1999). Narrative based medicine in an evidence based world. *British Medical Journal*, *318*, 323–325.

Greenlagh, T., & Hurwitz, B. (1999). Narrative based medicine: Why study narrative? *British Medical Journal*, *318*, 48–50.

Habib, S. (2003). *Queering the Middle East and the new Anti Semitism*. Retrieved December 18, 2003, from http://www.brunel.ac.uk/faculty/arts/EnterText/3_2_pdfs/habib.pdf

Hanrahan, M. (2003). May, challenging the dualistic assumptions of academic writing: Representing Ph.D. research as embodied practice. *Forum Qualitative Sozialforschung/Forum Qualitative Research [On-Line Journal]*, *4*(2), Retrieved June 18, 2004, from http://www.qualitative-research.net/fqs-texte/2-03/2-03hanrahan-e.htm

Heylighen, F. (2001). Memetics. In F. Heylighen, C. Joslyn & V. Turchin (Eds.), *Principia Cybernetica Web*. Brussels: Principia Cybernetica. Retrieved April 10, 2002, from http://pespmc1.vub.ac.be/MEMES.html.

hooks, b. (1989). *Talking back: Thinking feminist, thinking black*. London: Sheba Feminist Publishers.

Kundera, M. (1978/1996). *The book of laughter and forgetting*. London: Faber & Faber.

Luria, A. R. (1976). *Cognitive development: Its cultural and social foundations*. Cambridge, MA: Harvard University Press.

Mandela, N. R. (1994). *Long walk to freedom: The autobiography of Nelson Mandela*. London: Abacus.

Maranhao, T. (1991). Reflection, dialogue, and the subject. In F. Steier (Ed.), *Research and Reflexivity*. London: Sage.

Marx, K., & Engels, F. (1968). *The German ideology*. Chicago: University of Chicago Press.

Maturana, H., & Varela, F. J. (1980). *Autopoiesis and cognition: The realization of the living*. Dordrecht/Boston: Reidel.

Miles, M. B., & Huberman, A. M. (1984). *Qualitative data analysis: A sourcebook for new methods*. Beverley Hills, CA: Sage.

Morrison, T. (1970/1993). *The bluest eye*. New York: Plume.

Munro, P. (1998). *Subject to fiction: Women teachers' life history narratives and the cultural politics of resistance*. Philadelphia: Open University Press.

Noakes, T. D., Harley, Y. X. R., Bosch, A. N., Marino, F. E., St Clair Gibson, A., & Lambert, M. I. (2004). Physiological function and neuromuscular recruitment in elite South Africa distance runners. *Equine and Comparative Exercise Physiology, 1*(4), 261–271(11).

Okri. (1998). *Infinite riches*. London: Phoenix.

Oliver, M. (1992). Changing the social relations of research production. *Disability, Handicap & Society, 7*(2), 101–114.

Orland-Barak, L. (2002). The theoretical sensitivity of the researcher: Reflections on a complex construct. *Reflective Practice, 3*(3), 263–278.

Peta, B. (2005, 11 March). The burning issue that needs to be addressed: Corruption. *The Independent*, UK.

Pillay, M. (1992). *Zulu communication disorders: Beliefs and perceptions*. Undergraduate research study, University of KwaZulu-Natal, South Africa.

Pillay, M. (1997). *Speech-language therapy & audiology: Practice with a black African first language clientele*. Unpublished Masters Dissertation, University of KwaZulu-Natal, Durban, South Africa.

Pillay, M. (2003a). *(Re)positioning the powerful expert and the sick person: The case of communication pathology*. Doctoral Thesis, University of KwaZulu-Natal, Durban, South Africa.

Pillay, M. (2003b). *I-visibility as a theorising process*. Paper presented at Kenton Education Association & Southern African Comparative and History of Education Society conference, Cape Town, South Africa, 30 October–02 November 2003.

Price-Williams, D. (1980). Toward the idea of cultural psychology: A superordinate theme for study. *Journal of Cross-Cultural Psychology*, pp.75–88.

Ramose, M. (2002). *African philosophy through Ubuntu*. Harare: Mond Books.

Salomon, G. (Ed.). (1993). *Distributed cognitions: Psychological and educational considerations*. Cambridge: Cambridge University Press,.

Searle, J. R. (1969). *Speech acts*. Cambridge: Cambridge University Press.

Sedgewick, E. (1990). *The epistemology of the closet*. Berkeley, CA: University of California Press.

Skultans, V. (1999). Narratives of the body and history: Illness in judgement on the Soviet past. *Sociology of Health & Illness, 21*(3), 310–328.

Spivak, G. C. (1985a). The Rani of Simur. In F. Barker, et al. (Eds.), *Europe and its others (Volume 1)*. Colchester: University of Essex Press.

Spivak, G. C. (1985b). Can the subaltern speak? Speculations on widow sacrifice. *Wedge, 7/8*(Winter/Spring).

Tzu, S. (1998). *The art of war* (Y. Shibing, Ed.). Hertfordshire: Wordsworth Editions Limited.

United Nations Educational, Scientific and Cultural Organisation (UNESCO) Institute for Statistics. (2004). *Global Education Digest 2004: Comparing education statistics across the world*. Montreal, Canada: UNESCO.

Van Maanen, J. (Ed.). (1995). *Representation in ethnography*. Thousand Oaks, CA: Routledge.

Vernon, A. (1997). Reflexivity: The dilemmas of researching from the inside. In C. Barnes & G. Mercer (Eds.), *Doing disability research*. Leeds: The Disability Press.

Vidich, A. J., & Lyman, S. M. (1998). Qualitative methods: Their history in sociology and anthropology. In N. K. Denzin & Y. S. Lincoln (Eds.), *The landscape of qualitative research: Theories and issues*. Thousand Oaks, CA: Sage.

Vygotsky, L. S. (1978). *Mind in society: The development of higher psychological processes.* Cambridge, MA: Harvard University Press.

Vygotsky, L. S. (1987). *Thinking and speech.* New York: Plenum.

Wagner, E. L. (2002). *(Inter)Connecting IS narrative research: Current status and future opportunities for process-oriented field studies.* Unpublished paper, Working Paper Series, London School of Economics.

Winter, R. (1989). *Learning from experience: Principles and practice in action research.* London: Falmer Press.

Zimmerman, A. (2001). Looking beyond history: The optics of German anthropology and the critique of humanism. *Studies in History and Philosophy of Biological and Biomedical Sciences, 32*(3), 385–411.

RENUKA VITHAL

4. A QUEST FOR DEMOCRATIC PARTICIPATORY VALIDITY IN MATHEMATICS EDUCATION RESEARCH[1]

INTRODUCTION

The notion of *democratic participatory validity*, described, exemplified and developed in this chapter, emerged from a study that explored the question of what happens in a mathematics classroom when student teachers attempt to realise what may be referred to as a social, cultural, political approach to the mathematics curriculum, and especially one that seeks to integrate a critical perspective (Vithal, 2003). The issue of validity in research – most simply the question of: "how does a researcher know that she knows" in the knowledge generation endeavour – was brought into sharp relief through two main struggles that had to be engaged in this study. The first arose from the explicit and deliberate attempt to maintain resonance between the educational approach under investigation with its attendant qualities of democracy, equity, fairness and social justice, and the research methodology developed to study the approach in the processes set up and the research relations among researcher, teachers and learners to arrive at claims and themes.

To give meaning and substance to the criterion of democratic participatory validity in a more general sense here, I refer to and rely on this earlier study of theory-practice relations (Vithal, 2003) as I connect and critique the existing work in the field. The second struggle which strengthened the case for developing and considering this form of validity arose from the deeply unstable, widely transforming, and under-resourced context within which the study took place. The imperative to keep the study going in situations of student and teacher strikes and other conflicts and contestations in the research setting inherent to large multiple systemic changes, posed challenges for questions of rigour and scholarship (Vithal, 1998). To develop this second line of argument, I draw on debates about the importation and exportation of research, researchers, and their methodologies between and within countries: between those at the centre with wealth, privilege and power to speak and shape the world and those at the margin, who are dis-advantaged, and struggle to have voice. I make specific reference to mathematics education research (Vithal and Valero, 2003; Valero and Vithal, 1999) and retain a strong focus on issues of context.

R. Dhunpath and M. Samuel (eds.), Life History Research: Epistemology, Methodology and Representation, 67–81

Mathematics educators have increasingly been concerned with identifying scientific criteria for establishing quality in mathematics education research. They refer, for instance, to issues of validity, objectivity, rigour and precision, predictability, reproducibility and relevance (see, for example, Kilpatrick, 1993). Many of these are revisited in the International Commission on Mathematical Instruction (ICMI) study appropriately titled, *Mathematics education as a research domain: A search for identity* (Sierpinska & Kilpatrick, 1998) and other works such as the *Handbook of research design in mathematics and science education* (Kelly & Lesh, 2000). The discernible silence about what a critical perspective in mathematics education research could mean in these earlier writings is now being addressed, for example, in the *Second international handbook of mathematics education* (Bishop et al, 2003) and in edited volumes such as that by Valero and Zevenbergen (2004) on *Researching the socio-political dimensions of mathematics education: Issues of power in theory and methodology.*

The rise of new developments in mathematics education concerned with linking democracy, social justice, equity, human rights and related ideas to the teaching and learning of mathematics (both in theory and practice), has increased the imperative to examine the means by which such approaches could or should be studied. The need for "hard" evidence produced through research, to move innovative progressive ideas from the realm of advocacy and "imagined or theoretical practice" to actual and real practice at a systemic macro level beyond anecdotes requires intellectually honest and authentic interrogation and rigour at the micro level to support the development of critical approaches to mathematics education. To this end, mathematics education can and does draw from developments in general education and the social sciences. However, what still remains even in these works is the invisibility of the deeply diverse and unequal contexts in which research takes place and, in particular, the silence of voices from the "developing" or "third" world in discussions about appropriate criteria relevant to their context. The stability assumption built into mathematics education research methodologies, especially in rapidly transforming societies marked by constant wide-ranging disruptions (Valero & Vithal, 1999) justifies questioning existing criteria for quality and relevance and opens up new possibilities. The argument for developing or rethinking criteria is made with a caution against a ghettoising of research of "developing world" contexts in favour of creating opportunities for interrogating theories and methodologies developed at "the centre" which may be shown to unmask aspects rendered more visible at "the periphery" to improve research approaches for all settings. A parallel may be put forward for mathematics education research as is done for mathematics in which theories and propositions are continually checked and tested against outliers, a practice arguably and perhaps surprisingly relatively absent in mathematics education research.

As research methodologies are challenged and alternatives found, the debates around how "new" forms of research should be evaluated have led to developments in many aspects, but arguably and most notably with reference to the criteria of validity, reliability and generalisabilty. In this paper I focus on validity. First, I trace a path through the changing, perhaps exploding, conceptions of validity in different research paradigms and methodologies, then point to the difficulties of activating conceptions of validity, particularly those put forward in critical research, and arrive at what I call *"democratic participatory validity"*. I develop democratic participatory validity with reference to the aspects of choice, negotiation, reciprocity, responsibility, responsiveness and reflexivity within a critical approach to research and one that recognises the importance of context.

VALIDITY IN TRANSFORMATION

Validity and generalisability have their origin in the positivistic research paradigm where they take several forms such as internal or external validity, where the concern is with credibility of inferences drawn from a study and their applicability to other contexts. Developed and used in the positivist paradigm, such criteria are not only well established and well defined in research, they are intended to be uniformly applied across studies. With the emergence of qualitative research, the concern with validity in research has given rise to new questions and challenges. In the interpretive and critical paradigms, the problem of assessing validity in a study has become rather complex. However, across paradigms, validity, according to Eisenhart and Howe (1992, p. 644) may be

generally defined as the trustworthiness of inferences drawn from data.

Qualitative researchers have differed considerably in their response to the issue of validity. One extreme approach has been to ignore or dismiss validity as a criterion, where it is considered to be meaningless and even obstructing qualitative research (see, for example, Grumet, 1990). However, an earlier approach (see, for example, Goetz and LeCompte, 1982 cited in Eisenhart and Howe, 1992) has been to retain validity concepts developed in experimental research but to translate them into terms applicable to non-experimental designs like ethnographies. Internal validity in these non-experimental designs, it is argued, could be judged according to the extent to which research procedures led to authentic representations of reality and external validity requires careful and extensive descriptions of all aspects of the study – the context, participants, etc. Perhaps a more radical approach presented by Lincoln and Guba (1985) is that a completely different set of standards are required to judge the "trustworthiness" of qualitative research since the alternative naturalistic research paradigm has a different ontological and epistemological basis from that of experimental research. Reclaiming ordinary language terms, they point to different kinds of trustworthiness. Since naturalistic inquirers focus on reconstructing the perspectives of those being studied, the "truth value" of findings (analogous to internal validity) was interpreted as the researcher being able to demonstrate that the research findings are credible to those who provide the data. To demonstrate "applicability" (analogous to external validity), the main task of the researcher is to comprehensively describe the contextual conditions of the study, providing thick descriptions so that the potential audience of the research can decide whether the research findings can be transferred and applied to another context. In tracing these changing conceptions of validity (or generalisability) across paradigms, we observe that new meanings are being engaged through a different discourse. Some notions of validity retain roots in the positivist paradigm but their meanings are being reshaped, whilst others attempt a complete break from positivist notions.

That conceptions of validity are exploding can be seen in the range of criteria being advanced. For instance, Maxwell (1992) discusses five different ways in which validity has been understood and used in qualitative research: descriptive, interpretive, theoretical, and evaluative validity; and generalisabilty. In interview research, for instance, Kvale (1996) introduces the concepts of validity as quality of craftsmanship, communicative validity and pragmatic validity. Lather (1994, p. 40) argues in her paper on "Validity after poststructuralism" for "creating a nomadic and dispersed validity" which counters "prescriptive discourse practices of validity" and offers, for instance, the notion of a transgressive validity with four framings of validity as ironic validity, paralogical validity, rhizomatic validity and voluptuous validity. These notions are explored in relation to her study of women living with AIDS. In this lies both a justification and means for generating new and different conceptions of validity within mathematics education research relative to the theoretical base and practical concerns of a critical perspective in mathematics education.

No doubt, validity is socially constructed as Kvale (1996) argues, but the point to be made here is that the approach being taken by those who draw on critical theory, feminist and postmodernist approaches to research, reconceptualises concepts of validity (and generalisability) in forms that are relevant to their theoretical (including ideological) and methodological commitments in the research. Hence, while multiple discourses of verification have emerged, these are neither ad hoc nor random, but rather connected to the theoretical and methodological positions on which their research rests. Conceptions of validity are therefore anchored by the paradigm in which the research is located. Critical researchers are likely to reject notions of methodological correctness which can guarantee the validity of their data and findings (KincGracee & McLaren, 1994). They have devised different standards of verification relative to the theoretical underpinnings of their research. Not only are the forms and meanings of research criteria shifting from paradigm to paradigm, and within paradigms, but researchers are exploring alternative criteria for validation, rather than ascribing a unified or universal meaning.

What must be pointed out is that in distinguishing between these understandings of validity, there is seepage of use, meaning and discourse across paradigms in the untidy world of actual research. For example, the strategy of triangulation often used to establish the trustworthiness of claims in both the interpretivist and critical paradigms has its roots in the positivist paradigm. Within qualitative research, it is possible to observe how meanings ascribed to validity in the interpretivist paradigm have been carried through into the critical research paradigm, but here some of these ideas have undergone further change as several studies that include feminist and postmodernist perspectives demonstrate. For example, Lather (1991) describes, in addition to several forms of validity found in interpretivist studies, the notion of catalytic validity given the emancipatory intent of her research.

It is the last notion of validity (catalytic validity) that separates the interpretivist or naturalistic research from critical research. This has been explored within critical research (see, for example, also KincGracee & McLaren, 1994). It

represents the degree to which the research process, reorients, focuses and energises participants towards knowing reality, in order to transform it, a process Freire refers to as conscientization (Lather 1991, p. 68).

Recognising the critical researchers active involvement in the research process

the argument for catalytic validity lies not only within recognition of the reality-altering impact of the research process but also in the desire to consciously channel this impact so that respondents gain self-understanding and, ultimately, self determination through research participation (ibid., p. 68).

Focusing on the way in which power relations of the wider society are perpetuated in research practice, critical researchers take steps to ensure that research studies are democratically designed and findings democratically produced. Citing research by Roman (1989) and Roman and Apple (1990) in this context, Eisenhart and Howe (1992, p. 652) describe valid research as using a methodology that

resonates with the experiences of the participants; allows participant to understand and transform their experiences of subordination; reduces the separation between the researcher's intellectual world and the participants' descriptions and understandings of their experience; and allows the researcher's prior theoretical and political commitments to be informed and transformed through participants' experiences.

What can be noted is that each of the researchers are reconceptualising validity in a manner and language that is appropriate for their research, which resonates with their theoretical orientations and commitments, and extends beyond a concern with credibility and applicability of the claims of a study, to the research process and participants.

VALIDITY IN ACTION

The question that arises is how such validity concerns should be addressed in any research claiming to be an inquiry from a critical perspective. As a qualitative researcher, if located in the critical paradigm, one could draw on several of the above notions to develop a conception of validity appropriate and relevant to one's research. In particular, the researcher could engage the notion of catalytic validity, which is widely referred to by researchers working in the critical paradigm as the emancipatory and empowerment potential and consequences of research. Catalytic validity developed in critical studies requires the researcher to assess

the degree to which research moves those it studies to understand the world and the way it is shaped in order for them to transform it (KincGracee & McLaren, 1994, p. 152).

This also includes those doing the studying, given the inherently unequal distribution of power in the research relationship. But it is difficult to assess catalytic validity in a study for several reasons, such as: to what extent can a researcher make claims about what exactly has been transformed, the direction the transformation has taken, and the life span of that transformation? In my research, for instance, the goals of the study were not explicitly directed at changing the student teachers *per se* in the way critical researchers write about transforming participants in the research, hence my reluctance to locate my study firmly within the critical paradigm. This was despite the fact that I was aware of the trans-formatory possibilities of my work with them. I produced a wide range of data – through interviews, observations, written work and reflections, etc. – firstly within the teacher education setting of the university while introducing a social, cultural, cultural, political approach in which they engaged theories and practices related to ethnomathematics, race, gender, class, language and other dimensions of the relationship between mathematics education and society. Later, I produced additional data with teachers and learners as I followed them into the schools that the student teachers had chosen to use to practice their teaching (Vithal, 2003).

Although my focus was not on directly transforming participants, I was aware that some change, if not transformation, could be anticipated given that the student teachers were experiencing teaching and learning mathematics in a completely different way. To some extent, therefore, it was possible to consider catalytic validity in my research through what student teachers said in interviews and in their diaries, as well as by observing the enactment of their experience and reflections as they were engaging in a social, cultural, political approach to the mathematics curriculum through practices such as project work in classrooms with learners. It was, however, the problem of operationalising catalytic validity that drew attention to and enabled the proposal of a different form of validity – a "democratic participatory validity" – to be considered in relation to any catalytic validity. Clearly, the notion of research being a catalyst for change is important given the declared intentions of critical researchers; hence the need for evaluating this outcome. But in what sense could I say that these student teachers had been transformed? Perhaps as mathematics teachers, it could be discerned in their understanding of what it could mean to teach and learn mathematics in this critical approach and in the way in which they acted on that understanding. It may also be possible to obtain some indication of the substance of that transformation through observation of the nature and extent through which they incorporate this approach in their teaching. However, a range of further questions arise around the sustainability of transformations:

- When student teachers enter the school context after their exposure to the research, in the absence of the researcher and a research process, what is the status of that transformation?
- Could some aspect not being focused on in the study undergo transformation?
- What about transformations that impact significantly on other aspects of a participant's life, obscured from the researcher's sight? For instance, student teachers who demonstrate some change through their practices within their

mathematics classrooms, are sometimes considered to be subversive "troublemakers" which has consequences for collegial relations.
– Can a researcher know the impact of a research process on the whole life of a person?
– Could a transformation come to have negative consequences? For instance, a very high catalytic validity could result in completely opposite consequences from those a researcher intends.
– Could student teachers come to understand their position in schools, with the result that they prematurely terminate teaching as a career?
– Then there's the question of who recognises or decides on what constitutes an act of empowerment or emancipation?

Related to the above questions is the inescapability of the "imposition of emancipation or transformation", usually by a researcher who selects and involves participants in the research process. This selection is often based on the researcher perceiving and defining a group as being disadvantaged and oppressed. This lack of equity between the researcher and the research participants creates a space for considering another form of validity – focusing on the aspect of participation – that may be considered necessary (though not sufficient) for any transformation to take place. The problem of the researcher's authority can be partially dealt with by focusing on relationships in critical research.

I argue that there is a need for considering another form of validity in any critical research, which brings to the centre of its methodology the idea of democratic forms of inquiry. In such research it should also be possible to ask questions about: what is the extent of the opportunities created for democratic forms of participation in the research process, the extent to which participants actually come to own and shape the different parts of the research process in its entirety, and how far are the eventual findings from those that different participants agree to – "*a democratic participatory validity*". If a research study claims to be democratically designed and the results democratically produced, it should be possible to say something about the degree to which a study could be assessed as being democratic research. This is an important validity consideration, if

Democratisation of educational research is an important goal of critical education research (Eisenhart and Howe, 1992, p. 653).

DEMOCRATIC PARTICIPATORY VALIDITY

I use the term democratic to emphasise the aspect of "equity in participation" in the research endeavour. Rather than focus on the extent of emancipation or transformation which a critical research process attempts to offer, it seems more pertinent to consider the way in which participation is organised within a research project as a whole and its impact on the research process. This could include the participants, the researcher herself, and the outcomes of that participation. I do not claim that this resolves the many dilemmas identified above, but it forces and allows space for the researcher to doubt her own frameworks and interpretations, and gives visibility and voice to dissenting views and understandings. I maintain that this is an issue of validity because it relates to how a researcher could handle competing and contradictory claims in the analysis. A democratic participatory validity reveals the confidence with which a researcher is making particular claims, to show the extent to which they are shared or conflicting. In practitioner or insider research, democratic validity, according to Anderson and Herr (1999, p. 16),

> refers to the extent to which research is done in collaboration with all the parties who have a stake in the problem under investigation. If not done collaboratively, how are multiple perspectives and material interests taken into account in the study.

Participants or stakeholders cannot be "forced" into research but nevertheless the researcher has to open to scrutiny the processes for managing multiple and possibly conflicting interests in a research setting within a broader educational setting.

It is possible to argue for a democratic participatory validity not only on the basis of the concerns of a critical perspective in mathematics education research but also from the perspective of different research contexts, particularly those characterised by fundamental transformations, disruptions and instability. If disruptions and conflicts are taken seriously, in such research settings the researcher is forced to involve research participants in significant ways in the research endeavour (Vithal & Valero, 2003). The researcher may have multiple positions or may not be able to be consistently present throughout the process. One outcome is that if research participants experience greater ownership of the research process then it may be that the quality of data made available is enhanced, and therefore the possibility for making more critical and deeper theoretical reflections in the analysis is also improved; that is, it allows the researcher to access disruptive data, and such data could yield insights that may not otherwise be possible. The discontinuities may reveal aspects of the question under investigation that the continuities cannot (Vithal, 1998).

But let me attempt to evaluate the notion of a democratic participatory validity as it relates to my research with the student teachers. How did the research focus come about and who shaped the research question? I chose and initiated the inquiry. Student teachers were invited to participate in the study and their decisions were shaped by their vested interests in the project. The extent to which student teachers owned the process varied and could be assessed through the additional effort they made in setting up the projects, in collecting different data which they used to inform their own understanding, and in writing and presenting the research report. Not all of them could negotiate the same opportunities for implementation and hence also for data collection, analysis and writing. However, the student teachers were able to regulate their own level of participation in the processes. For example, only half the student teachers participated in writing the report. An implicit idea here is the degree of choice that participants can exercise and the extent to which that choice can be exercised in the research process (as opposed to the pedagogic process) within the constraints of their situation – in this case their positions as student teachers in schools, the organisational context of the school, etc. A democratic research process makes available opportunities of partnerships in research. Accounting for democratic participatory validity requires the researcher to make visible and assess the nature of collaborations. An immediate criticism this raises for my study is that the participation in the research was neither equal, consistent, nor uniform across participants – the teachers and learners and even the student teachers themselves.

Democratic participatory validity applies not only to the findings but also relates to all components of the research process, including the research focus and questions, data collection, analysis, and writing. Moreover, it may be considered with other forms and processes for establishing validity. Triangulation, for instance, may offer a useful means for establishing democratic participatory validity in critical studies, not in the sense of seeking to establish "a truth" but as a means of offering multiple perspectives and making visible the extent to which these may converge and diverge. My study relied on triangulation through multiple agents, methods, and through time and space. The realisation of a social, cultural, political approach which integrates a critical perspective into mathematics education was considered from the perspective of several participants, including the student teachers, the learners, the teachers in the schools and myself as the researcher, as well as through a variety of methods such as interviews, classroom observations and various documents (journals, learners' work, etc.).

The trustworthiness of the data and findings was confirmed through the negotiation of descriptions produced by the student teachers, and those produced by the researcher. The production of a paper after the student teachers' involvement in the data generation, which became a part of the research process as a negotiated reward for participation, increased the possibility for valid accounts. This is because descriptions and preliminary analysis offered in the paper could be disputed publicly by participants such as the teachers in the schools. Credibility of the descriptions and analyses was also increased by referring across the contexts of different schools. Student teachers could, and indeed did, disagree with some of my interpretations of events in the classroom, which are visible to some extent in the case descriptions that allow for critique and dissenting voices (what I refer to as *a crucial description* – Vithal, 2003). Yet, as sole author of this report, my findings are privileged even if I make explicit the teachers' and student teachers' readings. I also recognise that in discussion, my position as teacher educator and having an assessment responsibility may have diluted differences and forced some consensus.

Democratic participatory validity need not only be considered or applied in research that explicitly declares a democratic intent. It could be used more generally in research methodology to observe or declare the nature of the relationship between the researcher and the research participants as well as the extent of the involvement of the researched in the research process and the eventual claims made. For example, considerations of democratic participatory validity in a survey study may lead to the involvement of a sub-sample of participants in a partnership with the researcher in the construction of the questionnaire, its administration, data capture, analysis, discussion of findings and the writing of a report. Alternatively, it could involve partial contribution to the process (Singh & Vithal, 2003). Democratic participatory validity could be said to be high when democratic participation is evident or is the basis of the study throughout the research process, one in which participants can shape the nature and degree of their participation and have a voice in its claims. Democratic participatory validity could be said to be low when the participants have no say in any aspect of the research process and are only seen as subjects or respondents. It indicates whether co-learning agreements rather than data-extraction agreements are set up between the researcher and participants (Wagner, 1997). In my study, democratic participatory validity was high for the student teachers but low for mentor teachers and even lower for the learners in respect of my engagement as a researcher. The question of how such a form of validity might be extended to learners within a research setting is a major challenge for researchers investigating a critical education. Some movement toward this consideration is supported in the recent writing of Sfard (1998) who argues for the use of a "participation metaphor" in researching learning in mathematics and not only a focusing on an "acquisition metaphor" which currently dominates in mathematics education. She does not, however, go into a critical research paradigm.

In order for researchers and research participants to agree about the extent of democratic validity in any one study, they would need to agree on what constitutes a democratic partnership within research relationships. Democratic participation may be characterised by such features as negotiation, choice, reciprocity, responsibility, responsiveness and reflexivity while also recognising that these operate within inherent and inevitable power relations between researcher and research participants. Relationships with the learners and school also need to be considered. Within this setting, those who seek to realise and research a critical approach to mathematics education that is not widely available in the education system may intervene and act upon an existing current actual classroom or school situation, and arrange it in particular specific ways with ideas and inspiration from their imagined hypothetical understandings of theory and practices associated with such an approach. These *current actual, arranged and imagined hypothetical situations* are theoretical-methodological tools for researching mathematics education from a critical perspective (Vithal, 2003; Skovsmose & Borba, 2004), and they offer democratic participatory validity an important role and function in critical research.

FEATURES OF DEMOCRATIC PARTICIPATORY VALIDITY

An elaboration of several key components of democratic participatory validity in relation to the current actual, arranged and imagined hypothetical situations, and with recognition of the importance of contexts especially those characterised by change and uncertainty, could give this form of validity more meaning and depth.

Choice for participants in the research process means that they are free agents in the process in that should their experience of the research process become in any way exploitative, they could withdraw or change the nature of their participation. This choice, however, is not completely free since it is exercised within other constraints. For instance, their participation could be a prerequisite of their teaching practice requirement for their degree. Choice, in this research, allows the researcher to not fall foul of practices that are contradictory to the theory on which the research rests. Choice also serves to counter, in part, imposition that any negotiation might lead to, especially when the researcher is in an inherently more powerful position than the participants because of the unequal balance of knowledge and skills specific to the situation and to research itself. Choice is also essential if participants are to maximise their participation in the research especially in terms of the effort and commitment that any successful research project requires. The postulating of an imagined hypothetical situation, which offers a space for mediating between theory and practice, supports the element of choice in that the recontextualisation of theoretical ideas need not be uniform or consistent within or across research sites, though they may be negotiated.

It is *negotiation* that carries the potential and possibility for change. The potential for negotiation allows ideas propagated by the researcher and by the participants to be challenged, critiqued, reformed, transformed or discarded. This means that the quality of reasoning both in the practice and in the theory may be improved. Negotiation is essential and central to the relationships between the imagined hypothetical, current actual and arranged situation. Firstly, between the imagined hypothetical and the current actual situation, the researcher and research participants need to negotiate their creative pedagogical imagination to develop possibilities for action in practice, while keeping the actual situation in mind. Secondly, for a realistic interpretation of the hypothetical situation into the arranged situation, a collaborative transformation of the actual existing into the arranged situation is needed. Thirdly, negotiation enables theorising to occur from the ground in the arranged situation, back into the hypothetical situation, and to the *a priori* theoretical landscape. Throughout these relations, negotiations also serve to enhance the quality of the participation of research participants. However, negotiation is not without its problems. Given the inherently unequal power in research relations, negotiation itself can dilute different perspectives and contradictions in seeking consensus to act in a particular situation.

Reciprocity ensures that the goals and outcomes of the research process will meet the needs and interests of both the researcher and the research participants. Given the availability of choice and negotiation, reciprocity keeps at bay the possibility for the research process to collapse by helping to secure the commitment and participation of the research participants in the arranged situation. It assists in bringing equity to the research partnerships since both are seen as needing something the other can offer which in turn contributes to effort and commitment. All involved participants should have a clear idea about what is in it for them in the research process. Through reciprocal partnerships, participants are made accountable to each other even if that accountability lies in different domains and interests, be it theory, practice or both. It is in reciprocity that the ethics and politics of research are enshrined and the aspect of rewards and reasons for participation need to be dealt with head on.

The focus on participation as a validity concern, particularly in contexts of socio-political conflict, brings into sharper relief the principles of responsibility and responsiveness to the research participants and setting (Vithal & Valero, 2003). *Responsibility* refers to the researcher's capacity of being openly accountable to those involved in the research, about the questions being posed, observations, interpretations and claims being proposed. Accountability about what and to whom becomes especially important when the setting is dynamic and unpredictable and multiple vested interests may be at play. *Responsiveness* is the capacity to reply and react readily to the influence received from the research interaction. Responsiveness allows for flexibilty in shifts from questions and methods to remain relevant to fluidity in context. In contrast to traditional approaches in which researchers produce and remove data form a situation to use and analyse later outside the research setting, for knowledge production purposes, the responsiveness and responsibility principles require a constant and open "giving back" to the research participants or situation involved in the research. This contributes to the necessity of establishing a de-objectifying dialogue between researcher and participants, so that they can have a substantial understanding of the research purposes and intentions, and can also benefit intellectually from it (Valero, 1999; Valero, 2004; Valero & Matos, 2000). In other words, reciprocity is more than a negotiation of rewards for participation but is rather an active involvement and mutual accountability in the research.

This means that for any real notion of partnership to survive in research, deliberative dialogue is needed (Valero, 1999; Valero, 2004). Such dialogue has been operationalised in some research approaches through the notion of *reflexivity*. Choice, negotiation, reciprocity, responsibility and responsiveness are made possible through reflexivity because meaningful and substantial participation in a study is made possible through opportunities for reflexivity. Within contexts of conflict and change, a double reflexivity (Apple, 1995) is needed, one directed to the content or topic under research and one directed at the research process and relationships themselves. Reflexivity includes both group reflections of collectives – coflections (Valero, 1999) – and individual reflections, providing a means for managing conflicts, unequal power relations and hierarchies not only between the researcher and the research participants, but also among the research participants themselves: for instance, between teachers, teachers and pupils, and among pupils, as well as among a team of researchers who may also differ according to some dimensions (Smith, 1999). It may be argued that conflicts and contradictions are the lived realities of those who inhabit spaces of contestation, and hence, create an imperative for dealing with them in the heart of the research process involving researchers as a community and their relationships to research participants. Theoretical and methodological frameworks that prioritise systematicity, logic and coherence at the expense of the research participants' involvement in a study are unlikely to be able to capture the breadth and depth of the phenomena they seek to investigate in unstable settings, yielding processes and claims that may be disputed by the research participants or the broader community represented in the study. This is why participation and outcomes of research need to be problematised and raised as a validity criterion in situations of conflict.

Choice, negotiation, reciprocity, responsibility, responsiveness, and reflexivity are important features of any democratic relationship. And democratic relationships in the research process are likely to improve the quality and quantity of ideas and knowledge generated through the process because a diversity of interpretations and explanations are laid open which may be compatible or in conflict, be connected or discontinuous. The diversity valued in a critical mathematics education landscape also comes to be valued in the research landscape. A democratic participatory validity forces the researcher to bring resonance between the educational relationships and the research relationships. Democracy must be enacted in the research process as it is advocated within the educational processes. This does not mean that unequal power relations are neutralised in research (they clearly cannot be) but rather that democratic processes and relations are privileged and legitimated in the research enterprise.

CONCLUSION

Democratic participatory validity in research needs to be developed both procedurally and substantively, both in theory and in practice. It signals a key concern in research in mathematics education both from a critical perspective and with reference to rapidly changing education systems. In this conception of validity, the concern has moved very far from a focus exclusively on the validity of conclusions drawn from an analysis, to a validity concern that permeates the entire research endeavour which is both theoretical and practically grounded. It is a shift from a focus on the validity of the research process to include a concern also for the participants in that process and the nature of relationships embedded in the process. However, the need to remain sceptical toward this proposition of a democratic participatory validity must be maintained by asking the question: how valid is the validity question (Kvale, 1989), particularly in critical research? In constructing the notion of participatory validity, we must ask in what sense, then, are we still speaking of validity, and is validity in fact needed in a critical approach to research in mathematics education?

NOTES

[1] This chapter is based on and draws from two earlier sources: Vithal, R. (2003). *In search of a pedagogy of conflict and dialogue for mathematics education.* Drodrecht: Kluwer Academic Publishers; and Vithal, R. & Valero, P. (2003). Researching mathematics education in situations of social and political conflict. In A.J. Bishop, M A. Clements, C. Keitel, J. Kilpatrick, & F.K.S. Leung (Eds.), *Second international handbook of mathematics education.* Dordrecht: Kluwer Academic Publishers.

REFERENCES

Apple, M. (1995). Taking power seriously: New directions in equity in mathematics education and beyond. In W. Secada, E. Fennema, & L. Adajian (Eds.), *New directions for equity in mathematics education*. Cambridge: Cambridge University Press.
Anderson, G. L., & Herr, K. (1999). The new paradigm wars: Is there room for rigorous practitioner research. *Educational Researcher, 28*(5), 12–21, 40.
Bishop, A. J., Clements, M. A., Keitel, C., Kilpatrick, J., & Leung, F. K. S. (Eds.). (2003). *Second international handbook of mathematics education*. Dordrecht: Kluwer Academic Publishers.
Eisenhart, M. A., & Howe, K. R. (1992). Validity in educational research. In M. D. LeCompte, W. L. Millroy, & J. Preissle (Eds.), *The handbook of qualitative research in education*. California: Academic Press, Inc.
Grumet, M. R. (1990). On daffodils that come before the swallows dare. In E. W. Eisner, & A. Peshkin (Eds.). *A qualitative inquiry in education: The continuing debate*. New York: Teachers College, Columbia University.
Kelly, A. E., & Lesh, R. A. (Eds.). (2000). *Handbook of research design in mathematics and science education*. New Jersey, NJ: Lawrence Erlbaum Associates.
Kilpatrick, J. (1993). Beyond face value: Assessing research in mathematics education. In G. Nissen, & M. Blomhoj (Eds.), *Criteria for scientific quality and relevance in the didactics of mathematics*. Roskilde: IMFUFA.
KincGracee, J. L., & McLaren, P. L. (1994). Rethinking critical theory and qualitative research. In N. K. Denzin, & Y. S. Lincoln (Eds.), *Handbook of qualitative research*. California: Sage Publications, Inc.
Kvale, S. (1989). To validate is to question. In S. Kvale. (Ed.), *Issues of validity in qualitative research*. Lund, Sweden: Studentlitterratur.
Kvale, S. (1996). *Interviews: An introduction to qualitative research interviewing*. California: Sage Publications, Inc.
Lather, P. (1991). *Getting smart: Feminist research and pedagogy with/in the postmodern*. New York: Routledge.
Lather, P. (1994). Fertile obsession: Validity after poststructuralism. In A. Gitlin (Ed.), *Power and method: Political activism and educational research*. New York: Routledge.
Lincoln, Y. S., & Guba, E. G. (1985). *Naturalistic inquiry*. Beverly Hills, CA: Sage.
Maxwell, J. A. (1992). Understanding and validity in qualitative research. *Harvard Educational Review, 62*(3), 279–300.
Sfard, A. (1998). On two metaphors for learning and the dangers of choosing just one. *Educational Researcher, 27*, 4–13.
Sierpinska, A., & Kilpatrick, J. (1998). *Mathematics education as a research domain: A search for identity*. An ICMI Study. Dordrecht, Netherlands: Kluwer Academic Publishers.
Singh, S., & Vithal, R. (2003). Feminism's courtship with survey: Dangerous liaisons or close encounters of the feminist kind. *Academic Bulletin for Staff and Students, 13*(1), 19–35.
Skovsmose, O., & Borba, M. (2004). Research methodology and critical mathematics education. In P. Valero, & R. Zevenbergen (Eds.), *Researching the socio-political dimensions of mathematics education: Issues of power in theory and methodology*. Dordrecht: Kluwer Academic Publishers.
Smith, L. T. (1999). *Decolonizing methodologies: Research and indigenous peoples*. Dunedin: University of Otago Press.
Valero, P. (1999). Deliberative mathematics education for social democratization in Latin America. *Zentralblatt für Didaktik der Mathematik, 98*(6), 20–26.
Valero, P. (2004). *Reform, democracy and secondary school mathematics education*. PhD Dissertation. Copenhagen: The Danish University of Education.
Valero, P., & Matos, J. F. (2000). Dilemmas of social/political/cultural research in mathematics education. In J. F. Matos & M. Santos (Eds.), *Proceedings of the second international mathematics education and society conference* (pp. 394–403). Lisbon: CIEFC – University of Lisbon.

Valero, P., & Vithal, R. (1999). Research methods of the "North" revisited from the "South". *Perspectives in Education, 18*(2), 5–12.

Valero, P., & Zevenbergen R. (Eds.). (2004). *Researching the socio-political dimensions of mathematics education: Issues of power in theory and methodology.* Dordrecht: Kluwer Academic Publishers.

Vithal, R. (1998). Data and disruptions: The politics of doing mathematics education research in South Africa. In N. A. Ogude, & C. Bohlmann (Eds.), *Proceedings of the sixth annual meeting of the Southern African Association for Research in Mathematics and Science Education.* University of South Africa, 14–17 January.

Vithal, R. (2003). *In search of a pedagogy of conflict and dialogue for mathematics education.* Drodrecht: Kluwer Academic Publishers.

Vithal, R., & Valero, P. (2003). Researching mathematics education in situations of social and political conflict. In A. J. Bishop, M. A. Clements, C. Keitel, J. Kilpatrick, & F. K. S. Leung (Eds.), *Second international handbook of mathematics education.* Dordrecht: Kluwer Academic Publishers.

Wagner, J. (1997). The unavoidable intervention of educational research: A framework for reconsidering researcher-practitioner cooperation. *Educational Researcher, 26*(7), 13–22.

PART TWO: REPRESENTATION AS EPISTEMOLOGY

MICHAEL SAMUEL

5. RISKING AMBIGUITY: EXPLORING VOICE IN RESEARCH

Constantly risking absurdity
and death
whenever he performs
above the heads
of his audience
the poet like an acrobat
climbs on rime
to a high wire of his own making
and balancing on eyebeams
above a sea of faces
paces his way
to the other side of day
performing entrechats
and sleight-of-foot tricks
and other high theatrics
and all without mistaking
any thing
for what it may not be
For he's the super realist
who must perforce perceive
Taut truth
before the taking of each stance or
step
in his supposed advance
toward that still higher perch
where Beauty stands and waits
with gravity
to start her death-defying
leap
And he
a little charleychaplin man
who may or may not catch
her eternal form
spreadeagled in the empty air
of existence.   Lawrence Ferlinghetti

There is no such luxury as "freedom of speech". Perhaps only in that inner
dialogue with the self do we grow closer to understanding what that freedom

R. Dhunpath and M. Samuel (eds.), Life History Research: Epistemology, Methodology
and Representation, 85–92
© 2009 Sense Publishers. All rights reserved.

entails. Are we ever free to express whatever and however we wish, without suffering the consequences of censure, exclusion, marginalisation, or perhaps reaping the flattery of fame? Why have we continued to be fascinated with the world and language of our dreams, our imaginations? What degrees of censure can the "sleeping mind" ignore? What potential does this imaginative world release?

For centuries the creative artist has attempted to reconstruct this imaginative world, populated with both the taut realities of the logical and rational, and the species of inexplicable, intuitive, organic, non-directive and (some would describe) "natural" reflections. It is a fascinating world, revered by many but...do we consider these latter forms of reflections as worthy of entry into the hall of academia? Does the world of the imagination, supposition, dreams and fascination constitute research? How is Research defined, and by whom? What tightwire ropes do academic researchers walk? What is the pursuit of the poet and the researcher? Beauty? Truth? Beauty and Truth? Who defines?

In this chapter I will attempt to explore the realm of alternative forms of representation which are increasingly becoming the hallmark of researchers who feel stifled by the conventionality of traditional genres of academic research. I shall attempt to argue that this deviation from the traditional forms of representation can be understood theoretically, methodologically and pragmatically as social science research attempts to expand its contribution to knowledge production, development and dissemination. I shall first explore why alternative forms of representation are necessary in achieving this goal, but also point to the possible limitations of this approach within the present climate of academic research. Hopefully, this article will encourage others to explore the possibilities of using alternative forms of representation, whilst aware of what they would be signalling theoretically, and that this "re-looking" at academic writing would also impact on how data is collected, analysed and re-presented to its potential audience.

WHO IS WRITING?

My own foray into an alternative to the traditional form of academic writing, stemmed from my concern that after several years of in-depth research and reflection, my thesis would end up on a proverbial dusty shelf in some library. I believed that writing an academic thesis was not simply about my wanting to earn the titles and qualifications that accompany a successful candidate. I believed that the ultimate test would be in terms of how my writing would be able to influence others to think and act more deeply about how they became and continue to be teachers of the English language. The sub-title of my thesis, "On becoming a teacher of English", identifies clearly its target audience. They are teachers. They are individuals who have (on the whole) become sceptical of the world of academe, who label the lecturers at universities as "ivory-towered" and "theoretical". They thus became the co-writers of the thesis, unconsciously shaping how and what I wrote.

Perhaps we need to reflect on why teachers have become so categorical and vociferous in their opposition to the "academic perspective" on education and training. How have they come to label academics the way they do?

The starting point could be to challenge teachers. Not only "academics" perceive the world along theoretical lines. All individuals own and act out "theoretical" perspectives around teaching and learning; all of us have inherited and develop our own brand of principled positions which reflect our assumptions around many educational matters: about governance, about educational service, about language teaching and learning; about everything educational. These perspectives themselves may not often be articulated by teachers as "theoretical", but nevertheless can be inferred from the manner in which they act (or not) in relation to particular circumstances within the educational terrain (Eraut, 1996). Of course, even if one chooses to be anti-theoretical, this in itself is a theoretical perspective about how to view teaching and learning.

Another reflection could cast a gaze in the direction of the producers of the academic writing: those "publish-or perish" die-hard academics who have mastered the "art" of being seen, heard and read in academic forums, journals and books. What motivates academics to write and speak the way they do? Why has this language become so predictable (and unimaginative)? How often have you been to a conference where it is possible to switch off for several minutes, as homage is paid by the speakers to the gods of traditional academe? How often have you read a masters or doctoral dissertation where the level of predictability of what the students will say compares favourably with the likelihood that rain will follow a drought? Academic research has fallen into a formulaic pattern related to not only what one researches, and how one researches, but also why one researches.

Why have we landed in this predicament? These latter academics are themselves not independent actors; their freedom of speech is not unfettered. The world of academe has become saturated with communicative conventions in a language that is exclusionary, that dialogues with itself, with speakers and readers who have acquired this shared language. This is the language of formal propositions and precepts, usually using the world of numbers and abstract logic to represent the thoughts/experiences of its "speakers/writers". For the main, many authors are constrained by the conventions of what their audience considers to be academic research: methodologies of data collection, analysis and representation of "findings". Authors intent on being part of this community of "researchers" soon learn to speak/write its language. Their assimilation and acceptance is more likely guaranteed when they write and speak its talk. Writers can express an intention to set themselves outside of the established convention, but run the risk of being marginalised by the forces of the powerful regime that guard the gates through publications boards, conference organising teams, publishing houses, academic employers, etc. Using its language displays the academic's acceptance and arrival into a community.

The audience (community) of traditional research is not the practitioner-teacher whose worldview is (on the whole) concerned with the pragmatics of engagements with a learning community, a school staffroom and the parent body. The academic is not dialoguing with the teacher-practitioner when s/he writes or speaks. Maybe this is a harsh generalisation of all traditional academics...A softer claim: the academic is constrained by who s/he perceives to be the context, audience and purpose of his/her output. Ultimately, it is the audience who seems to be writing the text.

> Language lies at the borderline between oneself and the others. The word in language is half someone else's. Language is not a neutral medium that passes freely into the private property of the speaker's intentions. It is populated- overpopulated with the intentions of others (Bakhtin, 1981, p. 294).

In relation to academic writing, I believe Bakhtin to be saying that it is a crucial question who the writer of academic journals, articles, speeches and reports perceive they are dialoguing with. The writer academic has to consider in which circle his/her dialogue will occur and what purpose it is likely to achieve. For the academic who is constrained by the need to publish or present, the audience becomes the gatekeeper of the academe. Only when the status of belonging to the community is well accepted is the individual academic allowed the privilege to flout the terrain of conventions. But first it is necessary to arrive within the circle through a process of learning the rituals of the community, before attempting to step outside. Few "uitlopers" are granted sanctuaries within the borders. Perhaps the purpose and goals of transforming the circle recedes into the background as the novice is inducted into the academic research environment.

THE PROBLEM WITH LANGUAGE

However, even when the intention of the author is clearly explicated beyond the traditional confines, the text produced has only a potential for serving its original intentions. The readers will choose to make sense of it in ways that they deem fit. Language is a powerful yet also restricting medium of thought, since it is "populated" with the possibility of being ambiguous. Each reader can choose to ignore its writer's intended meanings. Texts therefore only have "potential for meaning". It is more likely that the writer's meanings and the reader's meanings will come closer when there is a shared degree of interaction between both, so that the intentionality of both can be understood, shared and perhaps agreed upon (Widdowson, 1984). Reading and Writing is thus a creative act!

If academic writing aims to develop **a dialoguing community** within the social sciences, it therefore has to consider seriously how the community of interlocutors present themselves to each other. Firstly, it needs to consider whether its language is a shared medium of thought and action. It needs to look at means of interactive exchange that illuminates the potential for meaning making. It needs to recognise the kinds of languages that both communities of theoreticians and practitioners share and understand, because no language is ever free from its embedded cultural and ideological assumptions about how to relate to the world. It also needs to explore the potential that inter-disciplinary dialogue can offer. Social scientists also need to look outside the realms of their parent disciplines within the humanities and explore the creative world of natural sciences research paradigms, which themselves are self-reflectively re-examining the possibilities and problems that traditional research paradigms yield.

RE-SEARCHING RESEARCH

This re-questioning is a paradigmatic question, which goes to the heart of the intention of academic research. The dominant convention of academic research which aims to pursue the development of explanations, that seeks to uncover patterns of certainty and control, that believes that objective distancing between the researcher and the researched is desirable, that believes that it is able to present sizeable and chunkable labelling of "the truth", would seriously need to be reconsidered. The empiricist conventions of objectivity, replicability and validity would need to be interrogated as the hallmarks of what constitutes research.

If we define research as a process of re-searching (re-looking) for available forms of illumination about phenomena that we encounter daily, then it is necessary that we look towards new ways of being illuminated. If we see research as a process of developing a democratic sharing of illuminations gathered from a variety of vantage points within and outside the research context, then it means that we need to populate our research reports with opportunities for different individuals to make sense of what we as researchers have come to understand. These opportunities should not only be restricted to those participants within the research environment, but also to the readers who will read the final reports. Each of these above positions reflects paradigmatic expectations about the purposes of academic research and therefore need different touchstones to measure the value of its research outputs. All of these positions will be greatly enhanced if they are permitted the opportunity to delve into the world of alternative forms of gathering information, of analysing and re-presenting the insight, knowledge and under-standing researchers have gained while involved in the process of re-searching.

LEARNING A NEW LANGUAGE

Making a choice for alternative forms of researching entails making a shift in how information is gathered, new ways of being illuminated. Do we restrictively rely on gathering data that presents itself in that problematic and powerful medium of language? We as researchers need to free ourselves to be able to be illuminated by the power of other forms of representation of understanding and experience: the visual forms of photographs, diagrams, maps, paintings, collages; of performance art in dance, music and rituals; through the treasure house of alternative "non-academic" genres of literature: poetry, letters, diaries, journals, etchings, drama. All of these forms do not necessarily escape the boundaries of a language, and it becomes the data-gatherer's responsibility to explore the territory with as full an induction into the cultural and ideological conventions of the language of dance, art and performance of each of the research communities s/he seeks to understand.

The cultural ethnographic researcher participates in the process of research fully aware of the limitations of his/her insider/outsider perspective, his/her (in)ability to speak the language of the participants in the research. He/she therefore needs, in representing his/her research, to uncover his/her subjectivity during the process of exploration, unearthing and representing of the languages to the world of academe. Researching in this perspective becomes an exercise of learning a new language, the language of the research context, not simply learning to speak the language of the audience of academic convention.

When a researcher chooses to explore alternative forms of knowledge within the research context, s/he relinquishes the status of superiority as knower. Nevertheless, when s/he chooses to write back to academe, the presence of the other participants in the research could also become silenced and marginalised. The democratic researcher is wary to impose his/her interpretations on the research context, and therefore allows the "data" to be interrogated by all participants. Often participants in the research context may not "speak the same language" as the researcher and may choose to communicate using a "language they know and use best". This language may also extend to a language beyond words and the researcher would need to include it in the final representation of the research. This allows for the research report to become a "thick description" (Geertz, 1983), layered with multi-possible data and interpretations. It is likely that when these various forms of data are assembled, the report becomes a field of blurry edges, a walk through a valley of reminisces and distortions, a peering out of a mountaintop with expanding vistas, a merging into a horizon whose margins forever move. It enters into the realm of uncertainty, unpredictability, and explores into the realm of possibility. It allows for new insights and questions to be asked. It does not keep doors shut inside the prison of convention. It asks itself and its readers to ask new questions even beyond the ones the writers have intended.

NEW AUDIENCES, NEW VOICES

In exploring this open territory, it invites a new and wider set of audiences to the research process. It allows different individuals to have power over who and how academic knowledge is produced. It evokes empathy from the participants in the research because it draws on their languages, their representations of their everyday world. It sees their world, its own meaning-making systems as worthy of being celebrated as "research", and they develop a vocabulary of their own to explain it. It ultimately challenges the powerful, the oppressive, the traditional researcher who claims to be the voice of the participants of the research context.

Using alternative forms of representation in research reports is not simply a matter of novelty, curiosity or cleverness. It is about providing audiences with a view of the complexity of systems being researched. Whereas traditional dominant educational research paradigms have tended to be reductionist in their quest to categorise and narrow down the realities into "biteable chunks", the use of several forms of representation of data gathering, analysis and reporting allows the readers (and writers) opportunities to think divergently and explore multiple interpretations which are more likely to exist within a community. Researchers exploring this latter divergent form of research are indirectly serving to expand the participation of a wider community of individuals engaged in "Re-searching", each recognising the value of several interpretations and understandings, and thereby enriching their engagement within their world. Perhaps this would provide more resonance with how individuals do experience their everyday world, unlike the staid conventionalised world of traditional research.

Another value of using alternative and multiple forms in the representation of research is that it allows access for those who have different ways of seeing, reading, interpreting and understanding their world. Not all individuals are enchanted by the possibilities of the language of words and numbers as a means of reading the world. "A picture paints a thousands words", said some lyricist…and music has often stirred the emotions, reflections, passions and thoughts of full-blooded humans without the need for words.

PRODUCTIVE AMBIGUITY

Nevertheless, Eisner (1997) cautions us about the "productive ambiguity" of alternative forms of representation in research: it has the potential to evoke insight and draw attention to various ways of seeing the world, yet it also has the potential to be read and misread in ways that are beyond the control of the authors of the composition. It is limited in that it is unpredictable in terms of the effect it is likely to have on the research community – besides providing the means to drink more deeply of the cup of life. It meanders out into a world that cannot claim responsibility for the journey it will lead the readers into. Its responsibility stops in the presentation of the possibility for pointing the direction the journey should embark on.

A simple pragmatic limitation of exploring alternative forms of representation in the academic research community is that the world of printed journals is not fully able to capture many forms of audio data, or data that reflects kinaesthetic ambiance of dance and ritual, of paralanguage systems in operation. To some extent this matter can be resolved with the advent of electronic computer journaling, or the presentation of research material in the form of CD-ROMs. But we crawl in this age of technology, because our feet have become accustomed to stamping the wet mud we know. Hopefully, as we become more confident about the potential of multiple forms of representation of research, we would see more researchers reporting using visuals, video clips, verbal transcripts of interviews, art works, and dance presentations on computer screens rather than relying only on the printed word to convey our thoughts and understandings of our research environments.

THE TIGHTROPE RESEARCHER

It is a tightrope we walk as academics: the "sea of faces" which sit in the audience within educational research include both the gatekeepers of the traditional research paradigms and the ardent teacher critics who devalue the abstract theoretical propositions that characterise the convention. The "sleight-of-foot tricks and other high theatrics" we perform as researchers exploiting alternative forms of representation is motivated by a strong passion for balancing the "taut truths" we know and experience in our everyday interaction in a complex unsanitised world. We constantly know that our "charleychaplin" antics can be fatal! However, we are driven not just by the applause of our artistic performances. We believe passionately, and as full-blooded humans, that the democratic right to perform our own walk, our own means of getting to the other side, is what drives us as academic researchers.

REFERENCES

Bakhtin, M. (1981). *The dialogical imagination.* Austin, TX: University of Texas Press.

Eisner, E. (1997, August–September). The promises and perils of alternative forms of data representation. *Educational Researcher,* pp. 4–9.

Eraut, M. (1996). *Professional knowledge in teacher education.* Paper presented at Finnish conference of Teacher Education, Salonlinna, 26 June.

Geertz, C. (1983). Blurred genres: The refiguration of social thought. In C. Geertz (Ed.), *Local knowledge: Further essays in interpretive anthropology.* New York: Basic Books.

Widdowson, H. (1984). Reading and communcation. In J. C. Alderson, & A. H. Urquhart (Eds.), *Reading in a foreign language.* New York: Longman.

RUTH BEECHAM

6. THE DANGERS OF TRUSTING THE WORDS
OF ANOTHER...

In this chapter I explore the notion of trust in the development of narrative knowledge creation. While I accept that motivational pluralism (Sober & Wilson, 1998) governs the initial thrust of the narrative research project, I also believe that trust-in-the-*t*ruth-of-the-word-of-the-other is the primary moral condition for its success as a research method. I equally believe that as researchers we do not necessarily explicitly examine the relationship of trust-making to truth-making as part of the narrative research enterprise. So as a starting point, I outline how and why I have come to worry about the issue of trust in narrative research, and then use several sources of researcher-ly experience to tease out what I consider to be three forms of dangerous relationship. The first of these concerns the dangers that arise from trusting in the linguistic skills of the researcher who simultaneously mediates and creates the conditions for narrative truth-making. Here I write about the ability of skilled fictive wordsmanship to serve as both marketer and manipulator of emotional response; a trust-making machine that holds within it the potential to exclude researchers not holding significant skills of English writing-as-fiction. The second dangerous relationship I examine concerns explicitly trustful speaker/hearer collusions in the narrative research relationship. I raise concerns about the epistemological and ethical issues that pre-dispose researchers and participants to trust-in-the-words-of-another, and how the potential exists to establish "insider-outsider", "us-and-them" polemics. And finally, I talk about the dangers inherent in a non-trusting research relationship; in particular the status of words that are spoken, heard, interpreted – and later denied.

INTRODUCTION

The notion of trust in narrative knowledge creation is of great significance to me. In part, this has occurred from developing understandings of my practice as a speech therapist. In turn, this has been influenced by my knowledge-border-crossing into narrative research as a method to deepen my understanding of the South African curriculum of speech language therapy. The learning from one context of practice has deepened the learning from the other. To me, engaging in either speech therapy or narrative research is equally dangerous. While both have textual outcomes, both domains are also founded (and founder) on the development of relationship. In this chapter I will be raising issues of concern learnt from both

R. Dhunpath and M. Samuel (eds.), Life History Research: Epistemology, Methodology and Representation, 93–113

practices. Along the way I refer to data from several contexts (South Africa and Australia), several sources (doctoral thesis and research papers), across several years (1999–2004), aimed at multiple audiences (speech therapists, educationalists, students, and qualitative researchers). And throughout, I shall be exploring a question that has come to haunt my practice in both domains. As a therapist or researcher plying my trade I silently ask, "What predisposes you to trust – or distrust – my words?"

For me, the significance lies in the unasked nature of the question. At one level, there seem to be risks of violating deeply held rules of communication in the public asking; of potentially tearing the web of social interaction by speaking the question directly. At a deeper level I remain unsure about what I mean by trust itself, about what kind of knowledge I am asking to be made explicit in a communicative interaction. At this beginning point, therefore, I am aware of the first danger: an attempt to rationally deconstruct trust – this-something-of-the-senses – as an arte*fact*. Avoiding the danger does, however, leave me in a quandary, as this chapter claims, by virtue of its presentation in an academic textbook, to be non-fiction. How, then, can I be sure you understand of what I am speaking?

TRUST IN THE WORDS OF TEXT

I presume you to expect an argument, a rational point of view, and that your trust in me is tied up with your expectation that this argument will resonate sufficiently with your knowledge so that you can make a judgement upon mine. Yet already I bend the rules by declining to offer a definition of my major term. If your trust of me is tied up with your judgement of my knowledge, then how are my words to arrive at the goal of a non-fictional commodity?

My sense is that the primary issue is not knowledge. Rather, I believe trust-in-text has much to do with another kind of knowing: that concerning my skill as a writer. My aim is to engage you, my reader, to persuade-you-by-participation that my journey and its discoveries have credibility. In a phrase, my aim is to win your trust. To do so, my words serve as a commodity – an actively persuasive commodity. The meanings I construct need to resonate with you, to stir within you the magical 'Me too!' of identification, perhaps of illumination. To do this I spin a web of grammar and lexicon to create a compelling discourse. I am a Selector, (a Manipulator?); a Mistress of the edit and backspace keys: I Choose the words; you Interpret them. I am, therefore, the Creative Manager of an advertising campaign – and acting thus irrespective of the claims of academic discourse that this book rests upon. Claims that include the knowledge that this book must be marketed, sold, and consumed, and that the research credit I receive from writing within it will help to keep me employed by my knowledge-as-marketable-commodity-University. I have, therefore, significant Interests in persuading you of my words.

A thought from the side (neatly boxed):

> *McDonalds is advertising heavily. It's difficult to escape the change of its menu to a Healthy Good Thing. But do I trust in the truth of their narrative? The narrative is credible of course – I can go and eat their salads to prove this. But do I trust in the truth of their actions? The repetitive form of their advertising narrative has to convince me that their motives are to be trusted. If they achieve this, I will be pre-disposed to interpret their narratives with sympathy – with a tendency towards belief. I think that if I were their Advertising Manager I would greet such an admission with a cheer, "The narrative was trusted, change in belief occurred. She knows differently now!" Of course, the opposite could happen and their narratives could fail to win my trust. In this case I may become irritated by the blanket-bombing advertising narratives. Irritation and distrust could, perhaps, solidify my belief in their profit motivation. In turn, and from being a fairly passive observer of McDonalds, I could become an outspoken critic. Then the Advertising Manager would cry, "The narrative was not trusted, change in belief occurred. She knows differently now!"*
>
> *Trust/distrust in the words of another play a pivotal role in the creation of new learning. It also seems that greasing the wheels are factors such as the constancy and repetition of the narrative form – as well as history.*

Having set out these understandings, are you inclined to trust me more – or less? Or do you perhaps think, "I could not care less – get on with it, woman!" While I cannot know your response, I need to judge you in your absence. Because of the topic of the book and this chapter I calculate you would like me to link trusting in the skills of the writer-persuader-academic to the representation of another person's story presented as narrative research. And I shall do so because I want you to trust me.

The compulsion to believe in the narrative research story lies not in the claim of the researcher to have immersed herself in this story. These claims lie outside the narrative, forming part of methodological justification for the narrative approach itself. Rather, the compulsion to believe in the representational narrative story relates more to the researcher's skill in writing it. One part of this skill involves mastery of form, content and use: wordsmithing. Yet the danger of trusting in mastery of form and content and use as the basis for creating new knowledge is not confined to the need for researchers to be skilled wordsmiths. More dangerous by far is that the word-smithing is located within the researcher's knowledge and skills with reference to a particular fictive tradition.

An example concerns the writing of my thesis. During the composition of the representational narratives within it I was intensely attempting to recall lessons learnt in university English 101; what *was* the structure of the English short story for goodness' sake – and, more importantly, given the pressures of thesis writing – was there a recipe for its writing that I could purloin from a book and reference nicely? This was an interesting experience, and a source of deep reflection, given that I had managed to write fiction short stories beforehand without this form of anxiety. On the one hand, writing narratives for a range of academic markers prompted me to believe that one should cover one's text-bases, and that there were Right ways and Wrong ways to engage in the writing. On the other, I experienced a sensation of my writing being funnelled to satisfy a particular brand of audience – an audience I experienced as having different rules of judgement to an audience who read fiction *as* fiction. I was, therefore, excessively keen to follow the fictive traditions of English, for I quite understood my supplicant role in the achievement of a doctorate. This uneasiness about there being some kind of difference in the rules – or perhaps rather the market forces governing the rules – accompanied the early part of the thesis writing, yet part way through two of the narratives were published in a mainstream academic journal (Beecham, 2000; Mpumlwana & Beecham, 2000). And what I learnt from these acceptances is that rational academic critique fails to pierce a narrative (presented in an artful form of English language fictive tradition), when this narrative is composed from the heated spaces of human relationship. I also learnt that powerful critics are powerless in this context, for if words are artfully skilled to reflect verisimilitude (Bruner, 1987), to create blanks of ambiguity (Iser, 1974) and 'novelness' (Bakhtin, 1981), one succeeds in stilling critique through the relinquishment of power. It is given to you, reader, because skilled fictive writing demands your trust; it is given to you to infuse the text with your personal meaning. When trust is gained, critique is largely suspended. You are engaged. You are part of the creation. And when critique is suspended, when the writer holds your trust in the palm of her hand, sometimes the reader can experience those illuminations that Denzin (1989) refers to as "epiphanies", moments of new learning that mark the reader as altered in some way. To remember the last good novel you read is evidence of this.

While my conclusion from these experiences was that that trust-making in narrative text is not different for different audiences, what remain(ed) are significant issues around who can succeed in being celebrated as a narrative researcher – and who would experience significant difficulty. For if a researcher is both competent in English and is *also* predisposed to English as a literary skill, would not the narrative textual result be more compelling as a vehicle for trust-making – and thus for *t*ruth-making?

Here I am talking about the relationship between stylistic, linguistic skill in English, and the dominant status of this language in academic writing and publishing; a relationship that in many countries continues to emphasise success as a "knower" (in terms of thesis production and academic publishing) with success as a competent speaker/writer of English. The danger would appear to be that in those nations that, through their organisational and social apparatus, pair competence in English with intellectual (academic) status, the representational "writing of lives" could become the specialised province of researchers owning particular skills; skills based on significant insider knowledge of English. And if (academic) judgements of success as a narrative researcher are based on competence in English as the basis for the *t*ruth of representational narrative, it is a very short step indeed to link the successful practice (in academic terms) of narrative research to some form of linguistic colonisation in these nations, perhaps contributing to a further divide of the world into the Have-Competence-In- English – and the Have-Nots.

Having raised this idea, let me complicate it by adding the issue of cross-linguistic narrative research representation. By this I mean the occasions when English-competent researchers co-author narratives of non-mother tongue English speakers. Nolwazi Mpumlwana, the Xhosa mother-tongue speaking participant in my thesis-adventure, and I, co-authored three representational narratives during the project. Yet I would contest the notion of *co*-authorship, for to me this term conjures images of two horses pulling one cart in one direction with a single motive and shared effort. In practice, and while the events of the narratives were Nolwazi's, my lack of performance (let alone competence) in Xhosa necessitated Nolwazi recounting these events to me in English, her third language. Nolwazi therefore translated her life events into a form that I could understand. I then engaged in a second translation, to encase these events in the English fictive tradition in order to serve an academic audience in terms of the higher degree (and publications). So while the two horses may have started their journey with the intent to share effort and motive, what took place was a process akin to Alice in Wonderland: the steady shrinking of the Xhosa horse while the English animal expanded exponentially.

What has continued to intrigue me is why Nolwazi and I continue in friendship to this day. Her answer to my anxieties has been to smile and say, "I trust you". Instead of accepting this as an artefact of a consistent relationship with many repeated forms, I have started to ask why Nolwazi's trust protected me (and in fact supported me) with research claiming to be interpretative – a claim that I have too frequently considered an essentially complex and interest-laden translation.

TRUST IN THE NARRATIVE RESEARCH RELATIONSHIP

This brings me to the second series of dangers in trusting in the narrative-research-words-of-another: that of the explicitly trustful speaker-researcher relationship, and how the potential exists to establish "insider-outsider", "us-and-them" conditions. My main point here is not that such conditions *do* develop between researcher and participant, but that the narrative research approach does not routinely account for the ease and speed of these conditions developing. I see dangers when the ethical and epistemological conditions for this pre-disposition to trust in the words of another are not explicitly recounted as part of the research approach. Here I am not talking solely of a description of the research context in relation to the research participants (although this sets the stage), or even the opinions and perspectives the researcher brings to the process (although this forms a part of what I am suggesting), but an in-depth exploration of the ethical and epistemological conditions within the wider context that *pre-dispose* researcher and participant to engage swiftly and trustfully in the research relationship.

There are two reasons why I believe this exploration to be necessary. The first concerns a need to explicitly understand the nature of the relationship between researcher and participant, an understanding that could only increase the rigour of the research approach. The second reason concerns increasing understanding of those occasions when relationships of distrust develop between researcher and participant. I shall return to this point later in the chapter, but at this stage just wish to indicate that exploring the epistemological and ethical pre-conditions could help to understand on what grounds words can be spoken, heard, interpreted – and later denied.

In returning to the first issue, that of increasing the rigour of the research approach, I would like to offer an example of such an exploration and present it as a bridge between Nolwazi's smiling "I trust you" and what I believe to be several dangers within an explicitly trustful narrative research relationship.

TRUSTING IN THE COMPLEX POSITION OF SPEECH THERAPY

Us

Nolwazi Mpumlwana and I are both South African trained speech and hearing therapists. My thesis was concerned with critiquing the South African curriculum of speech and hearing therapy. At the time, Nolwazi was a student failing to negotiate the complexities of this curriculum and who was pre-disposed to engage with me in its critique. Power, race and language differences aside, therefore, there were commonalities between us, commonalities located within a motivation to challenge the epistemological and ethical position of the South African speech and hearing therapy profession.

As a statement, this may help to give reasons for our swift and easy engagement in the research process, yet does not explain the almost immediate trust that developed. To reveal this it is necessary to explore what *drove* Nolwazi and myself to trustfully collude in this process, and, as the second face of the coin of trust, the epistemological and ethical conditions we were colluding *against*. As a preliminary answer to the first point, the first time I recognised there was a common foundation – perhaps a common motivation to our joint participation in the process – was when Nolwazi spoke the following words in the first narrative interview. I felt an immediate from-the-heart-resonance, an immediate connectedness to what I interpreted she was saying:

Nolwazi's reasons for participating in the research process:
(Interview Two, 12th August, 1999, text pp. 19–20; from Beecham, 2002)

> **Ruth:** …I want to ask you something to get on tape now. Why are you helping me with this research? What do you hope to get out of it for yourself?

> **Nolwazi:** From this research? (pause) Nothing (laugh). Nothing in the sense of, nothing personal, okay. But I also feel that if it's being done to improve the lives of the ones that are going to come after me, then let it be done. And also because I know that you're not doing that out of wanting to spite anyone, you know, it's not a matter of, "I want to show them", but it's a matter of, "Things are still not right". They need to be corrected, and I believe that…

I shall return to a more comprehensive discussion of the effects of this resonance on myself as researcher overleaf, yet at this stage need to complete the exploration of the ethical and epistemological conditions we were colluding against.

Them

The services of a speech therapist are bought and sold to citizens who either feel themselves to have difficulties in communicating their meaning of the world to others, or are diagnosed by others as having these difficulties. As a profession, we are located within public health and education. Our claim is, therefore, that we represent some small part of the Common Good to those nation states that accommodate the profession.

Because of what we do, the topic of the profession is the word of another – whether spoken, written, read or understood. Yet the profession holds a complex relationship to the words of human communicators by operating from two seemingly contradictory epistemological positions. The first of these is a strong understanding of itself as scientific, with therapists taught to pathologise words, to detail with microscopic lenses people who have difficulty in expressing their meaning in social interaction, and to understand the holes in the social web that result as multiple "disorders of communication". This term, elastic as the shifting discourse norms of any society, is subject to an industry of research determined to extend professional markets while simultaneously seeking to provide society with rigorous methods of quality control (Beecham, 2002; Kathard, 2003; Pillay, 2003).

Competing with this understanding of its practice is its second epistemological position. Linked to the promotion of its role within the Common Good, this position derives from its knowledge of itself as a "helping" profession. Yet the help it can offer has the same source as its topic: words. There is no other source of medication for disorders of communication other than words themselves (whether they be in the form of text, picture or spoken). Our Scientific Cure, therefore, lies in dialogic and narrative meaning-making: the stuff of relationship, of establishing rapport and trust in the words of the other.

In combination, these differing understandings need to be resolved into a single ethical practice: to help people understand and express their meaning in the communicative world. In many ways, the task is to reconcile a practical ethics rooted in helping a person's experience of making – and expressing – meaning, with an objectively rational moral certitude in the existence of Truth as Disorder of Communication.

Complicating this is the implicit commodity interface of "ethics" with "payment for services". This is taken for granted, and represents "common-sense". Without entering the power relations at the heart of this "common-sense" (Pillay, 2003), there is a consequence for trusting in the words of another that results from both these epistemologically divided positions as well as the "common-sense" acceptance that a (professional) helping relationship, based on a fee-for-service exchange, translates to one of trust-in-the-help-that-is-offered.

To aid in demonstrating this consequence, the following examples span two geographic contexts (South Africa and Australia), and three aspects of the therapeutic relationship (professional teacher-educator, student in professional training, and a citizen with communication issues who has sought therapeutic help).

Example from: 'How I have come to understand myself as a teacher of speech pathology' *(co-authored narrative Ruth Beecham & Libby Clark; 2004):*

… And I think a large part of my difficulty has been that I've been framing it [the subject] as "linguistics for speech pathology" as opposed to "linguistics for human beings in a world of language". It's not easy to break out of this pigeon-hole. It's like there are two roles I'm battling with – the one as teacher; and the one as therapist. A sort of, "Who am I?" in each role; what the fit is – and how comfortable I am with that fit.

Example from: 'The Monster of Professional Power' *(co-authored narrative, Nolwazi Mpumlwana & Ruth Beecham; 2000):*

In understanding what it is that lies between me and the helping of another person to communicate better; of the principles you have placed on the sharing of our humanness in this thing called therapy, I find the losing of my identity too big a price to pay… I don't want to be a part of your [professional] monster, I truly do not…. I will not make him stronger by practising your divided ideas about helping.

These examples point to a sense of division or "separation". The separation occurs as a result of different understandings about university-based professional education in relation to the practice of the profession. In turn, this separation appears to be perceived by a member of the public who has sought speech therapy services:

Example from: Clients as teachers: Power-Sharing in the speech therapy curriculum *(Beecham & Dunley, 2004)*

Tutor: I think to myself, "You're one of them!"…so they don't treat you any different…we don't get treated like one of "them". Which is good. Well, if I went to the office [speech therapy service] I would be a client.

The sense of being communicatively "separated" appears to be communicated within the therapeutic context. This indicates, in a preliminary way, that communicative separation deriving from competing epistemological and ethical positions may have an effect on the development of relationship as the basis for therapeutic practice.

In many ways, therefore, what is being suggested here is that a consequence of epistemological separation may be that professional communication is perceived as different to every-day communication. Bearing in mind that both Nolwazi and I had been socialised into professional language, at this point let me return to a consideration of how this epistemological exploration contributes to understanding the speed and ease of our establishing a trusting narrative research relationship.

Us in the Narrative Research Relationship

Earlier, I spoke of the impact Nolwazi's words had upon me in the research relationship. Given the epistemological and ethical conditions underlying the topic of our research, a theory of our trust-making could be that our collusion was motivated by a strong moral sense that since the "different" communication of the profession was not right, we were somehow bonded by duty to attempt rectification. Another way of putting this is that the "Truth" of the professional curriculum did not engender our trust in the *truth* of this position as furthering the professional aim of helping people express their meaning of the world.

From the Side: An Example of Truth and Truth from the Everyday World of War

> We can rationally assert the credibility of the statement, "The US has invaded Iraq". But some of us are not compelled to believe in the *truth* of the statement. In other words, we are not compelled to trust in the truth of the *action*. Perhaps it is that we do not trust that the statement is motivated by either consideration of the Moral Good, or aimed at promoting Good Will. So while credibility as Truth (as in "accurate reporting of the action") and *truth* (as in "I am compelled to believe in the rightness of these actions") are linked, I suggest that there is a great mediator that lies between them. Perhaps this may be called, "Trusting in the words of another because I interpret these words to be motivated by a Common Good".

So when Nolwazi spoke the words "Things are still not right", what resonated with me was our joint commitment to a mission-like purpose; a mission to make things right for the common (and Moral) Good. As became clear further along in the interviewing process, Nolwazi's primary communicative commitment lay within engaging with me (an ex-teacher of this curriculum) in a manner that stressed our inter-connectedness as human beings. However implicitly understood by her at the beginning of the research process, by its end, Nolwazi was able to articulate that her communicative resolve as a research participant was *not* to engage in the epistemological and ethical separation of communication from the human speaker that she believed lay at the heart of the speech and hearing curriculum.

For myself as both researcher and speech and hearing therapist, the effect of understanding the nature of the mission made me reflect deeply on what epistemological and ethical conditions I had thus far brought to the research process. There is no doubt about the self-interest that primarily motivated me (Sober & Wilson, 1998). I was a novice researcher coming to narrative knowledge creation with the expectation of doctoral thesis production. Epistemologically, I was confused as knowledge from speech therapy tumbled with that of narrative inquiry. Lodged with the fear generated from this confusion was a naïve faith that this uncertainty would be resolved as the research process unravelled. The source of this faith was my research participants, or rather, their words. Great words, I hoped; words that could resolve my confusion and result in a doctorate – for me. The trust I held, therefore, was not in the people who spoke these words, but in the words themselves. And what I trusted would result from these words would be a doctoral thesis full of new knowledge – new *t*ruth.

Yet when Nolwazi identified our joint mission, my motivation altered meaning-fully, as did our relationship. I need to emphasise, however, that it was only the relationship of trusting-the-words-of-the-human-speaker-of words with Nolwazi that changed. My trust in other participants remained linked to their words; words that fell from their lips as data. Before entering this dangerous terrain of dis-embodied truths, however, there are a number of dangers that I need to discuss in relation to an explicitly trustful research collusion.

The Dangers of Us and Them in the Narrative Research Relationship

Owning a joint mission of promoting a Common (and Moral) Good appears to presume that there is a Common (and Immoral) Bad. The mission itself, therefore, is at risk of being polarised. In turn, and as the words that are spoken between participants of this mission form the basis for knowledge, what is produced is polarised knowledge. At the time of interviewing, and influenced by a passionate level of theoretical re-positioning, I was a convert to the essential inter-subjectivity of the narrative exchange and experienced it rather as the cognitive removal of a boned corset. In the process I did not see danger in the passionate loyalty to the truth of our relationship that created an Us and Them that was very different to our prior, individualised, opinions and perspectives about the speech and hearing curriculum.

For example, in that past world I had interpreted a range of (admittedly narrow) shades of white to black to the hearts and minds of South African speech and hearing therapists engaged in developing or teaching the curriculum. Yet the view from Nolwazi and my fused world of trustful truth-making presumed a wholly dark view of the curriculum and its perpetrators with all their subtle and not-so-subtle injustices. What is encased, therefore, as a textual version of truth between faux leather thesis bindings is the legacy of this darkness. What I believe important to highlight, however, is an omission from the processes of illumination used to present this darkness as research.

During the doctoral research project, I understood illuminative processes Platonically:

...the problem for the subject or the individual soul is to turn its gaze upon itself, to recognise itself in what it is and, recognising itself in what it is, to recall the truths that issue from it and that it has been able to contemplate... (Foucault ,1984 in Rabinow, 1997, p. 285).

From this, I understood my tasks as researcher to explicitly reflect and document the origin and development of beliefs about the curriculum that Nolwazi and I brought to the research relationship, and how it was that we shared these beliefs during the research process.

My (retrospective) concern is that these are not sufficient to pierce the recesses of how the nature of a trusting research relationship serves to change the way both parties think about the research topic. What I believe is needed is some form of explanation of how a relationship serves to shape, colour and refine beliefs. Without this crucial reflexive exercise upon the effects of an explicitly trustful relationship on shifting beliefs, what can occur is a kind of blindness as to the truth of the mission itself. By this I mean that mindful embodiment of the words of a trusting relationship can come to represent the uncritically accepted truth of the joint research mission. And by virtue of this trust-in-the-other-as-representative-of-Mission, divisions can occur between this relationship and others in the research venture. Put simply, if the one (Missionary) relationship comes to represent the truth, then I believe the researcher is pre-disposed to interpret the words of the other relationships in reference to this truth. The trust, therefore, that lies at the core of this special relationship can become the arbiter, judge and jury of the hearts and words of others. The result can be, as I point out later on, a breakdown in trust between researcher and these other participants.

But before doing so, I think it necessary to make a better case for explicitly considering the nature of the relationship between researcher and participant as part of both narrative research methodology and analysis. To do this I shall build an argument for trust to alter the words that are spoken in a narrative research context. For if trust alters words, then so too, by extension, does trust change interpretation.

An Example of Trust-making Changing Word-making

Libby Clark, an Australian colleague (and now friend) and I began work on a narrative life history project several days after we first met. I was new to Australia and the university where we both work, and Libby was new to narrative life history research. The interviews spanned a period of 20 weeks, during which time our relationship developed socially and collegially. What follows is part of a single story that Libby related in two interviews, the first told right at the beginning of the research process, and the second in the final interview. Over the intervening months, Libby had forgotten she had told the story to me.

Verbatim text: Interview 2 (February 2003)

And then I was doing neuro. I was with a student who, on paper, was one of the brighter students from her year.

And she was incredibly patronising in the first few weeks.

And – but then it became clear that, you know, she was the one needing to do a lot more additional reading and what have you.

And that made me feel really good.

Verbatim text: Interview 4 (June 2003)

And then we did our adult neuro placement and I was shit-scared.

And I was with another girl who'd got HDs – she made sure I knew that (laugh) as they do! I was quaking in my shoes. [Name of] Hospital.

Anyway, after a couple of weeks, it became clear that she was actually having difficulty and that the supervisors were asking her to come in a bit earlier to go through her plans, and you know, having to re-do things a lot more than what I was, and so I started feeling pretty good – it was pretty nice, "Yep, I'm feeling pretty comfortable here, Yup!"

Critical Discourse Analysis (Fairclough, 1989) reveals that as textual sets, the first telling of the story includes little opportunity for interpreting the real impact of these events on Libby, whereas the second is significantly padded by her own interpretations, attributions and conclusions. There are several markers in the text that confirm this; for example in the first telling "I/me" are used only three times, whereas in the second, "I/me" are used seven times. In the first telling this may indicate Libby's distance from the story, or it may indicate her doubts of me, a virtual stranger as well as a foreigner, as a sympathetic interpreter of the story itself. In the second telling, however, and in addition to the increase in communicative turn-length that may indicate a growing perception of there being more equal distribution of power in the researcher/participant relationship, there are marked and clear referents both to feelings, as well as who, precisely, was doing the feeling. Libby's clear interpretation of events using terms such as, "shit-scared", "quaking in my shoes", "having difficulty", "feeling pretty good", "pretty nice", "feeling pretty comfortable", offer the interpreter clear direction in term of understanding the effects of the story upon her, as opposed to the first example that contains only one interpretation of how Libby felt about the events of the story. Another interesting difference between the two sets concerns the change in use of colloquial language. There appears to be an assumption of a similar value system between speaker and hearer with relation to use of swearing; a common system of believing that is further confirmed by Libby's assumption of communicative collusion in the use of "As they do!" In combination, therefore, the loss of formal speech conventions, the increase in interpretation of events with clear referents, together with the increased length of turn seem to indicate that growing trust between us was a causal factor in creating difference in the words. Yet to support my argument that trust can cause difference in narrative text interpretation, it is necessary to delve a little deeper.

The aim of the narrative life history research project as a whole was to explore how Libby, an Australian teacher of the speech therapy curriculum, had come to her understandings of her role as teacher of this curriculum. In the first telling of the story, I interpreted certain clues as to how Libby experienced a part of the world of this curriculum. Her linking of, "who, on paper..." and, "the one having to do more additional reading", as well as her use of "student" and, "in her year", appeared to locate her representation of reality within the frame of a university. My overall interpretation was that Libby, even though aware of its power, did not *personally* judge university based "text-success" as valid or legitimate in predicting professional competence.

Yet in the second telling of the story, Libby appeared to locate her representation of reality within a collusional, interactive, communicative, frame. References to university are replaced by markers of communicative attribution and interaction, such as "she made sure I knew that" and, "the supervisors were asking her to come in a bit earlier to go through her plans", as well as "girl" instead of "student". Ideologically different agency relationships were apparent, for example, in the first telling it was the student "...needing to do a lot more additional reading...", whereas in the second telling, "...the supervisors were asking her to come in a bit earlier to go through her plans and...to re-do things a lot more than I was". The use of "we" in line one is the first indicator of inferred collusion between the supervisors, Libby, and myself in holding a common viewpoint. In combination, my interpretation was that Libby, in common with senior practitioners (supervisors), and myself as researcher and practitioner, held a *common* (and common-sense) opinion that text-success is no guarantee of professional competence.

My hypothesis is that Libby's choice of words in the two tellings of the story not only reflects the establishment of a more trusting relationship between us, but also marks a shift in how she wished me to interpret the narrative itself. And as there is a core similarity between the two examples, here I would like to refer back to the comments I made earlier with relation to Nolwazi and my collusion in the formation of a joint "mission". For in Libby's second telling of the story, the inclusion of all participants – bar the academically clever student – in the interpretation that text-success offers no guarantee of professional competence suggests that this belief is widely shared; that it represents some form of (Australian) professional common-sense. Thus by re-formulating past events to support the present collusion between Libby and myself, not only does this serve to strengthen our relationship, but it also presumes the establishment of a joint mission. And in the context of our professional knowledge, the mission appeared to be the revelation of a Common (and Moral) Good about the curriculum: that text-success does not make a good therapist.

Libby and I "know" that this polarised hypothesis does not represent our *truth* of this aspect of the curriculum, and this is because the pair of us is immersed within its Australian spiders-web complexity. I can make the claim, therefore, that as a result of the multiple strands of this knowing, any representation of Libby's reality would explicitly account for these complexities. But what would have occurred if I, as researcher, had not been a teacher of the Australian curriculum; perhaps a South

African researcher exploring international speech and hearing curricula? A researcher, moreover, still passionately loyal to Nolwazi's truth of the curriculum. How would I have interpreted the "common" Australian view of "Text-success not making a good therapist", and how would this have been assimilated within my knowledge of the South African context, where the conflicts between mother-tongue languages and competence in English find the profession racially skewed in favour of the white colonisers of the country? Additionally, what form would the textual representation have taken if Libby or I had not been mother-tongue speakers of English – what translations would have occurred, and what accommodations would Libby have made for the different languages in her editorial control of the resulting narratives?

Posing these questions leads to a larger discussion regarding the pheno-menological essence of narrative research, a discussion too large to hold within this chapter. Briefly, however, and by virtue of its theoretical emphasis, my point here is that there is no claim to either judge the moral stances of researcher or participants, or to posit universality of aim or result – such as, for example, there being such an invention as a Common Good. Yet as I have attempted to point out, I believe that the increasing trust of communicative collusion in narrative as research leads to the co-construction of precisely these forms of judgement. In other words, I intuit that in the messy spaces of the research practice, the development of the trusting communicative relationship predisposes participants to identify an implicit Common Good that is particular to that relationship; a Common Good, moreover, that serves to form the mission of the research project itself. And as a result, collusional knowledge of the mission alters both the words that are spoken and how they are interpreted.

Having spent some time on developing the theme of trust in the research relationship, let me turn the coin and examine my arguments from the perspective of distrust. The following section refers to examples from my doctoral thesis where no common identification of purpose was present, where no collusion in the implicit formation of a Common Good was established, and what, as a result, occurred to the words that were spoken between researcher and participant.

NARRATIVE RESEARCH AND DISTRUST

I've already said that I entered the doctoral research process with certain understandings of what illuminative processes were needed to ensure the process would stand as narrative research. There were many other understandings that accompanied this, and while far too amorphous and confused to be definitively labelled a Research Process Checklist, there was a strong sense that there was some form of metaphorical pamphlet being formed in my mind, possibly titled "How To Do Narrative Research". This checklist was formed on the basis of outcomes; causal relationships of, "If-I-do-this, then-that-will-result". The primary outcome was, of course, a doctorate for me. Serving this (and inevitably aided by epistemological understandings from speech and hearing therapy), was my under-standing of words as data, with emphasis upon what was, precisely, to be done with these words in order to present them as research. Combined with this, and as I mentioned earlier, my trust in participants other than Nolwazi remained linked to their words – their words, not their hearts. An important motivator for this fundamental disembodiment of words from the speaking, feeling, creators of these words was loyalty to Nolwazi as representative of truth. Thus there were two layers of communicative interference in speaking with other research participants. One was an objectified judgement on words in relation to their outcome as data, and the other a passionate investment in hearing these words in relation to the truth of Nolwazi.

Here, I want to make the case for this multi-layered communicative interference to prevent the formation of a mission of Common Good. In the absence of the mission, I also want to problematise the status of the words that were spoken in this context.

The Context of Mistrust

An important part of introducing the speech and hearing student Nolwazi Mpumlwana to readers of my thesis was to ground her contextual understandings of the speech and hearing curriculum within her specific educational environment. Nolwazi had, at that stage, failed two years of study. As part of her reflections around the reasons for this failure, she was making claims to me that victimisation and racism were forming part of her educational experience. It seemed, therefore, vital to include the interpretations of her teachers as to the nature of her educational context. Complicating this aim was the fact that I had been a teacher within this department several years before. I had working relationships with many of the staff, and had close social and collegial relationships with two – both of whom are contributors to this volume. At the time of my employment by the University I had been known as an outspoken critic of the curriculum, and it had been clear then that not all members of staff agreed with me about the necessity, or range, of changes needed to transform it. In the research context of my thesis, all staff knew I was collaborating with Nolwazi to explore her experience of failing to negotiate the curriculum. From the perspective of the majority of staff, therefore, it could be expected that the research relationship I was hoping to establish with them was already infused with unsympathetic motives. From my perspective, I entered with competing levels of communicative interference.

With this context as background, and in order to support the arguments I have made about the foundation of a mission of Common Good to occur as a necessity within the narrative research process, I would like to offer two examples of what happened to the words that were spoken between staff members and myself. The first of these concerns a focus group of staff members, and the second refers to an individual interview I held with my friend and staff member, Mershen Pillay. The words-as-data results of both these conversations were edited out of the final thesis due to the levels of contestation that surrounded their status as research data. However I have asked Mershen via e-mail to re-construct how he understood what I was doing to, and with, his words, and what effects this had on our close relationship. With regard to the outcome of the focus group, and apart from explaining what I did to these words, the primary points I wish to make concern issues around collaboration and contestation.

Example One: A Focus Group

Earlier, I spoke of the scientific consciousness of the profession. I also discussed the epistemological and ethical separation that speech and hearing therapists bring to the practice of the profession, and made a case for this separation to occur between the partners of the communicative therapeutic exchange. I also suggested that while the resulting relationship is assumed to be one of trust, there seems no guarantee that this assumption is either credible or *t*rue.

The focus group was between speech and hearing therapists. To the majority of the participants, qualitative research was an unfamiliar paradigm of inquiry, as too was a narrative approach to data gathering and analysis. At one level, therefore, the contestation around the words that were spoken was around epistemology and my inadequate explanation of the research approach. At another level, however, the contestation was about me-as-researcher-in-relation-to-their-words.

There were two competing opinions expressed by focus group participants with regard to the historically derived stresses and strains of the speech and hearing curriculum. In attempting to represent these different voices, I set up the narrative writing as a form of argument in different fonts, yet retained the verbatim words spoken by participants. This was the document given back to each for their editorial comment. What occurred was that each participant made copious and yet *different* comments on virtually every line of the text. Most importantly for the status of the document as research reflecting a co-constructed *t*ruth, there were many comments such as, "I never said that!" and "This is not true!" There were even comments from participants denying the opposing side of the narrative argument. In other words, they denied the words that were spoken by others.

What is the status of words that have been heard, audio-recorded, interpreted – and later denied? In terms of this discussion, perhaps a more pertinent question concerns the nature of collaboration, and what predisposes participants to collaborate trustfully. Sen (2001) suggests the root of human collaboration rests upon a process of negotiation where individuals deal with one another on the basis of what they are being offered and what they can expect to get. Sober and Wilson (1998, p. 308) term this

> motivational pluralism [which] is the view that we have both egoistical and altruistic ultimate desires

that drive the need to collaborate. As I have argued in the preceding sections, my personal feeling is that collaboration flourishes when participants co-establish a mission of Common Good. In this focus group experience, and by virtue of the history encasing teachers, researcher and curriculum, either of these perspectives can help to explain what occurred to the words that were spoken. On the one side, there was little on the bargaining table to advantage participants, while on the other, the competing levels of communicative interference I brought to the process precluded the inclusion of focus group participants within Nolwazi and my co-established mission of Common Good.

While superficially collaborating in the production of new knowledge, therefore, new ideas did not flourish (Fullan, 2003). Neither did the relationships between the participants and myself. While this was an unhappy result, the emotional impact of these damaged relationships served mainly to strengthen my own perception that Nolwazi and I were engaged upon a just and moral mission. For myself as researcher, therefore, there was a sense of vindication in the loss of this part of the research process. This perception certainly did not accompany the results of the second example shared here; that of the interview with my friend and colleague, Mershen Pillay.

Example 2: My Friend

Mershen and I had been close friends for six years before I asked him for an interview as part of the thesis process. While we had both worked in the above speech and hearing therapy department in the early 1990s, after a period of time overseas, only Mershen had returned to work at the University in 1999. He was, therefore, employed there during the data gathering process, and he was also one of Nolwazi's teachers. Mershen's reaction to my interviewing him resulted in him sending me a long fax. The words of the fax made clear the level of betrayal he experienced as a result of my taking his words; a betrayal that ended the relationship itself for nearly five years. The fax is gone, yet over the e-mail, I have asked Mershen to re-construct his experience of what occurred (December, 2004). The draft of this chapter was not sent with this request; instead, I briefly outlined the thrust of the argument about trust, and posed the following question:

> **Ruth:** Are we on a Joint Mission in this, Mershen, and if we are, what are the parameters of this Mission and what is the Common Good we are motivated by?

> **Mershen's Reply:** Are we on a joint mission of some kind of Common Good? Yes. And No. Yes, in that we agree in fundamentals like the greater common good, social justice, liberty (and all things nice). But 'no' in the ways we get there. Now Ruth, you may not like the stuff I've written below – it's all "you-you" and lots of spitting and finger waving...but here goes.... Note I reserve the right to correct and withdraw things that I say here.

> I collude.

> You exclude.

> You CHOOSE when you want collusion (like now), and when you want exclusion (like then). So, it's just another ancient tired story of who-calls-the-shots, a simple power play, the usual stuff. But then, it FELT different. Let me remind you of how it felt. [It felt like] it was a "divorce". It felt like that –

the end of a love affair. I felt betrayed, fucked around with. I played the lover who'd been rejected for another. I actually said this same thing to you, in the same way I'd analogised now ("lovers"). I also said that I felt like the learner and you'd positioned yourself as the teacher. That I was the lightie, the boy. I felt little. I was made to feel little.

Unfashionably egalitarian as they may be, our lover-relationship – our "partnership" – like most others were/was based on collusions (strung-in by missionary motivations, like "goodness"). And these are the Very Precious Things (VPT's) that we loved about each other, that kept us together. Now, Ruthness, the way I see it is that you traded these VPT's for your own "space", for what you called "necessary distance". I diarised this/your concept of how you perceived the "research-researcher and non-researcher roles".... Now these VPT's were/are traded by you. You set the interest rates, and how others (me) may participate in working with these VPT's. You issued the currency that kept mainly/only your interests afloat...there was a block on what I could say, and how I could participate in what you called your distanced space (= your research)....I had no space to negotiate my meanings with you... You cramped me around, You & You (Pty) Ltd. You ran a tight business.

So you defined a free lover-ship as a one-way, open access for your business to flourish in. No imports from me were tolerated. You couldn't/refused to see/hear what I was saying...you re-theorised my mind FOR me; our friendship, our history of being together was annulled....And it's not like you weren't aware of it: I was direct in my telling of how I felt....I lost trust in you, the person. I found it difficult to reconcile what you were saying/writing about with our personal relationship. ... So the Common Good you strived for made sure I was caught in some pincer movement – where you opened the field to different, new ways of thinking that I wanted to be part of; but you barred me from participating – killing years of VPT's that I (and you) had take to build.

And then, I was part of the broad grouping of "the department". I was stereotyped as the "establishment" – part of the peoples against Nolwazi. So I became defrauded by default. And that hurt. (Specifically, you said that I was "One of them"). You also couldn't see how you too were one of "Us" – that even on the imagined outside – you're still on the inside.

Five years on, Mershen's words produce an almost identical result. At a deeply personal level I cannot argue with them because of a VPT: I am silenced by virtue of my trust in his *t*ruth.

On a different plane – that of the distanced "othering" gaze of the researcher, I fear – I need to ask from where, and from what motives, my silence derives. I can, without doubt, assert the credibility of his words, and how my actions and behaviour may have led him to write them – and also to feel them so keenly. My silence lies; I believe, in doubts as to my trust in the truth of his *actions,* in this case the result of my behaviours leading to his loss of trust in me, the person. So while I trust in the credibility of Mershen's representation of Truth (as in "accurate reporting of the action"), I don't accept the outcome of their *t*ruth (as in, "I am compelled to believe in the rightness of the punishing actions"). And this is because, from my own interpretation, I have a poor understanding of my crimes *as* crimes, and deeply question the degree of punishment that was meted out. There is, therefore, a dissonance between my personal judgement of my actions and an equally internally governed sense of what is Good, what is Just, and what represents Good Will. And one part of the result is that my trust in Mershen as sharing my ethical version of reality has been shaken. The second is that I remain silently locked within an emotion-laden conflict of personal epistemologies.

A solution would seem to lie within some form of epistemological mediation, a mechanism whereby perhaps Mershen and I could negotiate our personal positions. From there, with sufficient Good Will, we may be able to re-negotiate a joint sense of Common Good – and perhaps, even, a Joint Mission. This idealised scenario is, of course, merely a construct as, and from the excerpt above, I interpret little opening for negotiation five years after the events. Rather, what has been interpretatively activated is a resurgence of the conflict in my personal epistemologies. And this, in turn, simultaneously outlines the essential paradox. For how does one negotiate – through words – a future with a speaker, when the past has taught distrust of the speaker?

Casting around the world I know, I can determine that for several discourse communities this paradox does not appear to exist. For example, some politicians, journalists, and advertising companies seem to have little difficulty in negotiating "new" futures from distrusted histories, and presumably people come to trust these new constructions. Then again, South Africa's Truth and Reconciliation Commission (TRC) appeared to take the paradox itself as its starting point. While motivational pluralism may have nudged participants to become involved (the avoidance of formal legal charges and jail terms by participating would appear to me to be a significant motivational force), there is equally no doubt that the process of sharing stories led, in many cases, to changes in personal epistemological position. Did this, however, lead to the individuals concerned in the sharing of personal stories of grievous historical actions *trusting* each other? Could, for example, a change in epistemological position by a person who has murdered my mother be enough for me to trust the person to make different action-choices in the future?

And here, I return once more to Mershen's text, for explicit within it is the belief that the choices I make now are motivationally the same as the choices I made in the past: "*You CHOOSE when you want collusion (like now), and when you want exclusion (like then)."* It seems clear to me that I am not trusted to make different action-choices. Yet the problem remains that I did not understand the criminal nature of my actions then – or now. I do not understand, therefore, the ethical error of my ways. Without understanding the ethical foundation, and without external motivating forces driving the negotiation process, I am unable to change my epistemological position. Distrust remains, and with it, the paradox: How does one negotiate – through words – a future with a speaker, when the past has taught distrust of the speaker?

Or perhaps I am being too precious. After all, and as I have already mentioned, some politicians, journalists and advertising executives do not seem to even acknowledge the existence of the paradox. This implies that there are different practices of trust, almost like discrete yet linked disorders on a continuum of pathology, with each having slightly different rules of the game of truth, and with implicit knowledge of these rules held by the discourse participants. Indeed, perhaps these different trusts function as major determinants of the linguistic practices we engage with during the myriad context-dependent social practices of any day.

At this point it seems that I have come full circle, because as I hope to have explored, it seems insufficient, when playing with the World's of our research participants or therapeutic partners, to place ourselves in a similar position to the managers of a MacDonald's advertising campaign – trusting in the constancy and repetition of our/their texts over time. Rather, and when practicing either as speech therapist or researcher, I would like to know the rules of the game of trust I am playing.

CONCLUSION

I have made an argument for trust-in-the-*t*ruth-of-the-word-of-the-other to be the primary moral condition for the success of narrative as a research approach. Along the way I have explored this from the perspectives of text as well as face-to-face discourse. Where able, I've suggested ways researchers could explicitly examine the relationship of trust-making to truth-making as part of the narrative research enterprise. At one level, this is all I have to say. At another level – the level of the heart – this text has been an exploration of a haunting demon. It rises when engaging in therapy or narrative research projects. It listens to how I communicate – and with what motive. It digs deep into my flesh when for moments I forget it is there, constantly prompting the question: Why do you trust me – why *should* you?

REFERENCES

Bakhtin, M. M. (1981). *The dialogic imagination: Four essays*. Austin, TX: University of Texas Press.

Beecham, R. (2000). God's child. *Teaching in Higher Education*, 5(1), 127–130.

Beecham, R. (2002). *A failure of care: A story of a South African speech & hearing therapy student*. Unpublished Doctoral Thesis, Faculty of Education, University of KwaZulu-Natal.

Beecham, R., & Clark, L. (2004). *Averting the professional gaze from science: 'Connecting with care' as a model of educational development*. 26th World Congress of the International Association of Logopedics and Phoniatrics, Conference Proceedings, Sydney, August 29-2 September.

Beecham, R., & Dunley, D. (2004). *Clients as teachers: Innovations within the speech therapy curriculum at Charles Sturt University*. SARRAH National Conference Proceedings, Alice Springs, August 26–28.

Bruner, J. (1987). *Actual minds, possible worlds*. Cambridge, MA: Harvard University Press.

Denzin, N. (1989). *Interpretive interactionalism*. Newbury Park, CA: Sage.

Fairclough, N. (1989). *Language and power*. London: Longman.

Foucault, M. (1984). *The ethics of the concern for the self as a practice of freedom*. In P. Rabinow (Ed.), (1997), *Ethics: subjectivity and truth, selections*. New York: The New Press.

Fullan, M. (2003). *Change forces with a vengeance*. London: Routledge Falmer.

Iser, W. (1974). *The implied reader*. Baltimore: John Hopkins University Press.

Kathard, H. (2003). *Life histories of people who stutter. On becoming someone*. Unpublished Doctoral Dissertation, University of KwaZulu-Natal, KwaZulu-Natal, South Africa.

Mpumlwana, N., & Beecham, R. (2000). The monster of professional power. *Teaching in Higher Education, 5*(4), 535–540.

Pillay, M. (2003). *(Re)positioning the powerful expert and the sick person: The case of communication pathology*. Doctoral Thesis, University of KwaZulu-Natal, Durban, South Africa.

Sen, A. (2001). *Development as freedom*. New York: Alfred A. Knopf.

Sober, E., & Wilson, D. (1998). *Unto others: The evolution and psychology of unselfish behaviour*. Cambridge, MA: Harvard University Press.

DAISY PILLAY

7. A CUBIST NARRATIVE: PRODUCING DIFFERENT KNOWLEDGES WITH SUCCESSFUL TEACHERS

A metaphor … is now considered to be an essential process and product of thought. The power of metaphor lies in its potential to further our understanding of the meaning of experience, which in turn defines reality. (Mary Ann Stankiewicz, 1996, 4–5)

INTRODUCTION

In this chapter I employ a cubist metaphor as a heuristic device to understand and represent the lives of six South African teachers. Drawing from my research into teachers' lives, I employ the cubist metaphor from the field of Visual Art, to frame a constructive and deconstructive project to reveal the silences, blindspots and loci of teachers' lives. In constructing the life histories of participating teachers, I approach the task from four different positions, using the four different cubist principles. This approach enables me to enter teachers' "other worlds" within the discursive practice of "being teacher" and to celebrate possibilities for "being and doing teacher differently". Visual knowing reminds us that there is never a fixed story being told, there is no narrative closure. In constructing a variety of (re)presentations, teachers' stories are stirred around, generating the possibility for many more representations. The cubist narrative provides the alternative site of coming to know teachers, a frame to see again with fresh eyes.

Using the cubist metaphor inspired me to move from a fixed, linear position as researcher to one in which I explored reading, writing and representing teachers through post structural lenses which regard identities as multiple, fluid, non-linear and continually in a state of flux. In this chapter, I draw on poststructuralist theorising to understand teachers' identities and the meanings they constitute through the discourses and practices they adopt as a condition for and outcome of the changes, uncertainties and contradictions in different teaching and learning contexts. Drawing on multidimensional understandings of teachers' identities, challenged me to acknowledge that ambiguity, multiplicity and contradictions are inseparable to the form and substance of our identities. My research into teachers' lives may be regarded as a cubist painting, made up of different clues – yet it is a dynamic, harmonised composition of multiple viewpoints.

In this chapter, I will offer a description of the broader normative framework within which teachers think, work and act. I will explain *why and how* I sought the

R. Dhunpath and M. Samuel (eds.), Life History Research: Epistemology, Methodology and Representation, 115–133.

employment of a metaphor as a response to the interpretative dilemmas I faced in imagining different possibilities for "desirable teachers" (Pillay, 2003) and the opportunities I had to produce these possibilities differently. In expounding the cubist metaphor, I will discuss the four cubist principles that I drew on to create the analytical framework for the study and how it enabled me to explore my own role in the authorship of teachers' narratives. I also reflect on what constitutes "data" in the research process. Since the storied narrative is the researcher's construction, the power of the cubist framework lies in its ability to enhance the trustworthiness of the text, satisfying the rigours of plausibility and consensus. I offer selected aspects of the four different fictionalised narratives to demonstrate this.

REGULATING TEACHERS' LIVES

Education, like all facets of South African life, is undergoing large-scale changes as a consequence of the wider transition to democracy. As part of its social commitment to change, several pieces of legislation have attempted to regulate the roles and responsibilities of teachers in a consolidated effort to transform racist education. *The Norms and Standards for Educators* (2000), Outcomes Based Education, the South African Council for Educators (SACE) *Code of Conduct* (1997) and the Development Appraisal System (1998) were some of the government's initiatives aimed at engaging teachers to change. Overall, educational policies are envisaged to transform the educational legacy of the past into a democratic education system, which will contribute to the development of productive human beings in a country free from oppression, exclusion and prejudice.

Redressing inequities is thus a major political force of all policies in education. In South African schools, for example, the teacher's work and teachers' identities have been identified as a key focus to the transformation of the education system (Barasa & Mattson, 1998). The focus on all levels of educational change (macro, meso and micro) is an attempt to break decisively away from any absolute, singular and categorical framework of how to understand and practise being a teacher. It is in this context that the image of the patriarchal teacher has engendered intense debate and contestation, resulting in a range of policy initiatives. In light of different forms of regulation, teachers are having to re-negotiate what it means to be a teacher.

These emerging discourses, ideas and practices concerning the changing positions and identities of teachers have often become mired in fear and suspicion, domination and self-closure. Ironically, teachers continue to use the classroom to enact rituals of control that are about domination, unjust exercise of power or strategic mimicry. As products of the apartheid system themselves and having inherited particular identities as teachers, the spaces for change they carved involved uncertainty and risk taking. Without delving too deeply into the multitude of reasons that contribute to teacher dissatisfaction generally, many teachers have responded to the continued changes in a way that resulted in a sense of mis-alignment between their personal and professional identities. This misalignment has resulted in an exodus of teachers out of the profession. According to Ramrathan (2002, p. 127), the drive to leave is real and their reasons centred largely around structural issues (class size, work loads, rationalisation and redeployment), personal issues (better financial opportunities) and psychological issues (stress, morale).

The forces driving the issue of teacher resignation and the sense of disconnectedness that many teachers experience has impacted on their level of commitment. Many teachers continue to enact practices in their classrooms in a way that is less threatening, stereotypical and passionless. However, there are teachers who, while recognising the normative structures that regulate them, challenge and threaten the dominant forces and stereotypical images of being a teacher for possibilities of rejuvenating moments that enable them to commit themselves to their profession and enact practices that give their lives a sense of meaning, fulfilment and pleasure. It is the latter group of teachers that I draw attention to in this chapter.

PAINTING TEACHERS DIFFERENTLY

Given the postmodern turn, I feel that we need to explore different ways of representing the other and ourselves as researcher-author in life histories. At the moment, we rely mostly on realist tales that are author-evacuated texts. But what about creating impressionist tales, dramas, fictions and poetic representations of lives? (Sparkes, 1994)

Choosing to create a composition of teachers' lives is like a work of art, the choice of what to paint, how to paint it, where to place the figures/shapes and the focal points are a reflection of "who and where I am" (Pillay, 2003). I took my cue from Sparkes (1994) and, creatively using the generative matrix that Picasso has employed in the painting of five nude women (sex workers) grouped around a still life, I learnt to evoke different emotions and stories of possibility.

Producing the cubist framework was also as a result of my search for voice in response to feeling jettisoned and under-represented as a visual artist and art educator in the mainstream educational context. Over the years the Arts curriculum has been sidelined in the Teacher Education curriculum in response to the neoliberal agenda of financial austerity and its focus on the production of "hard skills". I declare my sense of personal and professional marginalisation here because I am fully cognisant that I am implicated in the construction of these teachers' stories as I bring into the research process as much of who I am, as who the research participants are. As Trinh Minh-Ha (1998, p. 28) suggests: [We need to]

inscribe difference without bursting into a series of narcissistic accounts of yourself and your kind.

The narratives of Grace, Barry, Danna, Lanna, Manny and Terry (pseudonyms for my research participants) were woven out of a combination of biographical excavations using life history interviews and a range of alternate data sources (written, oral and visual) that emerged during the interviews. While the multiple data sources gave me access into the teachers' lived experiences, told and experienced in terms of their race, class and geographical specificity, the experience of producing the data generated certain concerns for me relating to my use of life history methodology. This chapter focuses on only one of the participants, Danna and her narrative.

THE CUBIST METAPHOR: CREATING A "WRITERLY" TEXT

The painting, *"Les Demoiselles d'Avignon"* (Refer to Fig.1) was the occasion for working the hyphen of self and other, generated from the cubist matrix. As Fine (1994, p. 72) wrote:

> Researchers probe how we are in relation with the contexts we study and with our informants, understanding that we are all multiple in those relations…I invite researchers to see how these relations between get us better data, limit what we feel free to say, expand our minds and constrict our mouths, engage us in intimacy and seduce us into complicity, makes us quick to interpret and hesitant to write. Working the hyphen means creating occasions for researchers and informants to discuss what is, and is not, "happening between," within the negotiated relations of whose story is being told, why, to whom, with what interpretation, and whose story is being shadowed, why, for whom, and with what consequence.

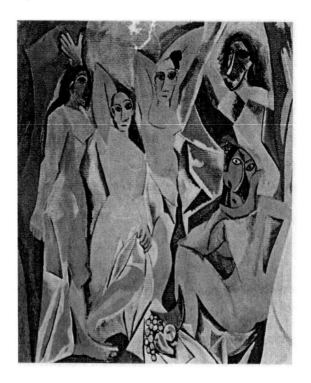

Figure 1. Les Demoiselles d' Avignon

Painted by Pablo Picasso in 1907, *Les Demoiselles d' Avignon* is:

> ... a painting that reveals his rebellion against the myth of beauty. In this painting he wants to destroy the whole of what Western Art stood for since the early renaissance. Not only the proportions but the organic integrity and continuity of the human body are denied here. ("Culture Shock: Flashpoints", 2002)

THE CUBIST FRAMEWORK

Closely exploring the discourses used in various texts and references (such as included above) to explain Picasso's *subject and meaning* of the painting and his *treatment of space and form,* I came to adopt four discrete yet connected positions (refer to Table 1) to generate my narrative knowing. The table describes the four cubist <u>principles</u> (column 1), mapped over by the four <u>perspectives</u> I adopted from the four principles (in column two), and the four factionalised <u>narratives</u> that I finally narrated in the cubist composition of teachers' lives (in column three). In this section I offer a **description** of my engagement with the painting and its generative matrix and then offer exemplars of the different **interpretations** to show how through continually adopting/ shifting positions, particular images, metaphors, story lines and concepts were made available and relevant.

Table 1. Producing Different Knowledge and Producing Knowledge Differently

	Principles	Perspectives	Narratives
Sources	**Les Demoiselles d' Avignon**	***Cubist Analytical Framework***	***Successful Teachers***
Levels	**Principle One:** *Three–dimensional figures and space reconfigured in a new dimension of time and space (two–dimensional picture plane).*	***Perspective One:*** *The storied narratives: "Freeze frames, coloured facets"*	***First person and third person narratives*** These individual stories are likened to a two-dimensional relief frieze, foregrounding the self, dispersed through the story, reconfigured in time and space.
	Principle Two: *Spatial ambiguity and multiple views*	***Perspective Two:*** *Storied vignettes: "Fluid images and potential spaces"*	***Vignettes:*** stories that offer a dramatic yet elusive discussion of particular positionings the six teachers take up within the ongoing

			shifts between the individual and society. This shift offers another view of the potential spaces for what there might be.
Principle Three: *The geometrical framework imposing a new kind of integrity and continuity*	*Perspective Three: Agenda for agency: Patterns of desire imposing a continued commitment for change and continuity*	**Ensembles**: Organised in thematic categories this view foregrounds the commonalities that unify the different teachers irrespective of where and how they perform their success.	
Principle Four: *Work in progress: Exhibits concepts of metamorphosis, of simultaneity and consecutive vision*	*Perspective Four: Cubist lives: An exhibit of metamorphosis*	Written as an overall **self-reflexive commentary** and synthesis of the data collected, the analogy of metamorphosis gives expression to the lives, of both teachers and mine	

Perspective One: Storied Narratives: Freeze Frames, Coloured Facets

Using the first cubist principle, *Three–dimensional figures and space reconfigured in a new dimension of time and space (two–dimensional picture plane),* I narrated teachers' constructions of self (re)configured in time and space. This principle offers the viewer a representation of five nude sex-workers painted in what many describe as "grotesquely distorted forms". This assisted me in developing perspective ONE of my narration of teachers' lives. I use the ideas and clues provided in the principle/painting to arrive at two different writing genres to represent the six teachers in my study.

In **Perspective One:** *Storied Narratives: Freeze frames, coloured facets,* I explore key descriptive words/phrases of the painting like, *"figures and background seem to form a relief", "the painting forgoes all pursuit of spatial depth", "close relationship to pictorial surface", "harsh angular planes shaded in a way that gives them a certain three dimensionality.* These constructs I employ to freeze and frame the storied narratives as a version of "a life" told and experienced, within a particular space and time. Likened to the five nude women, I realised at this initial moment that the re-constructed data of teachers' lives is offered as an act of creating one's self, told and experienced in a way that has no "intrinsic or immanent relations"(Freeman, 1993). Teachers had their own purposes for framing the stories in certain ways and I acknowledge in this representation that "a life" may be portrayed differently at different times with different audiences, with different purposes. I also acknowledge my own agendas and priorities in this process.

From a hermeneutic position, this version of the story reads as a "realistic version of a life", lived in all its colour and glory, pleasure and pain This fictionalised facet does not separate the figure from the background (the teacher from the socio-political context within which the life is lived); instead, it is written as a "relief", and submerged with the background which is silenced/not visible. While I did filter and colour the data as the orally generated stories were transcribed and transformed into "conventional" written texts, the inclusion of participant selected photos, poems, metaphors, illustrations, and favourite musical pieces captured the private, intimate experiences, thoughts, images, feelings and served as faithful representations of the "actual data" produced by the teachers. Like clues in a cubist painting, they provide the reader the spaces to experience this "life lived" sensually, without any attempt at categorisation – as a way of understanding what it is to be fully alive. While there is a sense of "flatness" or two-dimensionality that pervades the narratives in this version of teachers' lives, each storied narrative has an underlying tone (shaded) of other forces, muted and silenced discourses that inform such a telling. I realised then that one small shift and another view (three-dimensionality) of the facet was possible to understand the telling differently.

Like Picasso, this (re)construction narrated as storied narratives is in a sense "dislocated, inconsistent in style, in fact unfinished" (Culture Shock, 2002). I now offer you a glimpse of Danna's story, "The Adventurer" written in the first person narrative as a way to show how "the stories had to be "textualised" (Van Maanen, 1988, p. 95) for only in textualised form does data yield to analysis. This version of "a life" makes available to the audience the story of the self dispersed through discourse. While to some extent this may be regarded as an initial level of analysis, it is a crucial insertion in the whole constructive/deconstructive process signalled in Table 1 as Perspective Two, Perspective Three and Perspective Four.

The Adventurer

Danna is a White female teacher who came into South Africa with her family as a British immigrant when she was nine years old. She presently holds joint citizenship, British and South African. She teaches at the Technical College, a historically Indian institution offering a range of courses to school-leavers wanting to pursue a more "technically orientated' career. It services a predominantly African and Indian learner population. This college is one of five teaching and learning sites at which Danna has taught. Her experiences are diverse, ranging from teaching the physically challenged, to teaching at a Technikon for African students in the rural area of Edendale.

A bookworm
Mum never worked in England but when we came to South Africa she became a traffic warden and then the chief traffic warden. A real success story. She was very caring, loving and hard working and that rubbed off on us. But Lina, my twin sister, and I were very lonely. When mum started working she left very early in the morning, and came home late at night. I think that being left alone contributed in a

---

way to Lina "going off the track". I used to just bury myself in my books. I was a bookworm. I just read and read and read. I was an average student at school. I just loved reading anything from encyclopaedias to books . . . novels and stuff like that. By the time I got to standard three, I could read the entire children's Bible from cover to cover. I entered the Bible competition which I won hands down because I knew every story in the Bible.

I played teacher

Because we moved so much, we were never able to have friends. Mum bought us a chalkboard and Lina and I played school. I was always the teacher, of course, trying to help Lina learn. My father had a go at Lina all the time. *"Why can't you be like your sister Danna?"* We never knew then that Lina had a learning problem. I always covered for Lina. It was a very maternal or protective feeling, in a sense. My teaching really started out of the love of helping someone. My dad always expected a lot from me. I had to do so much more to make up for what Lina couldn't do. It became a competitive thing within me to do better all the time.

From England to South Africa
I am a British citizen . . .

Mrs. Blike was my standard one teacher and I didn't like her. She was an Afrikaner and she didn't like us British. When Lina and I came into her class she always pushed us aside. I remember the day a boy pulled my hair in class and I got the hiding because I slapped him. She actually shoved me out of the classroom. I thought she was very unfair. Mrs. Kamp, who was also Afrikaans, loved Lina and I. She loved all of us. I remember her teaching us about London. Lina and I had just come back and we were made to feel special. We had all these postcards and slides that we showed them about London. I enjoyed her and Lina actually did so well in the test.

High school: "A goody two-shoes"

In 1975 we moved into our very own home in Manor Hill in Durban and I attended Stamhill High . I remember my history teacher in high school. She made me love history. I also enjoyed Shakespeare. I was born 10 miles away from where Shakespeare lived in Stratford-on-Avon. Lina became deviant in high school, always in the office because she had detention. I was a goody two-shoes at school. There is a song that I had written during this time, which I called, "I was so confused".

I was so confused, I did not know what to do

I had so many fears in my life

I was growing so weary and tired

When I heard a voice say to me

I died on the cross

But arose again

Is that too much for you to believe? (Danna, 2000)

During my student teaching years, I never truly believed that I was made to be a teacher. If you ask my twin who has never trained as a teacher, to teach, she would be able to teach, but I don't think anyone can become a teacher. To be a teacher you have got to have that something inside, that caring and empathy. You must love what you are doing. Now I know. It was my destiny to end up in this school. I will always be a part of Townsend School for the Deaf.

My life changed in 1989 when I left Townsend to work at the Blairhill School for the disabled. I made the biggest mistake in my life leaving Townsend. My heart broke to tell the kids I was leaving. I cried. I sang the last song for them in the assembly, "Jesus loves me, this I know".

Open Flair: "I can and I will"
I hated Blairhill from the minute I walked in. I walked in to the staff room and "die hele vergardering" was in Afrikaans. From day one I was ostracised because I could not answer in Afrikaans. I felt very uncomfortable speaking the language. The staff did not make me feel welcome, especially Mrs Kemp, the head of department.

"Danna is here to join us in Economics," the principal announced. I was taken by surprise. I had never studied or taught Economics before. But again, I am the type of person who would just take anything as a challenge and do the best I possibly can. I was given a grade twelve class who had not been taught for the first half of the year because the teacher was ill. *"I will do my best,"* was a promise I made to myself.

The deputy principal, Mr. duToit, seemed to be the only person with whom I could get on. He was actually a very nice man, and I found him most approachable when I wanted assistance.

The first day I walked into the Economics class and I said, *"Good morning"* to the students and the students replied, *"Goeie more, mevrou"*. I was teaching a subject I didn't know on higher grade in Afrikaans. I was really frightened that the students weren't going to make it, but they did and they did well. I remember the kids were doing a section on Forms of Ownership (Business Economics), and I took them in their wheelchairs by bus to places like the sugar terminal and Toyota. The kids enjoyed it. It was real. For those kids who had a problem understanding, I was able to give individual attention after school and that really helped. I am thorough and I wouldn't accept a learner who said, *"I can't do it"*. The kids always laughed, *"Miss B, we can and we will"*. We had a lot of fun. (Complete version appears in the doctoral study-Chapter Four.)

While Danna's narrative illustrates my role as "ventriloquist", I also move on to explore the implications of Picasso's depiction of the two "mask-like" figures in my role as "interpreter" in writing up the narratives of Barry and Terry. The two narrative genres were inspired by juxtaposing the three figures on the left, painted as distortions of classical figures, and the two dislocated bodies and "mask-like" features on the right. The mask symbolically represents the "face" I give to the figures (as interpreter), asserting my perspective of the teacher's life, in my words, to a large extent. Narrating the story differently was enticing as well as challenging. However, as much as I acted as the vehicle for transmission (as messenger/bearer) of the narration, how I narrated the stories, and what narrative forms the stories take acknowledge my power in this relationship. Essential to the activist stance that I take in the research process, is also my critical awareness and sensitivity to the power relations in these conversations and the teller's vulnerability when they enter into this relationship with me. Danna's story in my thesis (the big picture) can more fully be understood in relation to the supplementary narratives of Barry and Terry: each narrative co-influencing the others.

In synthesising the data, in the form of stories within the two different representational styles, I had to provide the specific contexts and enough detail so that they appear as unique individuals (as hero/heroine) within particular situations, and I had to be able to differentiate one teacher's life story from the next (Polkinghorne, 1995), just as the five women (sex workers) foregrounded in the painting. The power of a storied outcome was therefore derived from its presentation of a distinctive individual, in a unique situation, dealing with issues in a unique manner.

Perspective Two: "Fluid, Multiple Images and Potential Spaces"

At this moment, I could have moved instantaneously to assigning categories and labels for the Danna narrative produced above. But a deep sense of restlessness and uneasiness pressured me to shift as Picasso did, to include the notion of multiple views, inviting the "reader" to move from point to point, to understand that there is no one reality, but an infinite number of momentarily caught glimpses, formulated and codified in the mind of the spectator. During these moments I realised that not asking questions about the individual stories and their connections to larger contexts (the "how" and "what"), the nature of these connections and alliances would leave open the possibility of solipsism and the elevation of the idiosyncratic (Goodson, 1992). **Perspective Two: *"Fluid, multiple images and potential spaces"*** arose out of this state of creative turbulence.

Taking my cue from the grotesquely distorted figures, each with features painted from multiple viewpoints (e.g. one eye painted in profile while the other faces front), propelled me to shift my gaze from looking up/front, to back, sideways and down as a way of mining the multiple positions teachers occupied as they continually reworked their meanings as African (male), or White (female), against the historically inherited narratives already codified by others (McLaren, 1993). Chunks of *"solidified spaces"*, I read as those threatening spaces teachers occupied to give meaning and open up the potential for difference and uniqueness. These motivated me to read between the lines and form alliances I would never have been able to form otherwise. Simultaneously, I read the *"fragments of translucent bodies" moving in spatial ambiguity"* as suggestive of the degree of fluidity and ambiguity between the figures and society (background). These *concave and convex* forms I read as those discourses (of apartheid/race/gender) that are codified by others and populated with others meanings and which continue to manipulate and subsume difference.

In reading teachers lives through the cubist principle of ***Spatial ambiguity and multiple views,*** I have written this version as storied vignettes. It is my attempt to show how making the shifts within the cubist framework, I am able to place the data (the storied narrative) under erasure and explore the multiple, fluid and tenuous relations between the individual and the socio-political context. However, as I began to understand this unidentified and unnamed data, I also needed to address my role – as the cubist artist would describe the moment of reconfiguration of space when:

> Background and foreground shapes integrate, blurring outlines, with the edges looser and opened . . . and a moment of final liberation from the imitation of visual reality that challenged the Renaissance world of nature observed by means of the arbitrary principle of geometric perspective. (Arnason, 1969, p. 129)

In foregrounding the self constituted through discourse, I shift my stance as narrator to a position where I critically explore the storied narratives (Perspective One) to make visible the multiple effects of particular relations and teachers' response to society's codes. To write up the vignettes from a critical point of view, I selectively identify particular discursive positionings within the framework of apartheid (ambiguous and tenuous relations between individual and society) in and through which the teachers in this study have been produced into relations of power. Teachers' personal biographies and experiences (of family, community life, schooling experiences) are shaped by specificities of race, class, gender, and have been identified as the crucial sites in these vignettes, to understand the construction and regulation of teachers' identities. In this fictionalised version, I offer a part of my interpretation of Danna's multiple, ambiguous and contradictory discourses. Using the same data in the storied narrative, the storied vignette shows how Danna consciously attempts to be "Exotic Other" in the contexts in which she chooses to work as a condition to be successful. In an attempt to represent the multiplicity of her private and professional identity, I offer three different views of Danna within the thematic category *"Seductive Spaces": Danna, the Outsider; Danna, the British woman;, Danna, the South African White woman.*

Danna, the outsider

Danna's story revealed to me the story of a stranger. For many years after her arrival in South Africa as a British immigrant, she found herself being part of another world that she did not inherently belong to, and was not fully part of, a world in which she often came up to be very different – very other. Being British, the type and degree of her strangerhood varied. Being British constrained as well as enabled her. She knows she can exercise power and decides when and how to use it.

Despite living in South Africa, the strong ideological umbilical cord between her British status and her South African residency had not been severed. She remembers with much fondness her life in England, her teachers and the blossoming of her singing career. When reflecting on her move from England to South Africa, there are signs that are symptomatic of a fractured and dislocated identity, described by her infantile desire never to give up her British citizenship, a duality which is referred to as the mind/body split. While her "British" identity enables her in learning discourses (Shakespeare and History) and made her believe that she had a sense of a special and sovereign identity, it also belies the dislocation she experiences by virtue of her gender and class. As little girls she and her sister were very lonely in the neighbourhood they lived in, because they had no friends and they were not allowed to play with the Indian children from across the road. She confessed, *"My sister and I spent our days alone until my mum arrived home at six o'clock every evening"*. While she experiences her race as something fixed and immovable, her idea of *"wanting to play with the Indian"* hints at alternate messages and provides the condition for exploring the unfamiliar and strange.

Wanting to be challenged is a seductive experience for Danna: to be able to explore her strangeness within and without her, to "cross-pollinate" ideas from within and without, from one to another, from one place to another. As a young girl, Danna explained how, together with her twin sister, she faced the wrath of their Afrikaner teacher. In this construction she described, *"Mrs. Lyon, my grade two teacher, was Afrikaner and she didn't like us British. When Lina and I came into her class she pushed us aside"*. Yet Danna leaves teaching at Townsend, School for the Deaf and takes up a teaching position in Blairhill, an Afrikaans speaking Institution. *I hated Blairhill school. From the minute I walked in. I walked in to the staff room and "die hele vergardering" was in Afrikaans. I walked in and the whole meeting was Afrikaans. From day one I was ostracised because I could not answer in Afrikaans. I felt very uncomfortable speaking the language. The staff did not make me feel welcome, more especially Mrs. Kamp, the head of department. An all Afrikaner medium school. I was an uitlander. I was teaching a subject I didn't know on higher grade in Afrikaans, a language I never really knew.*

However, there are contradictions to this deficit. Her position as British works invisibly as a claim to power (as historically privileged). Constructing herself as exotic other is reinforced further when she admits, *"I refused to nationalise and give up my British passport. There is no way under the sun that I would take allegiance to the flag and a country that I did not believe in politically"*. Her teacher position here also foregrounds her desire to be challenged by the unfamiliar and unknown, an appropriate description for an immigrant. This experience not only became the nexus for power to be exercised in productive ways, disrupting and resisting homogeneous and unchangeable notions of "the Afrikaner Identity" as well as stereotypical ways of thinking and working. This she points out when she says, "*I taught against all odds, I even took the learners in their wheelchairs to the sugar terminal*". Within these contradictions and tensions as "stranger", and challenged by the "strangeness" she locates herself in, Danna opens up spaces for disruptive moments to perform her success.

While these storied vignettes were thematically organised from the perspective that "I" have taken to explore teachers' lives, it is a text open to many different interpretations, purposes and audience. In reading between the lines, I was able to interpret the data in unexpected ways.

Perspective Three: Agenda for agency: Patterns of desire imposing a continued commitment for change and continuity

Placing the data once more under erasure, I shift/turn to view another facet of the cube from which I am able to read a different storyline. From the cubist principle of geometrical patterning, a new kind of integrity and continuity, I invented Perspective Three: "Agenda for agency: Patterns of desire for change and continuity". From this vantage point I am able to write and represent the different practices teachers enacted in their classrooms while simultaneously signalling the commonality across all six teachers irrespective of where, how, why and when they perform their success.

> The figures constitute a unique kind of matter, which imposes a unique kind of integrity and continuity on the entire canvas. Each individual figure is united by a general geometrical principle which superimposes its own laws onto the natural proportions . . . ("Culture Shock: Flashpoints", 2002)

Written as thematic ensemblings, I was able to draw on key constructs of integrity and continuity to create a storyline. Teachers' agenda for agency is organised to offer a deconstructive and pragmatic dimension to teachers' lives. Arriving at this position was just as persuasive and challenging. Key words like, "*Integrity*", "*Continuity*", "*United by a general geometrical principle*", "*the motif of the five female nudes superimpose its own laws on the 'natural' proportions*", "*the partial and fragmented figures contrasts strangely with a serene little still-life in the foreground* (pear, an apple, a slice of melon, a bunch of grapes) assisted me in reading the painting with greater depth and insight. I was able to transfer attributes by comparison, by substitution, or as a consequence of that interaction to the teachers and their daily practices. Organised as thematic categories, this view of teachers' lived lives foregrounds those shared practices in and through which teachers perform their success, within the constraints of the dominant discourses that seek to limit and oppress difference and better ways of thinking and working as teachers. The idea of the patterning assisted me to do that. In the sections below I offer a brief description of how the constructs were used to develop the idea of patterning in making sense of the messy process of reorganising, condensing, expanding, and synthesising the often disparate meanings.

The key words, "Integrity and Continuity" assisted me in developing the two key axes to develop the unifying framework, Agenda for agency: "Patterns of desire". In the main study teachers' potential for success is understood on two dimensions:

– Dimension One: Change as a space for moments of teachers' freedom **(Integrity)**
– Dimension two: Continuity as a space for affirmation and refiguration. **(Continuity)**

The first dimension which evolved from the construct Integrity, documents the conscious positions taken up by teachers and it foregrounds the creative and complex ways through which teachers' identities are forged in their daily practices. This dimension, *Practices of the self,* shows that teachers are agentic and powerful, and they are able to contest and change practices that are being used to block and constrain how they make sense of their lives and the world, for practices that give shape to their arbitrary desires and interests.

I have named these practices *Desiring knowledge,* which focuses on the subject discipline as a space to disrupt and challenge oppressive reason and for the transformation of prevailing ways of knowing and acting. *Blurring barriers* presents a description of different cultural investments teachers take up to rupture the traditional boundaries between teacher and learner, between the private/public lives. *Collective knowing* examines the fluidity of teachers' power relations in the different learning spaces. *Desiring difference* describes the shift from book learning to an emphasis on a diverse range of experiences. In these spaces, teachers create a range of unique experiences shaped by their own interests and desires. These unconventional practices and ideas to perform their success makes us understand the complexity of teachers' agency, and the possibility for decons-truction and reconstruction.

An example to illustrate one of the thematic categories, *Desiring difference: "It's not about methods, it's about who I am",* is provided below using the data from the storied narrative "The Adventurer".

The shift away from book learning by the teachers, to an emphasis on experiences as a resource for learning, is what I have described here as a shift from the "discursive to the figural" (Usher & Edwards, 1994, p. 199). Through different knowledges generated from a wide number of sources, a diversity of experience is constantly constructed and reconstructed. Associated with this is their desire for informality and the creation of different practices that do not do away with power but reconfigure and displace it in differing ways. The following excerpt is taken from Danna during the interviewing process:

"The Adventurer"

The first day I walked into the Economics class and I said, "Good morning" to the students and the students replied, "Goeie more, mevrou", I was teaching a subject I didn't know on higher grade in Afrikaans. I was really frightened that the students weren't going to make it, but they did and they did well. I remember the kids were doing a section on Forms of Ownership (Business Economics), and I took them in their wheelchairs by bus to places like the sugar terminal and Toyota. The kids enjoyed it. It was real. For those kids who had a problem understanding, I was able to give individual attention after school and that really helped. I am thorough and I wouldn't accept a learner who said, "I can't do it". The kids always laughed, "Miss B, we can and we will". We had a lot of fun.

For Danna, learning from experience meant engaging herself in a variety of teaching and learning sites, unfamiliar and without the relevant book knowledge or academic qualifications. In doing so she had consciously moved into "new territories" and created spaces in which she was able to reaffirm her potential to engage in new dialogues (different from her own), and simultaneously expand the possibilities for those dialogues. Within these bold moments, she became the author of her own script. Rather than assuming a kind of security within a context for which she has been trained, she moves into spaces where she takes the specificity of different contexts, geographies, languages, and of otherness, to recognise the otherness in herself (Giroux, 1994, p. 168). Her desire to explore other subject areas in which she has not been trained, meant that she was able to forge new links academically (she was excellent at cross-pollinating), spaces that enabled her to progress as an academic.

The construct Continuity I used to create the second dimensional axis, "Practices on the self". I explore particular practices teachers impose on themselves as a way of resisting the constraints and states of domination and for sustaining a continued commitment for their "own" voice, identity and unique ways of knowing and being. These moments of creative resurgence inflame particular practices and relationships that have been erased or silenced in the category "teacher". In the doctoral study I make available to the reader what I have named teachers' Biographical Investments. While I have loosely grouped the six teachers into three types of alterity practices; "the rehabilitators", "the soul seekers" and the "movers and the seekers" as part of the patterning, I offer as an example here the "category", "Movers and the Shakers" which begins to describe the power of movement in teachers' lives and the desire for continuity. Once again, I draw on data from the storied narrative to show how Danna moves out of one institutional site to another, and as that movement mentality grows it empowers her with capacities to cross-pollinate and germinate new ideas, practices and values.

MOVERS AND THE SHAKERS

Danna started her teaching career at Townsend School for the Deaf, where she acquired the skills of learning how to sign. Furthermore, she also taught them how to sing. She says:

> That was such an achievement and this made me all the more determined to "open the doors" for them.

> However, she leaves Townsend, with an exalted reputation. She expressed,

> My life changed in 1989 when I left Townsend to work at Blairhill School for the disabled.

Against all odds, her position at Blairhilloffered her the space to learn to speak and teach in Afrikaans. She also introduced the learners to different learning spaces, by taking the students to visit the sugar terminal even though they were confined to wheelchairs. She found this challenging, but left behind an exalted reputation when she decided to leave Blairhill at the end of 1989. The same can be attributed to her experiences at Pleasurehill.

She confesses:

1994 was a happy year for me . . . I became involved with many of their community projects and there were lot of friendships . . . Although the principal offered me the post as a deputy principal, no amount of coaxing was going to make me stay in Pietermaritzburg....

...Then to Cato Manor College... And this goes on...

For Danna the world is her classroom and moving from one geographical site to another (Pietermaritzburg to Edendale, Edendale to Durban) highlights that the potential to be teacher is found everywhere.

Agenda for Agency: Patterns of desire for Change and Continuity provides a dynamic framework in which a range of disconnected and fragmented data elements are made to cohere in a different but explanatory way. This understanding of teachers' lives imposes a new kind of integrity and continuity while working within the normative framework (representative by the traditional painting of the fruit in the foreground) of what it means to be a teacher within a South African context. Again, while these impositional forms are contingent constructions and fabricated ensembles that arise out of the dialogue between me and the teller, there are many other layers of interpretation, and many layers of truth in this dialogue.

Perspective Four: A Self Reflexive Narrative: "An Exhibit of Metamorphosis"

> Cubist Principle: The cubist work, an exhibition of all those concepts of metamorphosis, of simultaneous consecutive vision and the final liberation from the imitation of visual reality that challenged the Renaissance world of nature observed by means of the arbitrary principle of geometric perspective. (Arnason, 1969)

I developed the cubist framework in response to the interpretative struggles that I faced, knowing full well that there are multiple ways of making sense of the teacher's world. I see how the text I have composed over time was a way to inscribe reflexivity on different levels of the study. Infused into the non-linear structure of the text, the titles and the analogies, the cubist composition is a moment in my metamorphosis as researcher/learner exploring the lives of teachers in a particular moment of time and space. I move from an empiricist stance, to a hermeneutic space, to a critical interrogation of particular discourses that constitute teachers as agentic beings. Finally, I move to a deconstructive position to understand what it means in practice to be teacher. These simultaneous and consecutive visions and imaginings I reproduced as a consequence of the juxtapositions made possible through the metaphor. As a final liberation from the imitation of reality, the analogy of metamorphosis is used to explain how the play happens, between the teachers, my-self and the text that we have come to produce.

Composing the cubist narrative makes it impossible for me to come to any fixed understanding of teachers who commit themselves to their practice with some sense of pleasure and fulfilment. The nature of teachers' personal and social transformation is slippery. Just as unfinished as the cubist painting, I want to regard the slipperiness of teachers' identities as work in progress, as an appropriate place to embrace ongoing change. We are always in the midst of dialogue, open to resistance and change even in states of domination where teachers are temporarily silenced and imprisoned, to the resurgence of buried voices, to ongoing dialogue and transformation. If understanding the art of existence offers the space for better and different ways of being, knowing and acting, the question I advance is: "Can every teachers' life be a work of art?"

CONCLUSION

My meaning-making and representation of teachers' work in all its richness and complexity lies in the power of the metaphor and its potential to further my understanding of the meaning of experience, which in turns defines the reality I have manufactured. As a symbol system constructed of lines, shapes, form and colour and time and space, the cubist painting allows for texts to be composed, read and interpreted at different levels of sophistication (Branch, 2000). The framework that I found in cubism enabled me to explore my own authorship in an imaginative way. There is nothing particularly privileged about the multiple interpretations that I have explored and each one is no less plausible than the other. In using the cubist metaphor, I found that I am able to challenge the authoritative social and cultural scripts in the making of teacher culture. I am able to show how power, meaning, discourse and subjectivity actually work in practice. In this space "for play", I was able to envision revitalised academic and public discourses to guide my thinking and open up possibilities for the disruption of the linear narrative. Inclusion of self through the metaphor pressed me to exercise my power differently. Finally, my own valuing of an aesthetic response to the world is acknowledged within this research strategy. It acts as a way of bridging my world, the world of successful teachers and the different audiences who will read this work. It was about placing what I knew against the new. As a teacher educator I continue to look, listen and draw on meanings outside of my professional purview. Like the cubist work, I know that what I offer is an unfinished story, a work in progress... open to question, challenge and disruption.

REFERENCES

Arnason, H. H. (1969). *A history of modern art: Painting. Sculpture. Architecture*. London: Thames and Hudson.

Arnason, H. H. (1988). *A history of modern art*. London: Thames and Hudson.

Bach, H. E. F. (1998). *A visual narrative concerning curriculum, girls, photography etc*. Edmonton: Qual Institute Press.

Bach, H., Kennedy, M., & Mickelson, J. R. (1997). *Bodies at work: Sensory knowing*. Paper presented at the annual meeting of the American educational Research Association, Chicago, March.

Barasa, F. S., & Mattson, E. (1998). The roles, regulation and professional development of educators in South Africa: A critical analysis of four policy documents. *Journal of Education, 23*, 40–72.

Bloom, L. R., & Munro, P. (1995). Conflicts of selves: Nonunitary subjectivity in women administrators' life history narratives. In A. Hatch & R. Wisniewski (Eds.), *Life history and narrative*. London and Washington: The Falmer Press.

Bowe, R., Ball, S., & Gold, A. (1992). *Reforming education and changing schools: Case studies in policy sociology*. London and New York: Routledge.

Branch, R. M. (2000). A taxonomy of visual literacy. *Advances in Reading/Language Research, 7*, 377–402.

Bruner, J. (1984). The opening up of anthropology. In E. M. Bruner (Ed.), *Text play and story: The construction and reconstruction of experience*. Urbana, IL: University of Illinois Press.

Clandinin, D. J., & Connelly, F. M. (1994). Personal experience methods. In N. K. Denzin & Y. S. Lincoln (Eds.), *Handbook of qualitative research*. Thousand Oakes, CA: Sage.

Culture Shock: *Flashpoints: 'Vis…: Picasso's Les Demoiselles d'Avignon'*. Retrieved January 2, 2003, from http://www.geocities.com/rr17bb/LesDemoi.html

Eisner, E. W. (1998). *The enlightened eye: Qualitative enquiry and the enhancement of educational practice*. New Jersey, NJ: Prentice-Hall.

Ensor, P. (2000). *How do we grasp mathematics teacher educators' and teachers' tacit knowledge, in research design and curriculum practice?* Conference proceedings of SAARMSTE, Port Elizabeth, January.

Freeman, M. P. (1993). *Rewriting the self: history, memory, narrative*. New York: Routledge, and Cambridge: Cambridge University Press.

Giroux, H. A. (1994). *Disturbing pleasures: Learning popular culture*. London: Routledge.

Gitlin, A. (1990). Understanding teaching dialogically. *Teachers College Record, 91*(4), 537.

Goodson, I. F. (1992). Studying teachers' lives: An emergent field of inquiry. In I. F. Goodson (Ed.), *Studying teachers' lives*. London: Routledge.

Gough, N. (1994a). *Plotting research: Educational inquiry's continuities with detective fiction*. Deakin Centre for Education and Change Working Paper 35, pp. 1–35.

Gough, N. (1994b). Narration, reflection, diffraction: Aspects of fiction in educational inquiry. *Australian Educational Researcher, 21*(3), 1–26.

Grumet, M. R. (1991). The politics of personal knowledge. In C. Witherell & N. Noddings (Eds.), *Stories, lives tell: Narrative and dialogue in education.* New York: Teachers College Press.

Hargreaves, A. (1994). *Changing teachers, changing times: Teachers' work and culture in the postmodern age.* London: Cassell.

Hatch, J. A., & Wisneiwski, R. (1995). *Life history and narrative.* London: The Falmer Press.

hooks, b. (1995). *Art on my mind: Visual politics.* New York: The New York Press.

Krieger, S. (1991). *Social science and the self: Personal essays on an art form.* New Brunswick, NJ: Rutgers University Press.

McLaren, P. (1993). Border disputes: Multicultural narrative, identity formation, and critical pedagogy in postmodern America. In D. McLaughlin & W. G. Tierney (Eds.), *Naming silenced lives: Personal narratives and the process of educational change.* New York: Routledge.

Pillay, G. (2003). *Successful teachers: A cubist narrative of lives, practices and the evaded.* PhD Thesis, University of KwaZulu-Natal, South Africa.

Polkinghorne, D. E. (1995). Narrative configuration in qualitative analysis. In J. A. Hatch & R. Wisniewski (Eds.), *Life history and narrative.* London and Washington: The Falmer Press.

Ramrathan, P. (2002). *Teacher attrition and demand within KwaZulu-Natal in the context of HIV/AIDS.* PhD Thesis, University of KwaZulu-Natal, South Africa.

Rubin, W. (1988). "Primitivism" in 20th century art: Affinity of the tribal and the modern. In H. H. A. Arnason (Ed.), *History of modern art.* London: Thames & Hudson.

Singh, S. K. (2001). *Teacher resignations: Perceptions of teaching as a career.* MA Thesis, University of KwaZulu-Natal, South Africa.

Sparkes, A. (1994). Self, silence and invisibility as a beginning teacher: A life history of lesbian experience. *British Journal of Sociology of Education, 15*(1), 93–118.

Smyth, J., & Shacklock, G. (2004). Teachers doing their 'economic' work. In S. Ball (Ed.), *Sociology of education.* London and New York: Routledge Falmer.

Stankiewicz, M. A. (1996). Metaphor and meaning. *The Journal of the National Art Education Association, 49*(3), 4–5.

St Pierre, E. A. (1997). Methodology in the fold and the irruption of transgressive data. *Qualitative Studies in Education, 10*(2), 175–189.

St Pierre, E. A. (1999). The work of response in ethnography. *Journal of Contemporary Ethnography, 28,* 266–287.

Trinh Minh-Ha, T. (1989). *Woman' native' other.* Bloomington, IN: Indiana University Press.

Usher, R., & Edwards, R. (1994). *Postmodernism and education.* London and New York: Routledge.

Van Maanen, J. (1988). *Tales of the field: On writing ethnography.* Chicago: University of Chicago Press.

Vanhoozer, K. J. (1991). Philosophical antecedents to Ricoeur's time and narrative. In D. Wood (Ed.), *On Paul Ricoeur: Narrative and interpretation.* London: Routledge.

PART THREE: USING DATA METHODOLOGICALLY

MICHAEL SAMUEL

8. THE MUSIC OF RESEARCH: DIALOGUES OF PROFESSIONAL TEACHER DEVELOPMENT

This chapter constitutes a drama script written for three main interlocutors: the researcher and two research participants involved in a study tracking the professional development of novice student teachers as they journey from their own primary and secondary schooling, into the university and teacher education curriculum and into school during their Professional Practicum (school-based teaching practice) sessions. The study was conducted during the early stages of de-racialisation of South African schools when the new Outcomes–based Education curriculum was being introduced. The script reflects a variety of voices which constituted this climate of transformation.

The script should be read with the accompanying musical and visual textual material suggested to provide a holistic picture of the data production process and analysis phases of the research. The script captures the flavour of the idiolect of the participants to enhance authenticity. A more detailed discussion of the methodology used for this study is described in Samuel (1998) and in the opening chapter of this book.

A: Michael (Researcher)
B: Emmanuel (Bachelor of Education student)
C: Sanelesiwe (Bachelor of Education student)

SETTING THE SCENE

A: When I was about twelve years old, my father took me to a classical concert in the Durban City Hall. The memory of that event is vivid:

B: the somber consternation of Sunday Afternoon white faces, mainly in their late forties and fifties;

C: the smell of polished wooden floors did not dampen my brothers' and sisters' shuffling to find a seat;

B: the cacophony of musicians fine-tuning their instruments ahead of the arrival of the penguin-dressed conductor who took the podium after applause from the audience;

R. Dhunpath and M. Samuel (eds.), Life History Research: Epistemology, Methodology and Representation, 137–151

A: the presentation of the musicians to the audience by the conductor;

C: the players rearranging their sheets of music…

A: Only one place was not filled…

B: The string section was nodding approvingly to each other. Shiny gold brass instruments gleaming from the right back hand corner of the stage.

C: The wind section displaying a range of strange instruments I had not seen before;

B: The back of the stage was filled with an array of delightful noise toys: a childhood fantasy of percussion… But the centre space of the stage was not filled.

A: Now arrived the person I had been positioning to see:

B: the long-tailed starched pianist took his seat.

C: The hushed silence as he collected in the ambience of the occasion, the task ahead of him, the range of emotions that his fingers would have to deliver.

A, B and C: And then it began…

(Musical interlude: preferably a classical musical sonata with introduction by a piano.)

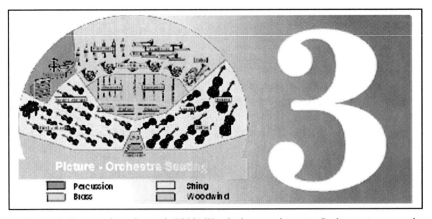

Figure 1. Excerpt from Samuel (1998) Words, lives and music: On becoming a teacher of English

A TEACHER OF ENGLISH

A: In this presentation I try to uncover the magic of that musical moment. The experience taught me profoundly that the process of playing music, whilst being liberating and entertaining, relied on the concerted and concentrated effort of many musicians.

B: Each of them was individual and separate in their voice and instrument,

C: but all were working towards deliberate interventions to achieve a common goal.

A: I see the process of becoming a teacher of the English language as an assemblage of many voices of different thinkers, players and actors. Together, like the musicians in an orchestra, we learn to become teachers of English, assembling the forces of influence of those whom we encounter.

B: We balance the forces of our own experiences as learners within the schools at which we were primary and secondary pupils.

C: We respond to the theories about language teaching and learning yielded through the teacher education programmes we attend.

A: Are we able to develop our own unique version about how to practice English teaching and learning? Or do we simply imitate the models that mentor teachers parade before us?

B: Is the pre-service teacher education programme adequate in shaping the images, experiences and actions of us as novice teachers of the English language?

(Musical interlude: preferably an extension of the above sonata concentrating on a section which draws in different instruments in dialogue.)

CRITICAL RESEARCH QUESTIONS
How do student teachers experience the teaching and learning of English over different periods of their lives?
- Within their homes and families
- During their primary and secondary schooling
- Within their undergraduate years at university
- During the Special Method English Class (SMEC)
- During School-based Teaching Practice as student teachers

THE RESEARCH DESIGN

C: Together, we will tell the stories of two student teachers as they journey on the road to becoming teachers of the English language.

B: We will look at only some of the milestones that we passed on this road.

C: The major milestones of this presentation recount specifically how student teachers experienced the pre-service teacher preparation English Special Method Course at the University of KwaZulu-Natal.

B: Both these students grew up in the rural area of Hammarsdale in KwaZulu-Natal, where they attended the same secondary school. Both are first language speakers of isiZulu and second language speakers of the English language.

A: Emmanuel *(pointing to B)* describes his journey of becoming a teacher of English as a journey of self discovery as a Rastafarian, about working with pupils who are both first and second language learners, about the demands of a challenging urban school environment.
      Sanelesiwe *(pointing to C)* describes the gendered identity that paints her interpretation of being a student teacher in an urban "Indian" school.

Figure 2. Suits and Ties   *Figure 3. Sanelesiwe at play*

UNDERGRADUATE YEARS

A: Sanelesiwe, can you recall your early years as a student in the university?

C: My school education had not prepared me for university. I could construct perfectly compartmentalised grammatical sentences, but I could not communicate effectively in the English language. After spending twelve years being taught English at school, why was I struggling to use English? It was now a matter of sink or swim. I resorted to all kinds of strategies to develop my confidence in the English language. I enrolled for a voluntary course in the Division of Language Usage on the campus where I learnt how to write an academic essay. I consciously attempted to exercise my English language skills with the non-Zulu speakers with whom I interacted. I still could not understand why my English language competence was so poor.

A: How would you describe your undergraduate years at the university, Emmanuel?

B: My undergraduate years at university brought a range of mixed experiences. I was for the first time exposed to people from different racial, linguistic, cultural, religious and class perspectives.

(Musical interlude: a Reggae musical piece)

Figure 4. University: a new dawn   *Figure 5. Emmanuel: Forbidden Fruit*

What I found strange was how females at university reacted to me because I am a Rastafarian. It was like them wanting to taste the forbidden fruit. I could easily have fooled around with many of them. But my Rasta beliefs tell me that one should be faithful to one sexual partner only. I have known many male teachers who abuse their status in schools and make sexual advances to the girls. I think this is very wrong. Teachers are like parents, and parents should not engage in sexual activities with their children. I know that young girls are attracted to me because I am a Rasta and this concerns me about how I will relate to them when I am a teacher.

A: What were your first experiences of the Special Method course, Sanelesiwe?

C: My first experience was novel. We were asked to write down our expectations of this course. Immediately, I realised that this course was going in a different direction. No other lecturers on campus had bothered to ask us what we wanted or expected from a course.

This exercise allowed the lecturers to gauge our prior conceptions of teaching and learning English. It was not surprising that many of us believed that the course would simply be about learning recipes for how to teach English. By this, most of us meant the strategies for understanding the grammar of the English language. We believed that the undergraduate English I, II and III courses had taught us how to study literature and this course would teach us about the English language. I fortunately knew that we would be learning more about how to organise the teaching and learning processes because of a forewarning I received from my teacher friend.

Figure 6. Sanelesiwe and University

This exercise also signalled the way in which we would engage as students and lecturers during the course of this SMEC programme. The lecturers were not simply going to force down our throats their versions of English language teaching and learning. Together, we were to negotiate what and how we learnt.

A: At an early stage in the course, you were asked to write an autobio-graphical account of your experiences of English language teaching and leaning. Describe this activity.

C: I had never before been asked to write so closely about myself. The experience of writing this autobiographical account was a useful way to get me to reflect critically on the kinds of experiences that I had gained during my school years. I was writing this assignment at the same time that I was studying about language acquisition. The two worlds of practical experiences and theoretical understandings of second language acquisition constantly interacted during my writing. I began to find in the theories explanations for why my school years had failed me as far as developing my English language competence.

I learnt what I considered to be the Golden Rule of other courses:

"When you say it, you forget it; when you read it, you remember it; but when you do it, you understand it!"

SCHOOL-BASED TEACHING PRACTICE

A: Emmanuel wrote this entry in his reflective journal the night before he went on school-based teaching practice:

B: Today is the 30th of July 1997; the night before my preliminary visits to Celebration Senior Secondary School. Various questions are "cropping up'"in my mind about this visit. What type of learners am I about to meet? I know the school I have to do my School-based Teaching Practice is a predominant "Indian" school, which now opens its access to "Black" (African) students. But how do educators deal with a multilingual, multicultural and multiracial context? What will be the teachers' attitude towards me – a Rastafarian? If in case I am asked to do something with learners, what is the first word that I am going to utter? But…what am I going to wear?

A: What were your first experiences at the school you went to, Emmanuel?

B: My first experience in this school was being witness to two students who were being sent home because they were wearing beards. This really amazed me. What were the reasons why they were not allowed to have beards? Who objected? Why? It reminded me of my own experiences in school when my principal forced me to cut my dreadlocks. I said nothing and just waited to be invited in to the principal's office.

A: *(taking on the role of the principal) "You must not be too friendly with the pupils because you will find it difficult to finish what you have started. You should be aware that you should not become too bossy and authoritative. Be friendly up to a degree and do not try and please them by sacrificing what is right".*

B: These mixed messages about how to handle the pupils in this school were the words of introduction by the school principal.

A: *(continuing in the role of the principal) "The context of this school is more challenging than the apartheid days. You are not only to be facilitators of pupils' learning, but also moulders and shapers of the new society in a non-racial, non-sexist and united nation. You must be certain that you are choosing this profession of teaching with open eyes: we are building the new society here".*

B: I was sure that I had heard this rhetoric somewhere and often before. Was this school going to prove any different?

A: What were your first experiences of working with a class of pupils, Sanelesiwe?

C: The first three days of schooling were lost during that week. Firstly, the teachers who belonged to SADTU agreed to go on strike. This, I think, was emanating from a dispute with the government over salaries. I felt sorry for the pupils. I think that the union is jeopardising the children's future. We did not go to school during the strike action that lasted two days. Instead, our student teacher team decided to meet on campus. I did not know what to do. Where was Michael, our university supervisor? How were we going to design a curriculum programme? We needed help.

A: What influence do you think your mentor teacher had over you?

B: At school, the mentor teacher communicated only through one of the female team members. We hardly spoke to him because he was always so busy. On one occasion he stated: "You are free to do anything you want". I was impressed by his flexible attitude. I realised that he was transferring a lot of responsibility to us to design a creative learning experience.

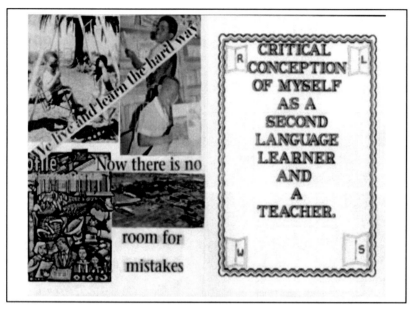

Figure 7. Sanelesiwe's collage: Book cover for autobiography

However, he also indicated that he was aware that the university expected us to implement "all those ideal theories". He told us that these "theories" don't really fit the reality of the school situation, but that it was necessary to experiment during the teaching practice session. As an experienced teacher now, he claimed that he did not use any of the "university's theories". He also indicated that when he was a student teacher he preferred being alone in the class without his mentor teacher.

I hardly saw him in my class when I was teaching during the whole teaching practice session. I did show him examples of the lesson plans I had designed, but he just said we must continue with the lesson; that there were no problems with the lesson design. He did offer us general advice about the discipline in the school: he felt that we should be harsh and firm with the pupils.

All of this confused me a lot.

A: What were some of the important learning experiences that you had, Emmanuel?

B: I learnt to be aware of the many different individuals in my classes. But I was most troubled by one group of pupils: the second language speakers in the class. I had even resorted to speaking directly to them in Zulu to ask them the simplest of questions. I had even tried to provide excuses for the pupils to make them believe that I understood the difficulties they may be experiencing in using English. I was not successful. They simply refused to participate in class. I don't know where it was coming from, but there was this sort of depression amongst African pupils that I could not explain. When I spoke to them outside the class, asking them why they did not participate, their responses were equally vague: they just laughed at my interest in them! I could not connect with them.

Figure 8. Emmanuel's collage: Book cover for autobiography

I think it is because their culture has made a deep impact on their thinking about how to relate to teachers. Even if they want to ask me a question, they don't. If they did approach me, it was usually after class and then, too, they would have this "formal" kind of way of relating to me. I saw that this has an impact on their learning, because they would ask questions about something that happened a long time ago in the class lesson. By not asking in the lesson, they are denying themselves the opportunity to be corrected straight away. I feel that African pupils are holding themselves back in this school because of their cultural views.

We can maybe become trapped in "apartheid discourse" to explain the African pupils' actions. We could say that the culture of submission that Verwoerd introduced with the Bantu Education in 1953 is responsible for pupils' passivity. Verwoerd, being a psychologist, saw a way to develop in Black people a sense of inferiority and self-doubt. This eventually leads to endless subordination and passivity. I believe that if I had more time with these African pupils in this school, I would be able to make a difference. Six weeks is too short a time to make any major impact.

A: What were your experiences of working with pupils in your school, Sanelesiwe?

B: I noticed that there was a difference in the way African pupils related to me as opposed to Indian pupils. Firstly, I believed that all pupils draw a line between us as student teachers and their resident teachers. They don't really accept us as teachers. But I think there is this respect that Indian pupils show us African members of staff.
        All Indian pupils called me "ma'am" which is the title I am used to because it refers to a married female teacher. However, I till believe there is this kind of distance with them as if they can't really believe that I, an African, am their teacher.

Figure 9. Sanelesiwe: Cherries, Misses and Ma'ams

        I found that the African female pupils tended to totally disregard me. They would keep their distance and would act as if I was not talking to them. When I approached them to ask for a reason why they did not do their homework, it was as if I was not there. With the Indian pupils, they would try and make some kind of excuse for not doing their homework. With the African female pupils, I felt that they did not accept that I was their teacher. They refused to answer me. I believe that this has something to do with how these African pupils are socialised in the township school. The female pupils do not show respect for female unmarried teachers.
        Generally I find that I experience more discrimination in this school because I am a woman than because I am an African.

A: What did you learn most from your pupils, Emmanuel?

B: During a lesson on inter-cultural views about marriage, one of the pupils began talking about Princess Diana. She seemed to know a lot about this individual, and this educated me about this world figure. I realised that my philosophy of life expects me not to concern myself with worldly things because anyway, we all leave this world one-day. I did not bother myself with watching the news, reading the newspapers, but I am a teacher, and I have to use what is common and interesting to most people to advance my lessons. But I also need to consider my spiritual world. Being concerned with what is happening on earth in my environment cannot tamper with where I stand spiritually. This is me, I don't move beyond this.

Figure 10. Emmanuel: The pupil teacher

A: Sanelesiwe, looking back on your school-based teaching practice experiences, what advice would you offer the Faculty of Education?

B: The University needs to develop a system of working a lot more closely with the resident teachers. I think that there is resistance from the resident teachers as to what we have to do during school-based teaching practice. They did not say anything to us directly but I think that there is generally a reluctance to change their practices. Resident teachers believe that we are "the OBE generation of teachers". They have a mindset against alternative ways of teaching and they simply say that it is all too theoretical and that it is un-implementable.

A: Now that you have completed school-based teaching practice, what are your views about being a teacher of the English language?

C: I was very pleased to see how well African pupils coped with the classroom activities. Their command of English was not that bad. This aroused a number of questions. Why are these pupils doing so well compared to African pupils in the townships? The methods being used in this school to teach English are different to the methods used in the townships. Pupils seem to like the English language. They regard it not just as a language of instruction, but a means of communication. Surely the teachers from township schools need to pick a leaf from the teachers at my practice teaching school, and stop wailing about the pupils being unwilling to learn. The absence of a learning culture should not be used as a scapegoat for the inefficiency of teachers.

FUTURE PLANS

A: Sanelesiwe, what are you future plans?

C: Overall, I feel that my experience of teaching in this school has taught me a lot about myself, my capabilities and about other people. I do, however, feel that my experiences involved my having to prove to pupils that Africans do have the capabilities that other races have.

        I do not think I would like to go back to the rural areas in which I schooled. It will be too difficult for me to work there as a lonely individual. I think one needs the support of several individuals to be able to change the system in those schools.

A: Emmanuel, what are your future plans?

B: Unfortunately I will not go back into the rural area to teach in my home village. I believe that my life will be wasted there, like my former principal who was shot and killed there. I think I will wait for things to settle down in my home areas when there is not so much conflict and violence in this area. In the meantime, I think I would like to teach in a multilingual school like my teaching practice school. I think I can make a contribution there.

CONCLUDING REMARKS

A: This study presented the argument that the development of student teachers identities is a complex set of several forces. The musical strains which reflect the lives of the individuals are juxtaposed, superimposed and sometimes silenced during the process of attempting to render their own development as teachers. Complex, complementary and contradictory messages characterise the musical notes and melodies you have heard.

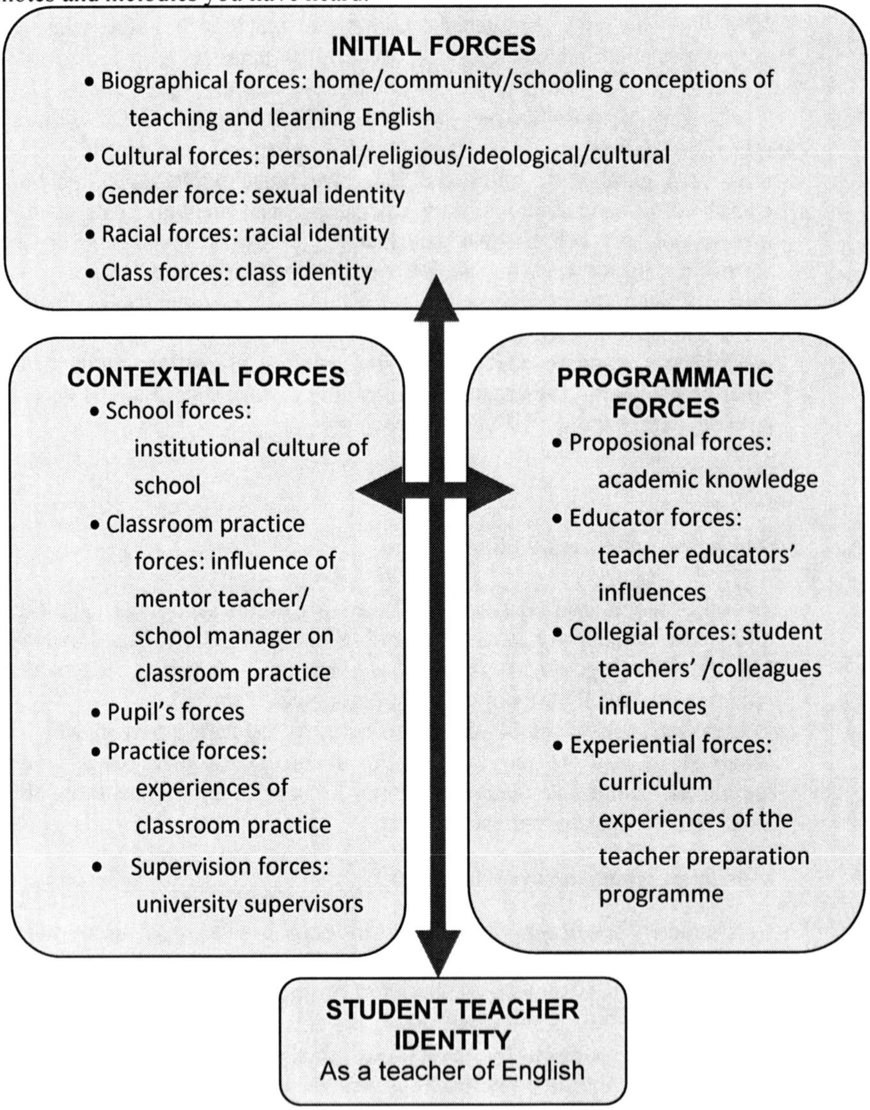

INITIAL FORCES
- Biographical forces: home/community/schooling conceptions of teaching and learning English
- Cultural forces: personal/religious/ideological/cultural
- Gender force: sexual identity
- Racial forces: racial identity
- Class forces: class identity

CONTEXTIAL FORCES
- School forces: institutional culture of school
- Classroom practice forces: influence of mentor teacher/ school manager on classroom practice
- Pupil's forces
- Practice forces: experiences of classroom practice
- Supervision forces: university supervisors

PROGRAMMATIC FORCES
- Proposional forces: academic knowledge
- Educator forces: teacher educators' influences
- Collegial forces: student teachers' /colleagues influences
- Experiential forces: curriculum experiences of the teacher preparation programme

STUDENT TEACHER IDENTITY
As a teacher of English

Figure 11. The Force Field Model of Teacher Professional Development (Samuel, 1998)

(Musical interlude; preferably a piece of jazz music which is derived from any of the earlier music pieces played.)

A: As conductor of this research design, I now step off the podium.

REFERENCES

Samuel, M. (1998). *Words, lives and music: On becoming a teacher of English.* Unpublished DEd Thesis, University of KwaZulu-Natal, Durban.

LABBY RAMRATHAN

9. THE ETHICS AND POLITICS OF DATA AS AGENCY

INTRODUCTION

The first recorded case of HIV in South Africa was in 1982. In 1990, National HIV prevalence rates were calculated for the first time through annual surveys of public antenatal clinic attendees and was recorded at 0.76%. In 1998 the prevalence rate was recorded at 22.8% nationally. In that year (1998) KwaZulu-Natal had a prevalence rate of 32.5%, the highest rate amongst the nine Provinces. Statisticians have reduced estimates of South Africa's average life expectancy from 65.4 years to 55.7 years. By 2010, this life expectancy will drop to about 48 years. In 1996, an Old Mutual Actuaries and Consultants survey forecast that the annual death rate in the workforce would rise from 5 to 30 in every 1000 workers. In KwaZulu-Natal, deaths outstrip births. (Marias, 2000)

Globally, the HIV/AIDS situation is considerably worse than that the world's worst expectations. Ten or twelve years ago it was projected that the year 2000 might see 15 to 20 million persons living with the disease. Today, we know that some 22 million persons have already died from AIDS related illness, more that 42 million adults and children are living with HIV/AIDS, and an estimated 14 million children under the age of 15 have lost father, mother or both parents. (Kelly, 2003)

These macro analyses of the HIV and AIDS pandemic based on the national demographics and medical/public health trends within South Africa and internationally are an alarming indication of the catastrophe we could be facing. These projected scenarios are certainly cause for concern, but what is the basis of such alarmist predictions? Do we actually know enough about the disease to make such predictions? How valid and reliable are these projections? Why should we believe them? Is there likelihood that these are exaggerated "doom and gloom" scare tactics used by activists and advocates demanding a systemic intervention for HIV and AIDS victims? These are some of the concerns expressed by researchers when the pandemic was catapulted into the public spotlight in the late nineties. In order to address some of these questions, this chapter introduces the concept "data as agency" as it explores how contextual issues around HIV and AIDS shape

R. Dhunpath and M. Samuel (eds.), Life History Research: Epistemology, Methodology and Representation, 153–172

research agendas and how the data produced and interpreted within these agendas are used as agency to command attention.

I explore the notion of data as agency within a critical discourse analysis framework, through an exploration of the death rate of teachers using what I call, "Interrogated Response" as a medium to explore how the context influences the interpretation of data produced on HIV and AIDS. Interrogated response is a construct borrowed from the domain of linguistics research within which research participants' responses are problematised and participants' ideological positionalities are exposed. The chapter concludes with an example of how researchers' voices could be mediated through a process of establishing a technical team of researchers to guide the research agendas and processes, thereby offering greater validity and reliability in the way data is produced, interrogated and utilised.

THEORISING DATA AS AGENCY

I began my doctoral study on teacher supply and demand as part of a larger international study on teacher education across five countries in a developing world context. Initially, I was quite comfortable with the research focus and worked on conceptualising the data collection strategy and analytical framework. As I went into the field to start with data production, what unfolded quickly changed the course of my study. Publicity around the HIV pandemic began to take centre-stage as the country began to grapple with the various reports on prevalence rates in general, and its influence on the teaching profession in particular. The media hype was amplified by the HIV and AIDS world conference hosted at the International Conference Centre in Durban, South Africa in 2000. At the same time, HIV activists used the conference platform to highlight the impact of HIV and AIDS on people such as the frail young Nkosi Johnson, an HIV-positive child pleading to the world for help in fighting the disease.

In the midst of this flurry, President Thabo Mbeki's stance on the relationship between HIV and AIDS and poverty, based on the findings of researchers accused of being "maverick" and "dissident", complicated the messages and confused the nation. What was intended to be a "simple" study on teacher supply and demand began to take on unanticipated dimensions as I became aware of the complexities surrounding the HIV and AIDS pandemic. Hence, teacher supply and demand became a vehicle to understanding a greater, more complex phenomenon – "*how do we come to know what we think we know*". In order to get a more reliable indicator of teacher supply and demand, it was necessary to first ask crucial questions around research methodologies used in generating data in a context of heightened emotionality. Introducing the concept of "data as agency" helped me begin to explain the varying interpretations emerging within the discourse on HIV and AIDS and its impact on society and systems.

The concept of data as agency takes on special significance in contexts where data is used in different ways to promote the ideological positionalities (or purposes) of particular individuals or organisations. That is, data takes on the form of agency when researchers interpret and use data in ways that serve to further their ideological and political agendas. In this instance, I argue that HIV researchers manipulated and portrayed data in ways that strengthened the images they wished to project to support their call for action on the HIV/AIDS pandemic. This phenomenon was also evident in Matthew's (1998) essay on "Flukes and flaws" where he cites several examples of studies done on the link between illness and an environmental factor, only to be challenged by another study. This kind of statistical manipulation is now used as a mechanism of agency by advocacy and activist groups frustrated with the government's reticence in addressing the AIDS crisis based on what has come to be characterised as a denial syndrome.

Data as agency can be theoretically located within an emerging framework of critical discourse analysis as it begins to explore the relationship between a particular discursive event, the situation, institution, social and historical context, and the embedded power relations that frame it.

CRITICAL DISCOURSE ANALYSIS FRAMEWORK

Although the field of critical discourse analysis (hereinafter referred to as CDA) is considered an emerging field, extensive seminal work has been initiated by researchers (Fairclough, 1989; Fairclough & Wodak, 1997; Janks, 1997; Toolan, 1997; and a range of work done in the Australian continent identified by Kamler, 2000). CDA espouses a critical sociological reading of the data that is consistent with the multiplicity view. Since discourse analysis has been explored elsewhere in this book (Dhunpath, Kathard, Beecham), I will not engage in an extensive theoretical explication of CDA. Rather, this chapter acknowledges Fairclough and Wodak's (1997) notion of discourse as being a social practice (through the use of language) framed by a dialectical relationship between a particular discursive event and the situation, institution and social structure and historical contexts that frame it. That is, a discourse is developed socially, is shaped and being shaped, sustaining and reproducing the status quo. Discourses may have ideological effects as a result of being socially influenced. They can help produce and reproduce unequal power relations that position people and things and can pass off any aspects of social life as common sense. The ideological loading through the use of language and the relations of power that underlie them are not always apparent and visible.

CDA attempts to make clearer, through intervention on social practice and social relations, the ideological loading and power relations within discourses. CDA is distinctive in its view of (a) the relationship between language and society, and (b) the relationship between analysis and the practices analysed through intervention and emancipatory interests (Janks, 1997).

Historically, CDA can be traced to the Western Marxism tradition where cultural dimensions of societies (emphasising capitalist social relations) are established and maintained in large part in culture and not just in the economic base (Fairclough & Wodak, 1997). These can be seen in the works of Althusser, Foucault and Habermas, elaborating on issues of power inherent in the ideology of the ruling class and how the structures and practices of ordinary life routinely normalise capitalist social relations (Fairclough & Wodak, 1997). Interrogating, amongst others, how ideologies position people, how knowledge systems propagate particular social relations and how philosophical heritage establishes and maintains particular social relations, leads to a clearer analysis of social structures and social relations with emancipatory interests.

Althusser (1971, in Fairclough & Wodak, 1997), for example, saw the central effects of ideologies as positioning people in particular ways as social subjects. He stresses the ideological effects of discursive formations in positioning people largely within a political context – positioning class struggles. Particular words and texts are associated with particular political voices. For example, the term *"comrades"* is usually associated with the political struggle by people against the apartheid regime within South Africa. The words (language) position people either for or against a dominant ideology like apartheid.

The term "critical" became associated with philosophers such as Habermas who seeks to re-examine the philosophical heritage from which the capitalist social relations are established and maintained. Habermas developed the concept of "ideal speech situation" which he describes as an utopian vision of interaction taking place without any power relations intruding into it. He argues that rational discourse overcomes distorted communication through critical engagement, while ideological discourse deviates from the ideal speech situation.

Acknowledging that CDA stems from critical engagement of the taken-for-granted social practices, it is the questions pertaining to the interests that relate discourse to relations of power. How is discourse positioned? Whose interest is being served by this positioning? What are the consequences of this positioning? These questions seek to understand how discourses are implicated in relations of power when we begin to interrogate data on HIV and AIDS. Discourse analysis provides the tools to unpack this evidence, presenting a multiplicity of views and arguments that can be made using the same data. CDA goes further than just unpacking the multiplicity of arguments, in that it exposes the power relations embedded within the various interpretations associated with how the data is used.

ACTIVISTS, DISSIDENTS AND ADVOCACY

Nkosi Johnson, a South African child who took centre stage at the 2000 World AIDS conference as he appealed to the world to take note of the disease, could have been regarded as just another child plagued by an illness that has no known cure. Why then did he become a world figure advocating and promoting a call to the world to help fight against the HIV and AIDS disease? The strategy seems to relate to the general sense of reticence of the South African government in acknowledging the enormity of the problem, linked to the maverick stance adopted by the president, Thabo Mbeki. Introducing this frail young South African Black HIV-positive child adopted by a White South African woman at this forum to funders, NGOs, academics, social movements and others was a tactical emotive call for help designed to have a more profound effect on the international community, and a means of challenging the apparent denial of the South African government.

However, the South African government rejects the allegation that it was in denial. President Mbeki's position on HIV and AIDS appears to relate to the problems and contradictions inherent in trying to understand AIDS in Africa. Influenced by strong dissidents like Peter Duesburg, a California-based scientist, President Mbeki has questioned the methods used in the public health system to test HIV status; the definition used to classify a person as having AIDS; and how the disease was identified as having caused the death of hundreds of thousands of AIDS victims. These questions stem from trying to understand why diseases that generations of Africans have been suffering long before HIV and AIDS are now being arbitrarily redefined as AIDS. His intentions, arguably, would be to shift the debates about HIV and AIDS from purely a medical/biological analysis to developing a socio, political, cultural understanding of health related issues. However, President Mbeki's stance was dismissed because the general public, including medical science researchers, opposition politicians, HIV and AIDS interest groups, were convinced that there is a causal relationship between HIV and AIDS.

In the case of Nkosi Johnson, the advocacy strategy of using a child in a public "academic" forum was intended to starkly and urgently bring into the international spotlight the HIV and AIDS pandemic. Nkosi Johnson's story became a more powerful vehicle than scientific data. In the second example, Thabo Mbeki heralded a shift in thinking about the disease from a purely biomedical phenomenon (controlled by medical science researchers) to an all inclusive socio, political, cultural and economic focus associated with unacknowledged causes of the disease such as nutrition and poverty. This, arguably, could perhaps only have been achieved through a person as powerful as the president of a country.

In the sections that follow, I explore two ways of interrogating and mediating the agency latent in data in the context of research into HIV and AIDS within South Africa. First, I propose *interrogated response* as a way of deconstructing the researcher's positionality in the research process and the way s/he uses the data to advance his/her agenda/s. Second, I explore the practice of *agenda mediation* through the appointment of a technical team of researchers to oversee the research process as a way of mediating different agendas.

FROM CRITICAL DISCOURSE ANALYSIS TO INTERROGATED RESPONSE

Specific studies predicting the transfer of HIV and AIDS into the teaching sector and school education have attempted to map the terrain dealing with issues like supply and demand for teachers and the impact on the education system (Coombe, 2000; Badcock-Walters, 2001; Kinghorn, 2001; Crouch, 2001). Many of these studies have presented a broad understanding of the systemic impact anticipated at the national level. For example, in 2001, Crouch indicated that South Africa would need as many as 55 000 teachers per annum to meet the demand for teachers due to attrition caused by HIV and AIDS (see Crouch, 2001). However, three years later, Crouch and Perry (2004) challenged their earlier predictions, indicating that South Africa would need between 9 000 and 11 000 teachers per annum based on a modeling technique which factors in low and high incidence of HIV and AIDS, teacher mortality, attrition and learner enrolment. The starkness of these variations in projection raises scepticism around the authenticity of these analyses and what variables are privileged in the modelling exercise.

In the first projection analysis (Crouch, 2001), the impact of HIV and AIDS was privileged based on an understanding of national demographics contained in several reports on impact analysis by key researchers within South Africa (e.g. Coombe, 2000, and Kinghorn, 2001). In the second analysis (Crouch & Perry, 2004) learner enrolment and teacher mortality were privileged – as the discourse on learner enrolment and teacher attrition patterns began to influence teacher supply and demand analyses (e.g. Ramrathan, 2002, and Badcock-Walters, 2001). The variations in the projections call into question how data are used.

A few additional points about data sources need to be introduced here. While there is acknowledgement generally that HIV and AIDS will have a major impact on the nation, the veil of secrecy that shrouds the pandemic presents a sense of scepticism about the accuracy and reliability of our knowledge and the extent to which this disease will impact on the nation as a whole. The accuracy of data is further compromised by the self-disclosure/denial syndrome: Declaring oneself as HIV-positive has sociological, psychological, cultural and moral implications which have been extensively documented and will not be explored here. Aside from the trauma one has to deal with, the social repercussions within communities are quite profound. There have been several reported cases of individuals believed to be HIV-positive being assaulted by members of their communities. For a community that values the preservation of virginity, the declaration of one's HIV status is a violation of a cultural norm. Fear of the social, psychological, cultural and moral repercussions of declaring oneself as being HIV-positive leads to this veil of secrecy around the disease and distorts the accuracy of the data.

The HIV and AIDS context is also influenced by the debates (mid 2000) on President Thabo Mbeki's initial stance on the relationship between HIV and AIDS, on the role of donor agencies and funding, and the roll-out plans for administration of the anti-retroviral drugs within South Africa (2003/4). His intention, as eluded to earlier, was arguably to shift the debates about HIV and AIDS from purely a medical/biological analysis to developing a socio, political, cultural understanding of health related issues, inviting other sectors to become involved in the process of addressing the HIV and AIDS pandemic.

Further, Kelly (2003) indicates that the epicentre of the HIV and AIDS disease is in Sub-Saharan Africa and there are fears being expressed that this epicentre will shift to more populous countries like India, China and Russia. This concern can be seen within the context of donor aid being dedicated largely to Sub-Saharan African countries in the form of support for the provision of anti-retroviral drug therapy, prevention of further transmission, as well as management and leadership. While HIV and AIDS research acquires the imprint of international commonsenses that direct policy, researchers have a responsibility to resist these essentialising impulses. In other words, rather than imbibing the dominant discourse and rushing to closure, there is a need to open up other avenues of enquiry to prevent dominant modes of enquiry from becoming reified. It is within this context that the rest of the chapter will focus on re-examining how HIV and AIDS research and reporting has been conducted, what happens to the findings, how they serve to illuminate and influence.

Generally, research methodologies are established (ostensibly) through rigorous processes based on particular assumptions, used as a basis for the production of new knowledges. Once these methodologies acquire a normative character, they are rarely questioned. However, methodologies that are tried and tested in one context (e.g. first world contexts or third world contexts) and imported into particular contexts (e.g. the exploration of HIV within society that is considered first world and third world simultaneously) may not necessarily take into consideration the specificities of that particular context. Normative methodologies (e.g. survey of state antenatal clinics) may not be appropriate to explore HIV within a population where the sampling is limited to the poor and largely one racial group that predominantly visits such state clinics.

Modelling and projection analysis, a common means of generating data on HIV and AIDS, draws its inspiration largely from development studies and econometric studies to understand social and economic dynamics across world contexts. For example, many of the conclusions drawn and statements made in Cawthra et al's (2001) *Development update* is based upon projections and predictions relating to how the economy and population will be affected by, for example, HIV and AIDS. The World Bank's intervention is another example of how it is influenced by research fuelled by projections and predictions based on modelling. Direct testing, on the other hand, gets its inspiration largely from a biomedical research agenda attempting to understand causal relationships. The aim is largely to find a cure to the disease.

Yet, the findings from such studies, which may be methodologically flawed, as a result of the rapidly emerging and expanding research in the field of HIV and AIDS within South Africa, together with the pandemic nature of the virus, may influence interventions, advocacy strategies for prevention of the spread of disease, donor aid and long term planning to manage the disease. Let me illustrate the point using the following example which demonstrates how "hard data" is used uncritically: Projection analysis, modelling and other statistical data are significant inputs in the policy making process. However, the validity and reliability of these hard data are seldom questioned, especially in the input variables that constitute the projection analysis, modelling and other statistical results. For example, the education management information systems database is usually used as an input variable. However, certain principals of schools are known to provide inflated pupil enrolments because pupil numbers are related to resources provided to schools, and this may result in flawed projection analyses. Further, in most modelling exercises, variables that are measurable are privileged over variables that are not measurable – like intervention.

Another example of flawed statistics used is modelling and projection analysis derived largely through analysis of African women attending antenatal state clinics in the country – and extrapolated to the rest of the population. The factor that is not considered in these projections is women who do not attend antenatal state clinics or women who do not believe in Western medicine. These variables affect the prevalence rates in a country co-existing as first and third world simultaneously and need to be interrogated and problematised to design defensible "scientific" methods of data production that influence policy.

INTERROGATING HIV AND AIDS RESEARCH: HOW THE SURVEILLANCE OF THE HIV EPIDEMIC IN SOUTH AFRICA IS DESIGNED

Ante-natal surveys are the most widely used strategy for obtaining information about HIV prevalence rates. The Department of Health in partnership with the Medical Research Council within South Africa has developed extensive protocols in antenatal surveys used annually. These surveys are conducted amongst women attending ante-natal clinics of the public health facilities in South Africa (Department of Health, 1999). In reporting on the result of the cross sectional surveys, a serious design limitation emerged in that sampling from the public sector has been found to under-represent race groups other than Black African women, because the number of White and Indian women using these public facilities is typically small (Department of Health, 1999). This was also acknowledged by Smith (2001) in his address to teachers at an advocacy conference on HIV and AIDS, adding that in cases where there were participants from other race groups, the data was excluded from the analysis.

Also recognised as a limitation, is the tendency for these findings to neglect providing direct information on HIV infection in men and infants (Department of Health, 1999). For these and other reasons, the surveillance of HIV within South Africa is being challenged, particularly because its restricted sampling process tends to exaggerate the pandemic by selecting certain sectors of the population into their sampling. The logic behind this sampling comes from contextualising the disease within South Africa by linking it to socio-cultural and socio-economic dynamics like poverty, migrant labour, income inequalities, financial insecurities and gender relations (Marias, 2000). These socio-cultural and socio-economic dynamics are largely prevalent in rural communities where economic constraints encourage labour migrations, leaving the women to bear the consequences of movement patterns of the householders, usually the men.

Modelling is a commonly used HIV and AIDS surveillance technique. The projections of HIV prevalence and impact analysis in South Africa is based largely on the Doyle model developed by the Metropolitan Life Insurance Group. Other life assurance companies have other modelling strategies to forecast, for example, annual death rates. The estimates of demographic impacts of HIV and AIDS produced by the Doyle model are derived from a combination of macro-simulations and micro-simulations.

A macro-simulation is calibrated in terms of inputs at a macro level, such as the reported HIV prevalence level at a national or regional level obtained through, for example, incidence studies at antenatal clinics. The limitations of data gathered in these studies are noteworthy: for example, the sampling of participants in the study is restricted largely to African women who access public clinics and who are usually working class women who value the input they receive from Western as opposed to traditional/indigenous forms of medical health care. Whilst this sample represents a large percentage of the target population, it excludes a broader representation of the South African population where trends concerning HIV and AIDS infection might possibly be significantly different. For instance, patterns of prevalence are known to vary according to gender, race, geographic location and socio-economic status. However, groups who are sceptical of Western medical intervention are not factored into the Doyle design which uncritically accepts the validity of the data sources driving a secondary data analysis strategy.

Micro-simulation is built on more comprehensive, scientifically defensible input parameters which consider, amongst others, risk behaviour of individuals and stratification within a given population, and aggregate their effects to produce projections of HIV and AIDS for whole groups or populations through complex iterative calculations. For example, a risk input parameter would consider the following four risk groups defined in the model: commercial sex workers and frequent clients; other people with a high incidence of sexually transmitted diseases; people at risk of infection; and people not at risk of infection. This risk group input parameter would influence the aggregate effects of HIV and AIDS prevalence within a group or population and ultimately influence projections through the modelling. These input parameters are more fine-grained, but based on unreliable data as the volatility of the HIV and AIDS virus has introduced significant variance, over time, of incidence patterns amongst different groups. In some micro-contexts successful intervention, such as educational awareness campaigns or changed sexual practices and behaviour, could be able to reverse the spread of the pandemic. The fluctuating impact of such interventions from the micro-contexts cannot be unproblematically generalised to the wider population. Therefore, prevalence rates determined by such modelling processes warrant a level of scepticism.

By combining the features of a macro-simulation model and a micro-simulation model, the Doyle model is considered by its proponents to be robust and better able to produce reliable medium and longer term projections at a macro-level without losing sensitivity to underlying micro-parameters which may be relevant to a particular group or population. While the Doyle model is considered robust and better able to produce reliable projections, this model relies largely on input parameters that have reliability and validity limitations. For example, teachers are almost always considered a homogeneous occupational category, implying that all types of teachers will be affected identically by the epidemic (Bennell et al, 2002). The reality is that teachers are not a homogeneous occupational category. A significant proportion of teachers are un- and under-qualified and this has implications in terms of socio-economic status and social behaviour patterns. Hence, the macro inputs across socio-economic status in this model may pose a reliability limitation. Furthermore, a micro-simulation input parameter may consider teacher mobility (migrant worker) as a risk factor. This parameter needs to be challenged by questioning the extent to which teachers within South Africa are actually mobile. Generalising the migrant worker as a risk factor in micro-simulation input renders the model suspect. This means that the Doyle model is using data that may not be reliable or defensible, yet it claims to produce projections that are reliable for the medium and longer-term analysis.

Yet another factor that undermines the accuracy of modelling data is disclosure. It is generally accepted that there is secrecy about death as a result of AIDS. When an individual dies, the cause of death is usually related to a medically known illness. Rarely are we likely to find AIDS reported as the cause of death even though there is a strong indication that mortality is a result of the immunity deficiency syndrome. In the absence of accurate data, it becomes extremely difficult to do grounding research on the HIV and AIDS impact with any degree of certainty. Studies like projection analysis through modelling, probability study, extrapolation, sector analysis, survey analysis, demographic analysis, etc. are used to illuminate the severity of the HIV and AIDS pandemic. These types of modelling studies claim that, to a reasonable degree of certainty, they are producing what the trends are in respect of HIV prevalence rates. Direct testing studies is another way of attempting to ascertain prevalence rates of HIV to a reasonable degree of certainty. Both these methodologies have been critiqued in terms of their research designs, research analysis and research reporting (see, for example, Ramrathan, 2002). However, these kinds of analyses continue to influence policy frameworks and interventions. Notwithstanding the probability of flawed research design, the data takes on the power of agency as it is used to generate models that in turn determine national and international policies. Are there other ways of establishing HIV prevalence rates that reflect a clearer understanding of this disease?

What follows is an exploration of data as agency through "interrogated response", set against a critical discourse analysis framework. Consistent with CDA, this section of the chapter explores how individuals position themselves in relation to the knowledge about HIV and AIDS in order to influence bureaucrats, politicians, donors, policy makers and the public understanding of the disease and its impact on society. This is explored through two concepts borrowed from the domain of linguistics research wherein CDA has been conceptualised, viz. semiotics and response.

In this approach, the death rate of teachers within KwaZulu-Natal (over a period of three years) is constructed as a sign depicted as a graphic representation or visual image. This sign is then interrogated within the framework of CDA in terms of the dominant discourse around HIV and AIDS prevalence rates. Using Semiotics, the death rate of teachers over a period of time is elicited through a multi-dimensional reading of this visual image (sign) against a set of conditions imposed by social factors: i.e. the veil of secrecy that shrouds HIV and AIDS and the methodological scepticism about the way data on HIV and AIDS is produced. These two concepts are developed in more detail in the following sections.

EXPLORING SEMIOTICS IN HIV AND AIDS RESEARCH

Semiotics comes from the realms of linguistic research – defined as **the study of signs** (semiology) or as others would say, **the science that studies the life of signs** (Chandler, undated). It has been derived from the Greek word *semeion* meaning sign. Two dominant views on semiotics emerged towards the end of the nineteenth century. In the Saussurean tradition, the Swiss linguist, Ferdinand de Saussure (1857 – 1913), the founder of what is now usually referred to as semiotics, argued that "a science that studies the life of signs within society is conceivable" and he refers to the study of this science as semiology.

> Semiology would show what constitutes signs and what laws govern them.
> Chandler (undated).

The Piercian view of semiotics, the second dominant tradition on the science of signs, was developed by an American philosopher, Charles Sanders Pierce (1839 – 1914). These two traditions differed in the understanding of signs.

In the tradition of Saussure, every sign is composed of:
– A signifier – the form which the sign takes; and
– The signified – the concept it represents.

In the Piercian tradition, every sign is composed of:
– The representamen – the form which the sign takes (not necessarily material);
– An interpretant – the sense made of the sign; and
– An object – to which the sign refers.

The difference, in these two traditions is that the Saussurian model excludes reference to an object in the world in its dyadic composition while in the Piercian model, the sign has a reference to an object. Hence, the Saussurian notion of a sign suggests that the relationship between the signifier and the signified is completely arbitrary and there is no natural link between the two. In this study, the Saussure's version of sign is used.

For example, what is inherent in the bringing together of three letters of the English alphabet (F, A, N), each with its own acoustic image to suggest that its combination is a device to create unnatural movement of air? There is nothing in its combination or its collective acoustic images to suggest a meaning associated with air movements, unless there is meaning making through convention. Signs are, therefore, negotiated within a context and through a meaning making process. While structuralism puts relationships among elements and structures at the centre and people at the margins (Tatto, 1999), meaning making puts people at the centre, and hence suggests a post-structuralist perspective. While one may claim that linguistics is an idealised system, it does not exist in a vacuum. The system had been created through a meaning making process and therefore is never value free (neutral) and hence cannot be separated from its uses. This also suggests that meaning making is a collective product developed through a system of social representation and therefore lends itself to interpretation.

In deconstructing this structuralist view of language, Derrida (in Sarup, 1988) indicates that the signifier does not yield a signified directly. In other words, there is no one-to-one harmonious correspondence between the signifier and the signified. They continually break up and reattach in new combinations, thus revealing the inadequacy of Saussure's model of the sign where language exists as a function of a system. This means that meanings derived from signs (language) will never be the same from context to context and interpretation to interpretation, as each signified would become a signifier for another signified, Thereby indicating that language (linguistic) is not as stable as structuralists would want it to be.

Encouraging ambiguity and multiplicity, opening up traditional boundaries and breaking out of frames are also hallmarks of post-structuralism which, inevitability, has the ability to theorise post-modernism (Rhedding-Jones, 1995). In theorising postmodernism, there are differences in meaning and there are differences in the writing of these meanings (Lather, 1991 in Rhedding-Jones, 1995). The interrogation of the responses to the signifier lends itself to this interpretation of differences in meaning as well as the differences in the understanding of these meanings, promoting multiplicity and breaking down traditional boundaries of structuralism. This leaves the traditional terrain of semiotics open to post-structuralist interpretation through deconstructive methods of enquiry, like "response".

RESPONSE – FROM LINGUISTICS TO ETHNOGRAPHY

Borrowed from the domain of literary criticism, where scholars are interested in the readers' response to text rather than the author's intention or the intrinsic meaning within the text, "response" has become a useful method of deconstruction for enquiry (St Pierre, 1999). Here the response of the reader, or in the case of St Pierre's ethnography – the response of the participants of her ethnography, is privileged above other traditional deconstructive methods of enquiry because it may contribute to new meanings through understanding (a) how response from a variety of relations to the phenomenon is being investigated that may radically interfere with each other; and (b) what the effects of this interference would be. In St Pierre's (1999) ethnography, she highlights "member-check" response and extends on this to explore a new response category – "imaginary response" within her ethnography.

St Pierre (1999), in her ethnography on a group of older, white American southern women in her hometown, identified two kinds of "response" data produced in her study. The first: **"member-check"** response data is produced when she gives back to the participants of the research, her (St Pierre's) representation of the data produced. This data was produced from the source and the kind of knowledge her participants used in constructing their subjectivities during the course of their long lives. The participants respond to this data constructed by the researcher. This St Pierre calls member-check response – an activity common to the fieldwork process for data production.

In this study, I made available my critique of the Coombe national study on HIV and AIDS to Carol Coombe, as author of the report. In the first instance, this was intended to serve as a "member-check" of my interpretation of her research report on HIV and AIDS within South Africa. In the second instance, it was hoped that her response to my critique of her study would produce another level of deconstructive analysis.

St Pierre (1999, p. 271) refers to the second response as "**imaginary response**". Imaginary response

> is the response we imagine our work (research) will produce, as well as others' response to what they imagine our work will produce.

Often, as researchers, we assume in our analysis that the research participants respond to the purpose of our enquiry and this is clearly articulated to the participants. We analyse the response to understand the author's intentions or the meaning implicit within his/her response. This raises several questions: Are we clear about the nature of this response from the participants? Is the participant responding to an imagined outcome of the research project? How can we tell whether there is a difference in the way they respond? What impact do these different kinds of responses have on the analysis? These questions are the central issue in St Pierre's ethnography on women's lives, which led her to conceptualise the second type of response – "imaginary response" – that leaves her hesitant about writing an ethnography that claims to be the final representation of women and their culture.

Through St Pierre's demonstration in her ethnography, a multiplicity of responses can be established. These could indicate, amongst others: (a) the different orientation one takes (positionality) in one's response, (b) the audience it is produced for, (c) the variables that one wants to privilege for interpretation, and (d) the impact one wants to construct. Deconstructing the response from research participants (including that of the author of the research project) can provide valuable information within the enquiry to construct new meanings. One of the ways to create new meanings might be through understanding that there is a possibility that "imagined response" exists and that it can influence meaning making as demonstrated in St Pierre's (1999) ethnography. Extending this logic, it might be concluded that there may exist responses motivated by a variety of other reasons than that of an imagined response. The challenge is to establish the tools that would make explicit the motivations behind the responses of research participants. One way of doing this is to interrogate research participants' responses in the data production process which I refer to hereafter as "**interrogated response**". Responses are interrogated through the use of a signifier. This strategy is used to deconstruct the positionalities researchers take in their reporting of research, as a way of constructing new meanings within HIV and AIDS enquiry.

INTERROGATED RESPONSE AND TEACHER ATTRITION

The interrogated response technique is a useful strategy to demonstrate how information about HIV and AIDS can be created/produced to signal different imperatives and motivations. This approach enables a re-examination of public knowledge around HIV and AIDS since different researcher positionalities will influence estimates of teacher supply and demand. In the following illustration of an interrogated response, conversations were held with HIV and AIDS researchers on selected data. This included Carol Coombe, author of several research reports on HIV and AIDS impact, and Anthony Kinghorn, a research consultant with an international association researching HIV and AIDS impact on society and systems.

In this instance, the sign used for the interrogated response was a graph of teacher death patterns. The graph indicates a peaking in the death rate of teachers within the 26 to 40 year age group. Whilst this trend might only be reflective of the age distribution within the teaching force, the question was whether the reason for such a large percentage of "early deaths" occurring within this relatively young age group could be attributable to HIV and AIDS since large numbers of deaths within this age group are unlikely to be attributable to natural causes.

The graph, together with leading questions, was presented to Anthony Kinghorn. His task was to interrogate the sign through the questions provided.

Carol Coombe, on the other hand, was given my critique of her research report on the impact of HIV and AIDS on education within South Africa. In summary, my critique of Coombe's (2000) commissioned (United Nations Economic Commission for Africa – UNECA) national report on the impact of HIV and AIDS on the education sector of South Africa report was:

The report is based largely on secondary data sources, like survey of women attending public ante-natal clinics; UNAIDS statistics; commissioned reports prepared for specific organisations, e.g. the SA National Council for Child Welfare; etc. While secondary data sources are, in itself, acceptable and useful in research, one needs to understand and take cognisance of how the personal agendas and biases of the various organisations are amplified and pushed through these reports. Also when secondary data are presented, the methodology used in obtaining the original data in the primary source is not presented, and it is taken for granted that the methodology employed is within the rigour of scientific research. Questions are raised on the incestuous inter-reliance on previous studies that seem to characterise the landscape of HIV and AIDS research worldwide.

Women attending state-provided antenatal clinics are usually the poor, with particular socio-economic circumstances and may exclude women that do not believe in Western medicine. Could these circumstances contribute to high prevalence of HIV infection? Are there comparable or contrasting statistics at private clinics or health care facilities frequented by higher earning communities? In doing an analysis at other health care facilities frequented by higher earning communities, one would get a more fine-grained analysis about whether HIV prevalence rates are similar or dissimilar across different classes and therefore to understand whether class dynamics leads to a difference in prevalence rates across classes. The HIV prevalence rates amongst the world nations are starkly different. The rich nations of the world, e.g. North America, have reported negligible cases of HIV (920 000) as compared to the poorest nations e.g. Sub-saharan Africa with 25,3 million cases of HIV (source of data – UNAIDS/WHO as quoted in The Daily News 3 July 2001, KwaZulu-Natal). This macro analysis indicates such large differences between poor and rich nations. At a micro level, can such a situation (difference in HIV prevalence) occur within a nation divided along similar socio-economic patterns? South Africa is a mixture of first and third world with rich and poor citizens. Is it likely that there would be similar prevalence rates pattern of the rich and poor world countries within South Africa where the two worlds co-exist? What are the dynamics within these world contexts and would these dynamics influence the prevalence rates amongst the rich and poor within South Africa?

The extrapolation from experiences elsewhere in the SADC region, reports of occasional studies, information from other sectors, demographic analysis, and anecdotal information, do not present a holistic and relevant picture of the impact of HIV and AIDS on the education sector in South Africa. While Carol Coombe has chosen to analyse an accumulation of research already conducted to provide a synthetic record of past studies, she does not problematise the validity and reliability of these studies. However, she chooses one set of strategies to collect data and does not problematise them, yet she uses this data to project the impact of HIV and AIDS on the education system. Her intentions would, thus, seem to be to bring to attention the impact of HIV and AIDS on the education system in the hope of getting donor agencies, bureaucracy and other influential individuals and agents to act on this impact analysis. We cannot continually use the excuse of "best data available" to inform scenario projections. Coombe's reporting seems to be driven by the need to immediately act upon the impact of the disease. Therefore, in her report, the dissemination to influence the action phase of managing the impact of the disease on systems overrides the research methodological concerns of establishing HIV prevalence rates and its impact on systems (e.g. education system). This is perhaps why, people like President Thabo Mbeki, would call to question our knowledge about the disease and its impact on society.

The language used in the report suggests the tentativeness and uncertainty of the analysis presented in the report. It is anticipated that ...; Probably due to ...; extrapolate ...; may...; due to ...; set to increase/decrease ...; bound to ...; more likely ...; etc. are some of the terms and phrases used in the analysis. This report, with its tentative and uncertain conclusions, may perhaps then be used as a basis for further reports, policy formulation, implementation strategy, focus areas, etc, which may lead to disastrous consequences.

Coombe was then asked to interrogate this critique using her experience and knowledge in the field. These interrogated responses were then analysed to establish the changing patterns of positionality the research participants assumed. The response by the research participants are indicated in *italics* and blocked followed by an analysis of these responses.

ATTRITION OF TEACHERS BY DEATH – WHAT DO HIV AND AIDS RESEARCHERS SAY?

One set of responses by the research participants (Kinghorn and Coombe) through interrogating the graph representing the death rate phenomena of teachers and my (researcher) critique of Carol Coombe's report, indicates a **changed position** (emancipation) adopted by the researcher participants. That is, there is acknowledgement by the research participants that there is an element of doubt in the projected HIV prevalence rates amongst teachers. Anthony Kinghorn makes this explicit by indicating that the death of teachers within the age group 26 to 40 could well indicate AIDS mortality. He says that:

> *If the death rate is similar across the bands over the three-year period as indicated in the graphs, this could well indicate AIDS mortality. In the absence of AIDS, death rates are usually very low in people aged 20–40 than in older ages where death due to "disease of lifestyle" and older age become significant.*

Carol Coombe, responding to observations and interrogation of patterns, is convinced that obtaining information through more formal structures (meaning scientific enquiry) is a big problem. She demonstrates this by quoting the Bennell et al. (2002) report on Botswana where people observe and experience things happening in their communities but structured data production processes indicate differently. She argues that until we are better informed, we need to rely heavily on soft information (information not supported by scientific enquiry) and observable conditions unfolding in reality:

> *Dr Bennell used structured interviews in a limited number of schools and districts in Botswana, and came up with the conclusion that nothing was happening. A second team composed of teacher educators visited villages, parents, communities and NGO's. They threw away their structured interview pro formas, and asked people and the chiefs what was happening in the village lekotlas. Police, nurses, teachers, family welfare educators and counsellors answered from their own observation and experience. They say a deadly disease is stalking their communities, and they are burying their families.*

Another set of responses by interrogating the signifier is a justification for the current public information that is made available through estimates, projection analysis and scenario mapping. These kinds of responses suggest a **defensive stance** taken by the research participants.

Anthony Kinghorn and Carol Coombe emulate their defensive stance by the rationality they offer in support of their data produced on HIV and AIDS prevalence rates and impact analysis. They indicate that:

- *Projections have very real limitations in reflecting "reality". They make incorrect assumptions about a lot of things, including the timing of the epidemic. Assumptions become potentially more problematic for population sub-groups which differ from the general population.*
- *None of the generally available projections (e.g. the commonly used the Metropolitan Doyle projection model) take antiretroviral use into account.*
- *We cannot wait for perfect data to start to understand the texture of the pandemic, and its likely consequences. We must do what we can with what we have for now, and must move ahead on this basis.*
- *Teachers with HIV and AIDS may have access to antiretroviral drugs which could at least delay mortality. As around 50% of teachers nationwide are on medical aid this could be of significant influence.*
- *Mortality rates are always a lot lower than the prevalence rate as many infected people will still be well or only have minor ailments.*
- *It is the picture of people dying young that the demographers fear.*

Taking an emancipatory stance suggests a tentative view of the data produced and that there exists a level of scepticism, while the defensive stance suggests confidence in the data produced on HIV prevalence rates. If we map this emancipatory stance on understanding the demand for teachers, the projected figures for teacher demand is significantly different from that of a defensive stance. For example, by taking an emancipatory stance, other factors are viewed and considered in relation to the patterns emerging from our observations and our experiences. In the example presented to the researchers for interrogation, the death patterns of teachers indicate a large number of teachers dying within the 26 to 40 year age group. Also evident from the signs is that increasingly more women are dying than men. Based on the understanding of HIV and AIDS disease, our (the research participants and myself as the researcher) reading of the signs depicting the teachers' death phenomenon indicates a strong link between death of teachers in this age group and HIV and AIDS.

Having made this claim that teachers within the age group of 26 to 40 are more likely to have died from AIDS, a more plausible understanding of the impact of HIV and AIDS on the teaching force is possible. This means that, for example, it is more likely that teachers within this age group (26 to 40) are at risk and that:
- The number of teachers needed to replace those that die or become medically boarded as a result of HIV and AIDS would be approximately 312 (0.4% of 77900 teachers in KZN) teachers per annum (calculated from the teacher attrition in KwaZulu-Natal using death rate and medical retirement figures within the 26 to 40 year group expressed as a percentage of the teacher population in 1999) per annum.
- There is an understanding that 0.4% of the teachers, after qualifying, would only provide between 3 and 15 years (based on the assumption that the average age of a newly qualified teacher is 23 years; that a student will take four years to qualify as a teacher; and that the average school leaving age is 18 years) of the human resources for the school system.

This estimate of teacher demand as a result of HIV and AIDS is significantly different from the estimates generated through taking a defensive stance. Taking the defensive stance, the estimate for teacher demand as a result of HIV and AIDS would be 9348 (12% of 77 900 teachers in KZN) teachers over a period of 7 to 10 years, calculated on 12% of teachers being infected with HIV, and that a person having contracted this disease will die between 7 to 10 years later (Coombe, 2000). This means that between 935 (1.2%[1]) and 1335 (1.7%[2]) teachers would die of HIV and AIDS per annum within KZN. This stance (the defensive stance) differs almost three-fold from the earlier stance (changed position). That is, taking a defensive stance on the current HIV and AIDS prevalence rates, the estimates may defer by almost three times that of taking a position that begins to read what actually happens in reality.

Interrogated response has its limitations in that the reaction to the interrogation could lead to two possible responses. A defensive one emulating positionality and power over the information presented (as demonstrated in the second set of responses from the research participants) or one that emulates a shifted positionality (emancipation) of the respondents (as demonstrated in the first set of responses from the research participants). The dilemma is in the reading of the response in terms of its intended purpose and intended audience. This analysis of changing and defensive positionality is, therefore, not attempting to provide "discovery of the truth", but more importantly show how a "multiplicity of truths" co-exists within the research terrain, reflecting positionalities/ideologies of the researcher in relation to the phenomenon being studied.

MEDIATING THE VOICES: A WAY OF ADDRESSING DATA AS AGENCY

In the above discussion, I have suggested that data has the power of agency in troubling numbers, shifting dominant discourses, and caucusing emotive responsiveness as we begin to unpack what we take for granted through interrogated response.

A way of mediating the different and competing agendas in research, is perhaps, demonstrated by a research in progress by the Human Sciences Research Council (HSRC) commissioned by the Education Labour Relations Council (ELRC), focusing on determinants for teacher demand. The research process includes the setting up of a technical task team comprising various stakeholders interested in the area of teacher supply and demand and HIV and AIDS impact analysis. The technical task team's role is to guide the research process as it progresses through the phases of the research. Competing voices are mediated through interrogation within the forum so that the research intention and process is guided with a common agenda.

Through this process of engaging in research, I am advocating a shift in the discourse of participatory research agenda where the dominant focus of the relationship is between the researcher and the researched to include an ethical responsibility of researchers amongst the community of researchers through mediation of the research agendas particularly in research that informs policy.

CONCLUSION

This chapter explored theoretically the concept of data as agency through critical discourse analysis and conceptually through an example of interrogated response, using HIV and AIDS research as a medium. Through interrogated response, the underlying motivations for producing data and reporting on HIV and AIDS are exposed, thereby influencing our knowledge about this disease and supporting the scepticism theory on HIV and AIDS prevalence rates and impact analysis. In the example above, the positionality implicit in the responses of the research participants presents different scenarios for teacher supply, and demand and these could be interpreted and used in ways sensitive to the images one is attempting to portray. Through exploring data as agency, this chapter motivated for the acknowledgement that the public perception about the pandemic nature of HIV and AIDS disease and its impact on the people and systems must be treated with scepticism. In addition, it presented a glimpse of the contextual issues surrounding the disease and the impact it has on researching HIV and AIDS. In concluding with an example of how data as agency could be mediated through a process element in the research design, the chapter reaffirms a fundamental ethical principle: that research designs, strategies for data production and analytical frameworks can no longer be based on "flukes and flaws", and that understanding a disease that is said to be consuming a continent deserves a more ethically prudent and reliable mode of enquiry.

NOTES

[1] Percentage of teacher deaths per annum if death occurs 10 years after initial infection with HIV (9348/10 years)
[2] Percentage of teacher deaths per annum if death occurs 7 years after initial infection with HIV (9348/7 years)

REFERENCES

Bennell, P., Hyde, K., & Swainson, N. (2002). *The impact of the HIV and AIDS epidemic on the education sector in Sub-Saharan Africa*. Sussex: Centre for International Education, University of Sussex, Institute of Education, UK.

Cawthra, H. C., Helman-Smith, A., & Moloi, D. (2001). Development update. Annual review: The voluntary sector and development in South Africa 1999/2000. *Quarterly Journal of the South African National NGO Coalition and INTERFUND*, 3(3).

Chandler, D. (n.d.). *Semiotics for beginners*. Retrieved from http://www.aber.ac.uk/~dgc/semiotic.html

Coombe, C. (2000). Managing the impact of HIV/AIDS on the education sector. Pretoria: UN economic commission for Africa (UNECA).

Crouch, L. (2001) *Turbulence or Orderly Change? Teacher supply and demand in South Africa – Current status, future needs and the impact of HIV/AIDS*. Abridged and edited by K. M. Lewin; Multi-Site Teacher Education Research Project. Centre for International Education, University of Sussex Institute of Education, UK.

Crouch, L., & Perry, H. (2003). Human resources development review 2003: Employment and skills in South Africa. Human Science Research Council. Cape Town: HSRC Press.

Department of Health. (1999). *Summary report: 1998. National HIV sero-prevalence survey of women attending public antenatal clinics in South Africa*. Pretoria: Health Systems Research and Epidemiology.

Edgar, A. (2006). *Habermas: The key concepts*. New York: Routledge.

Fairclough, N. (1989). *Language and power*. UK: Longman Group.

Fairclough, N., & Wodak, R. (1997). *Critical discourse analysis*. In T. A. van Dijk (Ed.), Discourse as a social interaction. London: Sage.

Giddens, A. (1987). Structuralism, post-structuralism and production of culture. In A. Giddens, & J. Turner (Eds.), *Social theory today*. Stanford University Press.

Janks, H. (1997). Critical discourse analysis as a research tool. *Discourse, 18*(3), 329–342.

Kamler, B. (2000). *Critical discourse in educational inquiry*. Material prepared for a Masters module. Deakin University, Australia.

Kelly, M. J. (2003). The HIV/AIDS context for the leadership response. In B. Otaala (Ed.), *Proceedings of a workshop on HIV/ AIDS – Government leaders in Namibia responding to the HIV/AIDS epidemic*. Windhoek: University of Namibia Press.

Kim, J. (n.d.). *From commodity production to sign production*. PhD candidate at The Annenberg School for Communication, University of Pennsylvania.

Maclennan, B. (2000, March 19). Dissent over AIDS cause. *Sunday Tribune*. KwaZulu-Natal.

Mamaila, K., & Brand, R. (2000, September 15). State in a bid to quell AIDS row. *The Daily News*. KwaZulu-Natal.

Marias, H. (2000) *To the Edge: AIDS review 2000*. Pretoria: University of Pretoria.

Matthews, R. (1998, November). Flukes and flaws. *Prospect*.

Ramrathan, P. (2002). Ways of knowing: Teacher attrition and demand in KwaZulu-Natal in the context of an HIV/AIDS pandemic. Doctoral Thesis (unpublished), University of Durban-Westville, South Africa.

Rhedding-Jones, J. (1995). What do you do after you've met poststructuralism? Research possibilities regarding feminism, ethnography and literacy. *Journal of Curriculum Studies, 27*(5), 479–500.

SADTU National Education Policy Conference. (2001). Education transformation: From policy to practice. Resource documents: A decade of struggle for quality public education and job security; Conference help 17–21 April 2001, Gallagher Estate, Midrand, Gauteng.

Sarup, M. (1988). Derrida and deconstruction. *An introductory guide to post-structuralism and post-modernism*. University of Georgia press.

Smith, A. (2001). *Trends in HIV and AIDS surveillance*. Paper presented at the National Teacher's Union Advocacy conference, held at Durban College of Education, 21 June.

St. Pierre, E. A. (1999). The work of response in ethnography. *Journal of Contemporary Ethnography, 28*(3), 266–287.

Tatto, M. T. (1999). *Education for the rural poor in the context of educational reform: The case of Mexico*. Paper delivered at The Oxford International conference for Education and Development; 9–13 September, Oxford University, United Kingdom.

Toolan, M. (1997). What is critical discourse analysis and why are people saying such terrible things about it? *Language and Literature, 6*(2), 83–103.

Volmink, J. (1998). Who shapes the discourse on science and technology education? In P. Naidoo & M. Savage (Eds.), *African science and technology education into the new millenium: Practice, policy and priorities*. Kenwyn: Juta & Co. Ltd.

Welman, J. C., & Kruger, S. J. (1999). *Research methodologies for the business and administrative sciences*. Oxford: Oxford University Press.

RUBBY DHUNPATH

10. THE ETHICS AND POLITICS
OF ORGANISATIONAL ETHNOGRAPHIES

Evaluation studies in South Africa have been criticised for focusing inadequately
on the ethnographic and anthropological dimensions of organisations. It is alleged
that the dominant approaches to evaluation have been structuralist and empirical-
rational in orientation, serving narrow bureaucratic functions for funders and
donors, based on self reports by programme participants (see Jansen, 1996). Jansen
argues that one way of resolving the dilemma of unreliable evaluation reports is to

> set a new standard for evaluation studies, for example, producing the richly
> contextualised narratives which bring to light powerful findings on impact –
> beyond statistical summaries" (Jansen, 1996, p. 3).

What are the potential benefits of an organisational ethnography, and what are the
epistemological and ethical implications of such an endeavour?

I shall attempt to address these concerns in this chapter by drawing on an
organisational ethnography of a South African non governmental organisation, as I
trace its mutating identity over three decades. I use insights derived from the
traditions of empowerment evaluation (Fetterman, 1999) and illuminative evaluation
(Parlett & Hamilton, 1976) as theoretical lenses to appraise the value of narratives in
understanding organisational behaviour. Further, I appropriate discourse analysis to
interrogate selected narrative data, as a methodological lens in organisational
analysis. I make a few generic observations about what an alternative mode of
organisational evaluation might look like and reflect on my experience of engaging
in such a project. But such an approach is necessarily complicated by ethical,
representational and epistemological hazards. In the latter part of the chapter, I revisit
the methodological wisdom of engaging in an institutional biography, highlighting
some of the dilemmas in negotiating a non-conventional approach.

EXCAVATING THE IDENTITY OF THE ENVIRONMENT AND LANGUAGE
EDUCATION TRUST

My interest in an organisational ethnography was motivated by my interest in the
mutating identity of the South African NGO, the Environment and Language
Education Trust (ELET), founded in the apartheid years as an alternative agency
for language teacher development. At the time, the organisation was somewhat
curiously positioned: It was an NGO, funded by a multi-national corporate
enterprise, but it provided a teacher development function, which was then the

R. Dhunpath and M. Samuel (eds.), Life History Research: Epistemology, Methodology
and Representation, 173–197

domain of higher education. As the demand for language teacher development increased, universities began to appropriate ELET's services to deliver in-service teacher education courses. After the installation of the new democratic regime in 1994, many NGOs found it difficult, if not impossible, to survive the substantially reduced funding quotas – as funds that were once accessible by NGOs for development projects were redirected to the new democratic government. The crisis was exacerbated as organisations such as ELET, which once enjoyed a symbiotic relationship with higher education institutions, were now under threat from their counterparts in higher education, as they too were forced to reconfigure their own institutional arrangements to respond to a changing policy environment.

How ELET was able to prevail at a time when several similar NGOs submitted to fiscal fatigue was a question that commanded my attention. As I pursued the enquiry through the typical evaluation routines of document analysis and interviews, it soon became apparent that the answer to the question was not going to be as simple as the question itself, and that conventional modes of enquiry would be inadequate in excavating the delicate contours of an NGO's life. Part of this methodological limitation may be ascribed to the theoretical frame within which the tools of enquiry are constructed. There appears to be an enduring trend amongst a community of organisational theorists, which believes that organisations exist in a relatively tangible ontological sense. Located within field theories derived from the wider background of classical management and administrative theory, attention is devoted to discovering essences in organisations, as a by-product of the search for improved efficiency and optimal performance. The prevailing canon inhibits looking beyond particular "legitimised" forms of knowledge through a limited set of epistemological preferences. These legitimised forms of knowledge act as "conceptual filters", or interpretative schemas inhibiting the exploration of features not readily accessible by empiricist modes of enquiry alone. But more importantly, these "filters" shut out the prospect of acknowledging and affirming the lay (profane?) ontologies[1] of organisational members as real and legitimate and intrinsically implicated in the construction of organisational identity. Hence, these theories were unable to illuminate for me, the organisational dynamics of non-profit organisations, which in my view, evince distinctive organisational characteristics. How do we transgress the conceptual filters?

One approach is to build an integrative theory that attempts to formulate propositions on the relationships between organisational development, the influence of neo-liberal organisational discourses and the lay (tacit) ontologies[2] of organisational members which are embedded in their narratives. In this regard, I want to consider Calori's (2002) proposition that theory building in organisation studies can be informed by

> a double extension, or stretching, towards both philosophy and practitioners'
> lay theories.

Similarly, Bergson (1983) emphasises the necessity of grounding philosophising in life experiences of members. Cognisant of this orientation, I will attempt to illustrate the links between philosophy and practice, and show that the analysis of participant's narratives can be used to elicit their "lay" ontologies as a way of making explicit their philosophical and ideological orientations. Accordingly, if an individual's thoughts and actions are held to be manifestations of her ontological beliefs and assumptions, then these are expressed or embodied in performance, thoughts and narratives, all of which find expression (implicitly or overtly) in the identity and behaviour of an organisation.

In exploring the potential of narratives in organisational ethnographies, I am influenced by Lather's (1991) "praxis of the present", which draws on feminist research, neo-Marxist critical ethnography and Freirean-empowering-participatory research, each of which is premised on a transformative agenda in relation to social structure and methodological norms. Hence, this post-positivist[3] conception of research and evaluation advocates modes of enquiry which recognise knowledge as

socially constituted, historically embedded, and value based (ibid).

It recognises in organisations, the pervasiveness of ambivalence, not as a contradiction but a signal of the coexistence of multiple identities, some emergent and prioritised, some diminished in importance (Blumenthal, 1999). It requires that the researcher make a concerted effort to resist the inclination to impose her own constructions of reality on the researched in favour of a reciprocal dialogue. It also calls for researchers to resist discounting ideas that do not fit into pre-established conceptual boxes. The goal of emancipatory evaluation research is to encourage self-reflection and deeper understanding on the part of the research participants at least as much as it is to generate empirically grounded theoretical knowledge.

WHY PURSUE AN ORGANISATIONAL ETHNOGRAPHY?

My choice of an organisational ethnography was motivated by the prospect of an approach to organisational evaluation which had the potential to satisfy my own intellectual curiosity, while simultaneously providing illuminative/emancipatory insights for members of the organisation, as a stimulus to interrogate their praxis, and to reflect on their philosophical and ideological inclinations in the context of the work they do. My interest in an organisational ethnography found resonance with Empowerment Evaluation (EE)[4], and Illuminative Evaluation (IE), which have their roots in an anthropological conception of organisations and institutions.

Empowerment evaluation is a form of participatory self-evaluation, which aims to create conditions for members of an institution to critically reflect on their praxis, with a view to affirming good practice and instituting mechanisms for change where necessary. EE is the use of evaluation concepts, techniques, and findings to "foster improvement and self-determination" (Fetterman,1999, p. 12). It comprises numerous inter-connected capabilities such as the ability to identify and express needs, establish goals and a plan of action to achieve them, evaluate short and long-term goals and persist in the pursuit of these goals. Employing both qualitative and quantitative methodologies, EE can be applied to individuals, organisations and communities, although the focus is usually on programmes. EE is necessarily a collaborative group activity, not an individual pursuit. Fetterman (1999, p. 9) suggests that an evaluator does not and cannot empower anyone; people empower themselves, often with assistance or coaching.

Empowerment Evaluation shares a kinship with Illuminative Evaluation. Illuminative evaluation research purposes a substantive understanding of the milieu as crucial in gaining insights into the lives of individuals who constitute the organisation (see Parlett & Hamilton, 1976). The crucial question that illuminative evaluation poses is: how do we discard the "spurious technological simplification of reality", by acknowledging the complexity of the organisational process (ibid., p. 101), while the crucial question that empowerment evaluation poses, is: of what pragmatic value is the emergent evaluation exercise if it does not inspire critical self-reflexivity among research participants? One of the most important guiding principles of EE is the attempt to understand an event in the context of multiple worldviews (ibid., p. 13). The aim is to understand what is going on from the participants' own perspectives as authentically as possible, to document this in a credible and legitimate way and make this accessible to participants as a stimulus for self-appraisal. The illuminative experience enables participants to find new opportunities, see existing resources in a new light and redefine their identities and future roles.

A powerful means of inspiring illuminative experiences is the use of narratives. Narratives facilitate the reconstruction and interpretation of subjectively meaningful features and critical episodes of an individual and organisation's life, allowing us to see the unities, continuities, and discontinuities, images and rhythms (Cortazzi, 1993, p. 5–9). Attempting an organisational evaluation using narratives and subjecting these to rigorous discursive analyses unveils those multiple, competing discourses that members of an organisation construct. The focus is not to pre-structure the reported experience with pre-determined categories, but to elucidate social-structural-institutional understandings from narrative data. Whilst the reported experience and knowledge of our participants is the primary source of data, our analysis invariably goes beyond these accounts, locating them in structures and cultures that are usually broader and more abstract than the understandings of our subjects. The challenge for the researcher is to clarify how the social contexts which frame our participants' narratives are constituted, what are their most causally significant features, and in what respects they are typical of a historical moment or of a distinctive social space. In effect, we move outwards from an individual life, to a model of a localised social-institutional structure in which the life is situated, to the wider societal context (see Rustin, 1999).

This mode of analysis resonates with Robert Chia's (2000) framework for analysing organisational behaviour. Challenging the canonical structuralist-functionalist mode of organisational analysis, Chia argues that social objects and phenomena such as "the organisation", "the economy", "the state", do not have an unproblematic existence independent of our discursively-shaped understandings of such phenomena. It is anomalous therefore to speak about "organisational discourse" as discourse **about** some pre-existing, thing-like social object called "the organisation". Hence, for Chia, discourse analysis **is** organisation analysis.

DISCOURSE ANALYSIS AS ORGANISATION ANALYSIS

The question of *discourse*, and the manner in which it shapes our epistemology and understanding of organisations, is central to an expanded realm of organisational analysis. It is one which recognises that the world we live in, and the social artefacts we rely upon to successfully negotiate our way through it,

> are always already institutionalised *effects* of primary organisational impulses" (ibid, 1).

My conception of discourse here is based on Fairclough's (1992) proposition that language is not random or individual, but that institutions and social groups articulate their meanings and values *systematically*. Hence, discourse is a mode of action, enabling individuals to act upon the world and especially upon each other. It is simultaneously a mode of representation. Secondly, it implies that there is a dialectical relationship between discourse and social structure, there being more generally a relationship between social practice and social structure: the latter is both a condition for, and an effect of, the former (Cohen & Musson, 2000).

This conception reaffirms Bakhtin's (1981) position that discourse must be seen as both shaped by and reflective of social structure, and simultaneously constitutive of this structure:

> Discourse is a practice not just of representing the world, but of signifying the world, constituting and constructing the world in meaning (Fairclough, 1992, p. 64).

Discourses do not simply represent reality, as experienced by a particular social group or institution, but they are also dynamic, serving to construct versions of reality. Furthermore, discourses are carriers of ideology, ideology being understood as a relatively coherent set of assumptions, beliefs and values about aspects of social reality, which is illuminated in a selective and legitimising way, restricting autonomous critical reflection and sometimes favouring sectional interests (Cohen & Musson, 2000).

However, while ideology and discourses "frame" the way individuals see the world, this does not imply that they are rigidly trapped within this framework. Neither are they constrained from creatively reworking the specific discourses and ideologies which characterise their particular realities. On the contrary, individuals appropriate specific discourses according to their particular circumstances. Discourse is a hegemonic process, where dominant social groupings exert power and influence over others through a variety of mechanisms, including normative and coercive strategies. In this way, organisations derive their stability from generic discursive processes rather than from the presence of independently existing concrete entities. In other words, phrases such as "the organisation" do not refer to an extra-linguistic reality. Instead, they are conceptualised abstractions to which it has become habitual for us to refer as independently existing "things". Consequently, discourse creates a coherent world with a semblance of stability, order and predictability, to what would otherwise be a nebulous, formless undifferentiated reality (see Chia, 2000). It achieves this by inscribing into language and utterances, the material, codified forms that constitute the foundation of language and representation. This then becomes regularised and routinised through social exchanges, leading to the formation and institutionalisation of codes of behaviour, rules, procedures and practices. In this way, the world we have come to inhabit achieves an apparent familiarity and regularity, which is consistent with our consciousness, through the internalisation of these discourses. In the ensuing discussion, I engage in an analysis of the discourses of key members associated with the organisation to illustrate the effects of their singular and collective identities on the organisation.

WHAT NEW KNOWLEDGE DOES AN ORGANISATIONAL ETHNOGRAPHY GENERATE AND HOW IS IT DONE DIFFERENTLY?

I will attempt to answer this question by focusing on a research project spanning more than three years, involving the production of narrative data with individuals associated with ELET, which I represented in an organisational biography entitled *"Archaeology of a language development NGO"*. The biography documents the subjective experiences of members of the organisation, attempting to capture the nuanced meanings of their experiences and interactions as they reflect on the life of the organisation in its mutation over three decades.

The selection of data for analysis is intended to serve two purposes: Firstly, it signals elliptically, through the eyes of members of ELET, the limitations of the dominant econometric mode of evaluation which the organisation is routinely required to conduct, highlighting the angst this causes and how this potentially compromises the work of the organisation. The same data is used to demonstrate the potential of narrative research to act as a catalyst for the generation of heightened empiricism (Gough, 2001), both for the analyst as well as for participants. As Rustin (1999, p. 115) suggests, in some cases, narrative data illuminates

> instantiated knowledge of an institutional pattern or strategy that we had not previously understood in an elaborated form.

The data also provides insights into the ways in which individuals are constrained and shaped by their particular contexts, and the ways in which they are able to devise strategies to enact their agency. The most significant advantage of the approach is its potential for grounded theorising by being sensitive to participants' own capacities to generate social meanings and how different agents, as an outcome of their professional trajectories, construct the lived life of the organisation, and conversely, how the institution circumscribes their individual identities.

At this stage, I want to introduce the four protagonists who have had an influential role in shaping the identity of the organisation. **Mervin** is the founding director. A former educational manager and academic, he was disillusioned with the state of language teacher development and the non-delivery of in-service professional development programmes within higher education institutions. In response, he launched ELET as an alternative agency for language teacher development through a grant from Anglo Vaal, a corporate donor. By the year

2001, the neo-liberal season of mergers and takeovers resulted in a more inward looking Anglo Vaal which announced the termination of its 30 year long social responsibility funding- lifeline to ELET. At this point in the organisation's history, Mervin finds himself walking the tightrope of competing demands. On the one hand, he has to steer the organisation towards financial self sustainability to ensure its survival. On the other hand, he is committed to preserving the humanitarian mission of the NGO. These incompatible demands, it would seem, are the source of tension he is required to manage within the organisation.

Cecil, a former teacher educator and school principal, is a senior manager deeply committed to the creation of ecologically conducive learning environments to supplement and complement ELET's teacher development programmes – especially in rural schools. Using a bouquet of indicators to determine the characteristics of an "unloved school", he institutes programmes to rehabilitate schools through a holistic development of the physical and psycho-social environment, using a variety of activities based on the Freriean model of participatory action. This is done within the context of language development by integrating environmental issues into literature, and poetry, using drama and role-play. However, in recent times, Cecil feels increasingly alienated from his work as the organisational discourse increasingly takes on an econometric flavour.

Tracy is the programme manager of the Project for Health and Sanitation (PHASE)[5]. Like Cecil, she is committed to rebuilding schools ravaged by apartheid. Trained as a creative artist and graphic designer, Tracy believes that effective learning cannot take place in hostile ecological environments. Driven by a developmental impulse, she chose in the earlier years of her career, to apply her aesthetic skills to materials design and curriculum development for NGOs. Like Cecil, she now experiences an existential dilemma as a result of the progressive erosion of the organisation's developmental mission. Because of a persistent sense that she is unable to assert her values and have them taken seriously, she desires disengagement from the organisation whose identity she helped shape.

Rene occupies a somewhat invidious position in her dual roles of development consultant to AngloVaal (the core funder) and as chairperson of the ELET board of governors. Rene, who has her roots in the NGO sector, moved into the corporate domain in an attempt to exercise its espoused social responsibility mission. Rene is the architect of the new organisational discourse as she nudges the organisation to be more receptive to changing market forces as they impinge on the organisation's survival. Her discourse, grounded in economic pragmatism, appears to be at odds with the developmental inclinations of the other members in this conversation.

Before we direct our attention to analysing the discourses of these four individuals, it might be useful to situate these discourses within some of the commonsenses that have come to typify the NGO sector as articulated by Eade et al. (2002, p. 3) who argue:

> Corporatism, strategic planning, and formal accountability became the order of the day; a way to contain if not to understand the complex environments in which development and humanitarian programmes now had to function. Having discovered a particular brand of corporate management, however,

many Northern NGOs and official development agencies began to seek spiritual and practical guidance not from within their own unique and multicultural experience, but from the orthodoxies of the for-profit sector (Powell & Seddon, 1997). Ironically, many observers and insiders feared that in nailing themselves so firmly to the mast of strategic planning and market-led approaches, NGOs risk casting their central values and accumulated wisdom – their distinctiveness – overboard.

The Normative and Coercive Power of Organisational Discourse

An analysis of the discourses of the four key participants in this study reveals interesting consonances as well as cleavages in relation to what might be considered commonsense orthodoxies reflected above. The central focus of this section is an analysis of organisational discourse and how it is articulated by individuals working in NGO environments, as they construct and reconstruct material practices and their psychological identities. The essence of the argument is that, even if organisational members do not consciously embody the values of the organisation, they inevitably reproduce it through their agency. Further, I contend that these discourses do not simply reside in the realm of public knowledge, but are consciously mapped on by individuals who control the strategic resources to do so. The normative and coercive power of these discourses can be formidable in neutralising dissent and co-opting individuals to be consenting agents, particularly in a context characterised by resource dependence.

All four individuals identified above are representative (to greater or lesser degrees) of the traditional NGO world which symbolises humanitarian values based on a developmental mission. At this stage in the organisation's history, ELET finds itself in a crippling financial crisis as a consequence of inadequate student fee recovery, compounded by the announcement that its core funder is terminating its support. The context of this debate is a strategic planning workshop intended to map the future of the organisation. Rene, in her capacity as the chair of the board, warns that unless ELET exercises fiscal austerity and adopts econometric principles, it faces demise.

> ...can I afford to continue keeping the item on my shelf if no one is buying it? I'm sorry if that sounds like a tough line, but if people are not paying for the courses, then ELET must make some tough decisions about the courses. Each one of us here, and not just the managers, should be wearing a marketing hat, to promote the services we offer. If we still are not able to sell what we have to offer, we must stop selling it. If the courses are not profitable, we must discontinue them. We need to abandon the spirit of entitlement (which some NGO's are guilty of) and adopt a spirit of entrepreneurship where every individual within the organisation adopts a corporate ethic and works to promote the interest of the whole organisation rather than individual interests.

In response, Cecil, who manages the teacher development courses (which are implicated here), argues:

If this [ELET] were a grocery shop, we would have closed it down a long time ago. But we are not a grocery shop. We offer teacher development courses. Our experience is that students may not pay up when we want the money, but in the end, just before graduation, they pay their dues. We've experienced financial crises before and we've bounced back. There is no reason to believe that we won't bounce back again.

These transcripts articulate the dilemma experienced by two managers, negotiating the tensions between development ideals and the realities of development practice. Cecil subscribes to the belief that in order for the NGO to fulfil its developmental mission it has to retain its humanitarian identity, which he believes is compromised by the adherence to a corporate rationality. Cecil languishes in the belief that there is some self-perpetuating philanthropy that will ensure that ELET bounces back. The difference between Rene, in her capacity as chair of the board, and Cecil is that Cecil has the luxury of dreaming lofty dreams without being unduly concerned with matters of fiscal austerity. Such matters, it would seem, fall within Rene's province of responsibility.

Rene cautions against this idealistic posturing. She does this with the benefit of hindsight (from her experiences with the NGO world) and foresight (from her involvement with the corporate world). She makes a conscious choice to infuse into the neo-NGO world, an agenda influenced by a corporate ethic, because she believes that ELET can no longer seek refuge in corporate handouts as she articulates below: Significantly, she infuses into the strategy debate the "standard neo-liberal toolkit" (Giroux, 2004) which seeks to neutralise the assumptions of corporate ideology, silencing its social implications. These commonsense assumptions relegate the developmental idealism of agents like Cecil to the level of expensive rhetoric. Here, agency is stripped of an ethical language, and fails to recognise a politics outside of the realm of the market. In this view, social developmental impulses are romanticised as activism – an occupational hazard that the market has to tolerate – reflected in Rene's response:

I think that it is important that we maintain dreamers like Cecil and it is perfectly reasonable that there will be people who will not be comfortable with the new rationality. We do need to keep the dreams alive, but with a consciousness of the reality we ultimately have to face. There were times when an organisation would fall into the crevice and some Good Samaritan would come along and rescue it. The days of organisations bouncing back because of good Samaritans are forever gone. These days, organisations bounce back because they respond creatively and strategically to their predicaments. Today, we no longer have the comfort of expecting a lifeline every time we are in trouble. We have to dream with the consciousness that at the end of the month we will have to pay the rent or face eviction. We cannot sit back smugly, hoping that we will bounce back as we always have.

On the one hand, Rene has an obligation to maintain the social mission of the NGO, which implies resisting the coercive power of the corporate rationality that she symbolically represents and overtly advocates. On the other hand, she has an obligation to ensure the survival of an organisation, which finds itself struggling as a consequence of a changed and ever changing development arena. Although she consistently urges ELET to adopt the less insidious attributes of corporate rationality, one is inclined to ask (at the risk of hatching another conspiracy theory) whether in fact Rene has not acted in a "sinister" way towards ELET by asking Anglo Vaal **not** to renew its funding grant as might be inferred from her comment:

> ... and I could quite easily secure another three years of funding, but I have nothing to benefit from a disempowered ELET, and equally, I have nothing to benefit from a totally patronising Anglo Vaal

It would hardly be surprising if she did dissuade Anglo Vaal from renewing the grant, since she believes quite firmly in the principle of autonomy and sustainability of the organisation without the bondage to a donor. She sees no fundamental dichotomy in the way the NGO conducts its affairs in relation to how the corporate world manages itself:

> It is really about exercising a few basic business principles: prune what you don't need, acknowledge that there are limitations to what you are able to handle and temper your dreams with the reality that to survive, NGO's will increasingly have to operate on the same principles as successful businesses.

Managerialism, Professionalism and the Ethical Divide

Rene is cognisant of the benefits to be derived from adopting the language of the corporate world. In that sense, her intention may not be insidious, but strategic, a consequence of her belief that the post-apartheid South African NGO is caught in something of a time warp:

> In the post 1994 era, I don't think the issue is whether NGOs are relevant... It is about everyone, the NGOs included, recognising the need for a changed and changing role. Where we have failed as the NGO movement is interpreting what its new role is. For many years, NGOs were THE alternative, to a point that the alternative became the mainstream. People entrench themselves into particular modes of thinking and acting and when circumstances change and there is a need to reconfigure their identities and find a new role, they tend to struggle with making that shift. It would appear to me that because NGOs were central to the whole development agenda in this country, they expect that the mainstream should come to them, rather than their joining the mainstream. Now we face a situation where funders and donors regard the democratic government as legitimate (whether it actually delivers or not) and find it more appropriate and proper to work with the government directly rather through the NGO movement.

Tracy by comparison, with a relatively limited exposure to the NGO world, endorses the need to bring the agenda of the traditional NGO into dialogue with the agenda of the corporate world for its survival. She does not consider it anomalous to infuse the corporate rationality into the NGO world as long as the social goals pursued are clearly defined. Like Rene, she believes that the NGO should not carry the baggage of ELET's historical roots into the new order – simply because of its success in a bygone era.

> *We must remember that we are operating in a very different context now. We have witnessed a dramatic shift in the funding scenario. Funders are no longer only funding NGOs; they're also funding consultancies, non-profit organisations, universities, research units and others. So, on the one level we have to compete with them. They go in, wearing their smart business suits and gold earrings and woo funders with their PowerPoint presentations. Funders are very impressed by that because funders are more interested in giving work to people whom they know are going to get the job done, rather than people who have a history of development work. There is certainly a culture of entitlement amongst NGO... and I think ELET to some degree is guilty of this. Funders no longer respond to the "cap in hand" approach. No longer can we go to a funder and say, "Look at the work we have we've done for the last 15 years... so please give us some money so we don't collapse". Funders are not interested in giving money just because the NGO has a good track record. That's what used to happen. Now, NGOs have to respond to competition and a results-orientated development environment. Therefore, cultivating a positive image and marketing an organisation aggressively is vital. Funders are favourably disposed to an NGO which has a social bottom line, but which acts like a business.*

There appears to be a significant consonance between Tracy's and Rene's discourses. Their conceptions of organisational "structure" and identity are located in a corporate discourse, despite their different disciplinary backgrounds (Tracy gave up a position in the corporate sector to join the NGO world; Rene left the NGO world to join the corporate world). Although Tracy echoes Rene's marketisation discourse, it does not suggest that she is blindly compliant in her advocacy of a new organisational identity (as we will observe later). Tracy's position is borne out of her belief in the need to rethink management strategies at ELET to make it more responsive to changing market conditions. This is different from Rene's call for a fundamental ideological reorientation of the organisation to imbibe the new corporate rationality. However, despite their differing philosophical and disciplinary orientations, collectively their discourses (in the context of this strategic planning meeting) have a profound performative impact on the organisation's strategic orientation.

Significantly, both discourses evince a submission to the inevitability and inescapability of resource dependency. From a resource dependency perspective, the advantages of non-compliance flow from the ability to exercise relative autonomy over decision-making, the ability to adapt to new contingencies and the latitude to alter or control the environment in pursuit of organisational objectives. Organisational dependence theorists argue that organisational responses to institutional pressures will

vary from conforming to resistant; from passive to active; from preconscious to controlling; from impotent to influential; and from habitual to opportunistic expectations (Oliver, 1991, p. 151).

Oliver identifies five possible strategic responses to pressures for conformity from the institutional environment. The range of responses varies in the degree of agency, as is illustrated in the following table:

Table 6. A Typology of Strategic Responses to Institutional Processes (Oliver, 1991, p. 152)

Strategies	Tactics	Examples
Acquiescence	Habit Imitate Comply	Following invisible, taken for granted norms
		Mimicking institutional models
		Obeying rules and accepting norms
Compromise	Balance Pacify Bargain	Balancing the expectations of multiple constituencies
		Placating and accommodating institutional elements
		Negotiating with institutional stakeholders
Avoidance	Conceal Buffer Escape	Distinguishing nonconformity Loosening institutional attachments Changing goals, activities, or domains
Defiance	Dismiss Challenge Attack	Ignoring explicit norms and values Contesting rules and requirements Assaulting the sources of institutional pressure
Manipulation	Co-opt Influence Control	Importing influential constituents Shaping values and criteria Dominating institutional constituents and processes

The table identifies (in ascending order) the broad repertoire of active organisational responses that organisations may exhibit in response to institutional pressures and expectations, based on the assumption that organisations will both choose to conform to or resist pressures on the basis of their self interests. Their desire to conform is often linked to issues of legitimacy, organisational capacity and the organisation's desire to retain control of resources. For example, an organisation is more likely to acquiesce when the probability of attaining legitimacy from conformity is high, while the strategies of compromise, avoidance, defiance and manipulation are more likely responses when anticipated legitimacy are low. In general, the exercise of power is proportional to the need for legitimacy and control of scarce resources, which in turn dictates the scope of active agency. The implication of the above discussion is that conformity is neither inevitable nor invariably instrumental in securing longevity, while the exercise of agency is not arbitrary. It may be argued that in the scale from acquiescence to manipulation, Rene and Tracy occupy extreme ends of the continuum, but that the commonsenses inscribed into the language achieve the effect of consensus rather than contestation. The following transcript (the author of which is Tracy, but might equally be of the words of Rene) captures the tension between acquiescence and agency.

Let us accept the reality that the generous handouts NGOs once received is dead. But having said that, I don't think there has to be a contradiction between operating in a professional, competent and businesslike way with maintaining a humanitarian mission. This is not to say that business is always professional and competent, but I'm just linking the means to the end. The challenge for us involved in humanitarian work is to reach our social bottom line but not at the expense of our financial bottom line. We're not missionaries out there waiting for the funders' god to deliver. It is a fact that we have to compete in an environment that's getting far more difficult, and I don't think by responding to competition, your essence is corrupted by it. It's just a different way of looking at how you work and how you see yourself in your work.

Again, this transcript suggests, implicitly, that there is consensus between Tracy and Rene on the inevitability of the organisation's need to professionalise. However, Tracy's reflections in the following transcript disrupt this assumption:

Over the past month, I spent so much time on what I regard as complete waste of time and energy simply to satisfy USAID's obsessive demands for senseless statistical reports they call evaluation and accountability. We generate vast amounts of data for the funder that I find rather shallow because they really say nothing about the real impact of the programmes. Having said that, I must emphasise that I fully endorse the need for rigorous, creative modes of evaluation for accountability, I'm just opposed to the highly technicist quantitative approaches that funders seem to favour over more meaningful qualitative approaches ... Sometimes you have to take a step back and say, "No I don't actually care, I want real action projects, not numbers". But these officials often create the impression that they are really powerful, and behave as though they are parting with their personal fortunes. Relating to them is a very stressful experience, and I sometimes feel my throat closing up with tension when I have to talk to them. I don't mind the rigorous demands from funders, but the USAID management style is very heavy handed, to the point of becoming demoralising...

In an apparent attempt at reclaiming her integrity as a development professional, Tracy concedes that the professionalisation of NGOs needs to happen, but not on the terms of the evidence-driven model that is presently demanded by funders. For Tracy, the tensions between bureaucratisation and professionalisation are a consequence of superimposing a narrow corporate economic rationality on the NGO, putting an inordinate amount of pressure on NGOs to satisfy technocratic requirements as a means of accountability, and in the process, dislocating their centre of gravity. Yet, in order to survive as an NGO, it is required to submit to these coercive forces; an NGO cannot operate outside the corporate framework since its survival depends on the benevolence of funders.

Hence, while individuals within the organisation might appear to share a common language, they derive different meanings from it. Tracy's discourses are consonant with those of Rene on fundamental issues of systemic reorientation and strategy. Both Rene and Tracy submit arguments, which few individuals within the organisation can convincingly dispute. However, while both Rene and Tracy argue for a more robust corporatist and managerialist organisation, Tracy is in fact circumspect about her allegiance in her practice. She is aware of the danger in funders' prescriptions for evaluation and reporting which reorientates accountability upward (away from the grassroots, supporters and staff) towards donors. For Tracy, without meaningful accountability to their beneficiaries, scaling-up could seriously distance NGOs from their clients and compromise their raison d'être – as the following apprehension by Tracy reveals. Note that this declaration was made to me in an interview outside of the strategic planning meeting.

There are times when I feel I'm not doing enough as manager. I'm not referring to management of the bureaucratic aspects of the programme – there's far too much of that in my opinion. I want to be able to refine the programme and add value to it. I want to take it beyond its weaknesses, particularly weaknesses in its implementation. I think I'd like to be able to have more of a presence, to be able to have more contact with trainers in districts. It is often frustrating when one has to deal with having to compromise your dreams of what you know you can achieve, to satisfy the unreasonable demands of the funder, who often has little knowledge of pragmatic realities one has to deal with. Are these evaluation reports an honest, authentic, useful tool? We generate vast amounts of data for the funder... I find that rather shallow. It's a game I don't enjoy playing....but...

The fact that Tracy chooses not to make public the above sentiments is significant. It might be argued that her choice of silence makes her complicit in her own oppression as she submits to the coercive influence of the dominant discourse. However, her silence belies a profound disillusionment with the instrumentalist and technicist nature of development work resulting in a conflict between the unitary "personal" self and the "false" organisational self, requiring compromises to private aspirations. The personal and private are suppressed and subsumed under the dominant discourses of the organisation as the avoidance of conflict takes precedence over personal inclinations. Thus, the boundaries between public and private are increasingly blurred as the organisational identity increasingly colonises all the spaces in the manager's life, diluting or confusing the manager's sense of self. Her disillusionment is further compounded by her sense of being devalued as she articulates below:

> *The tone at management meetings and even in informal discussions was starting to become quite combative: that there was a winner and a loser. I realised that I was investing so much in the outcome of the process that there was a danger that if my proposition wasn't taken seriously, I was going to feel undervalued and undermined. It was then that I decided that it was time to disinvest.*

Unable to maintain the buffer between external demands and her inner self, Tracy expresses a strong desire for disengagement from an organisation whose identity she helped shape, but which no longer gives her the kind of fulfilment she desires at this stage in her life.

This discussion has attempted to demonstrate how power relations are sustained within the micro-politics of interaction, where individuals, notwithstanding their own ideological inclinations, are complicit in imbibing and perpetuating a corporate culture which, in the first instance, derives its legitimacy from their willingness to be consenting agents and, in the second instance, is perpetuated by what Marx refers to as "false consciousness" of agents. Individuals are induced to become consumers of corporate culture as they are presented with opportunities to express their individuality in forums such as strategic planning sessions. Their perceived autonomy is affirmed as "engineered" opportunities are created for individuals to enact their agency. In this way, the normative framework designed by the management is internalised, co-opting agents insidiously into realising corporate objectives.

However, the above discourses are in variance (not necessarily in the performative sense) with Mervin's development discourses. As director of the NGO, Mervin concedes the necessity for the professionalisation of the NGO, in as far as acknowledging its obligation to deliver high quality emancipatory teacher education programmes to support the reconstruction of education. Yet, he is reluctant to submit to a corporate-managerial mentality, which he believes is in conflict with the spirit of the developmental enterprise and will necessarily undermine its values. He laments the decline in ELET's work to that of a development sub-contractor with little to show by way of substantive development.

> *...we often have to compromise our principles because all they [funders] want NGOs to do is provide a prescribed service in certain areas such as train teachers using materials and modules that were not prepared by us- we just have to deliver. They use the word "deliverables". You deliver a number of workshops, you deliver a number of school support visits and you leave. You have certain time frames and time lines and log frames and logjams and a series of bureaucratic and technical requirements. As a result, our core business, language development, is degenerating into a facile indulgence...[But] It is better to light one small candle in one dark corner,*

than to curse the darkness. So we try and achieve a balance between what we call needs driven and supply driven by matching the skills we offer with the actual need in schools.

Mervin resists cooption into the funder's modus operandi, because of his commitment to language as a disciplinary mechanism for development. He is acutely mindful of the prospect of ELET's *"jetting in, jetting out, consultant model of operation"* degenerating into *"a facile indulgence"*, where linguistic deficiency is compounded and the gap between those who are linguistically "privileged" and those who are not, is widened, resulting in the cultivation of *"a new generation of confident illiterates"*. It is this social development mission that has propelled him in his professional life, which he is now reluctant to abandon.

These competing discourses signal the duality that characterises the lives of those struggling with the ambiguity surrounding their roles. An NGO in South Africa no longer has a clearly defined, developmentally focused function, but is a contested entity, having to reconcile fundamental issues about professional identity while simultaneously redefining itself pragmatically to ensure its relevance as a means to continued legitimacy. These competing discourses are debilitating for some, empowering for others, but collectively they constitute a vital ingredient to maintain a vigilant balance between pragmatism and managerialism, a balance that determined the survival of few and the demise of many NGOs in the post-1994 period.

I return now to the question of ELET's success as an alternative site of knowledge production at a time when the legitimacy of the NGO in South Africa was being contested. This contestation occurred in a climate of state hostility and a changing higher education sector, which found itself in competition with NGOs for diminishing resources. An analysis of the interview data reveals that ELET's survival can be attributed to its evolution as a distributed knowledge system in which all necessary knowledge is not possessed by the single mind of the strategist (Spender, 1996; Tsoukas, 1997 in Calori, 2002). This view proposes the adoption of a democratic perspective of organisations, affirming and valuing the knowledge held by organisational members (not only senior managers). The essence of organisational capability, according to Calori, is the integration of individuals' specialised knowledge, which can generate new combinations of existing knowledge. Organisational capacity is strengthened by the assimilation of members' lay ontologies and tacit knowledges as well as craft knowledges which are the essence of what Calori calls **creative dialectical evolution**. Calori suggests managers need to mediate pure reasoning by being attentive to common sense from which intuition emerges, as Mervin illustrates:

We are victims of the new "Thatcherite philosophy" where we only get paid for the work we do, and we are expected to take care of the resourcing on our own. We are forced therefore to outsource some of the work such as materials development. However, we are also blessed in the sense that we have staff members who are developmentally sensitive, who have accumulated a range of home-grown, contextually sensitive strategies for meaningful language development. It has taken us several years to achieve that amidst our ups and downs. Now we have a fairly young team supported by some senior personnel, especially women, who are altruistic and non-careerists and who enjoy their work. I suppose there will come a time when they will not be satisfied with job satisfaction alone.

Organisational members who have internalised the principles of creative dialecttical evolution can stimulate organisational development through their routine interactions (ibid.). Leaders, for example, enable the process of creative evolution by managing strategy debates in a way that enhances knowledge integration and consequently organisational development. In so doing, they create the conditions of metaflexibility. Under the leadership of its founding director, ELET has demonstrated this metaflexibility, which has enabled it to redefine literacy beyond the narrowly conceived definition of literacy as language.

The main reason why we have survived is that we have been able to reinvent ourselves to respond to changes in the country, strategically. We realised also that, internationally, there has been a shift in the mode of teaching English from a purist notion of teaching the language structurally, to using other modes of intervention and delivery. For instance, people like Cecil and Tracy realised that it was futile to begin teaching a language like English in contexts that were totally under-resourced. We had to take into account the poverty and under nourishment in these contexts. We had to consider the levels of health and sanitation. So we made a conscious choice to select the extremely poor and under-resourced schools in the remote rural areas where we knew we could use our accumulated skills to make a real difference to people's everyday lives in a tangible way.

Mervin's capacity to accumulate the distributed knowledges in the organisation enables him to preserve the energy of an organisation in perpetual motion. His strategic leadership is enhanced by his ability to submerge his own ideological and philosophical orientations in favour of pursuing organisational goals. He is able to dialogue with the different worldviews in the organisation, and by not taking definitive ideological positions, particularly on the issue of language development, about which he feels passionately, he is able to guide ELET through its mutation.

MULTI-PERSPECTIVAL READINGS OF ORGANISATIONAL DISCOURSE

In reflecting on the usefulness of an ethnographic approach to understand an NGO, I am able to say with some degree of confidence that the approach has yielded insights that empiricist methods alone could not. However, this "reading" of the organisation was achieved through a psycho-social analysis of members' discourses. It may be argued that such a reading does not, in fact, transcend paradigm insularity and does not generate multiple perspectives of the organisation, particularly since this reading has been mediated by my own positionality and ideological orientation as a researcher. In the process of documenting the institutional memory of the organisation, the memory has become part of my psyche in as much as I am implicated in its construction. Hence, my capacity for evaluative integrity might be considered as being compromised and diminished, especially since discourse analysis is as much a reflection of my discourse as it is of my research participants. How might we transcend what Cherryholmes (1993) calls the threat of "textual fundamentalism"?

Carl Rhodes (2000), in his methodologically astute paper entitled: "Reading and writing organisational lives" uses an approach proposed by Cherryholmes (1993) in which he argues that texts do not speak for themselves and that rather than being fixed, the meaning of any text resides in the interpretative act. He argues for a pragmatic reading of the same text through multiple conceptual frameworks. For example, the discourses of ELET members cited above might yet be read (among a host of others) from a feminist perspective, a post structuralist perspective and a Marxist perspective, each generating nuanced interpretations, illuminating different facets of the organisation. Ideally, this reading is undertaken by "independent" critical readers in an attempt to generate alternative perspectives. While none of the readings are privileged as providing a more correct, more real or more essential interpretation, they alert us to the fact that we can better understand organisations through particular forms of discourse created by language, constructed from narratives of key organisational members. This meta-theoretical approach to organisation studies is seen both as a way to break from the dominance of systemic structural-functionalist approaches to studying organisations and to promote new opportunities to excavate the less visible and accessible dimensions of organisational life.

Deconstructing the biographical method in organisational studies shows how the

> understanding of organisations is inseparable from the organisation of understanding (Rhodes, 2000, p. 17).

and how attention must be paid to the

> organisation of writing rather than the writing of organisation (Cooper, 1989, p. 501, in Rhodes, 2000, p. 17).

> Each text we use to under-stand the world produces new texts and new understandings as the texts dissolve into one another and we become aware that we use the same means of making sense of our world as our 'subjects' use in making sense of their world, and in both our making sense of their world, and our making sense of their sense making (Burrell, 1996, in Rhodes, 2000, p. 17).

The approach proposed by Cherryholmes and Rhodes challenges epistemological foundationalism which rests on the premise that a final truth can be determined,

> but at the same time recognises that we must still choose strategies for understanding the world without the possibility of final knowledge of whether we are right or not. (Cherryholmes (1993)

In this regard, the emancipatory approach to evaluation research has the potential to channel respondents towards gaining self-understanding through their active participation in the evaluation act. However, an emancipatory intent is no guarantee of an emancipatory outcome (Lather, 1991). Too often, Lather suggests, researchers who conduct empirical research in the name of emancipatory politics fail to connect their doing of research with their political commitments (ibid.). If the underlying outcome of evaluation research is to encourage self and social understandings and to promote change enhancing action, then our research designs need to resonate with our espoused missions. To what extent has my emancipatory intent yielded my espoused outcomes?

It would be naïve to ascribe any definitive causal effects of the research experience for the organisation or its members, and the question of emancipatory outcome is perhaps best left to the individual participants in the study – who have declared in our many conversations that they have benefited significantly from the experience of narrating themselves. However, this self declaration is not a self evident indicator of outcome. The two questions that remain are whether the illuminating experience at the individual level has set the stage for liberation at the institutional level and, secondly, whether Fetterman's (1999, p. 16) suggestion that empowerment evaluation can "unleash powerful forces for self-determination" has been enacted or realised in any significant way.

With regard to the impact of the exercise at the individual level, Rene, the chair of the Board, announced that she would relinquish her position at the next board meeting because her continued dual roles within the organisation was no longer tenable. Shortly after the strategic planning meeting, Tracy the programme manager resigned from the NGO, citing irreconcilable differences between her developmental goals and those of the organisation. An immediate consequence of the evaluation at the organisational level was ELET's resolve to change its name, a symbolic precursor of other changes that were to follow, as the organisation reconfigured its identity. Among the many changes proposed, was that the newly conceptualised organisation would devote greater attention to establishing a stronger public profile by establishing a marketing and public relations wing. Additionally, it would infuse a mandatory research component in all future projects. It also proposed an organisational ethic that was more responsive to the dynamic environmental realities in which it operated, such as the opportunities and challenges of working in an environment plagued by the HIV and AIDS pandemic.

However, ascribing unqualified optimism for the above developments is a giant leap of faith in the value of strategy, since strategy is a social and, in particular, a linguistic construction, a particular kind of rhetoric that provides a

> common language used by people at all levels of an organisation in order to determine, justify, and give meaning to the constant stream of actions that the organisation comprise (Hardy, Palmer, & Phillips, 2000, p. 3).

Ultimately, the real test of performativity will be how effectively ELET's strategic discourse can galvanise the organisation into tangibly furthering the mission for which it was conceived, a necessary task of subsequent evaluations.

Thus far, I have chosen to approach the issue of organisational studies obliquely, by problematising conventional evaluation research, arguing that it is in itself inadequate for substantive institutional analysis. As signalled earlier, an organisational ethnography is riddled with epistemological, representational and ethical hazards, one of which relates to the perennial conundrum around validity and subjectivity and related ethical dilemmas. In the rest of this chapter, I reflect on some of the inherent hazards of using an institutional biography and how this might undermine its potential to count as an authentic alternative mode to traditional evaluations.

DISENTANGLING THE METHODOLOGICAL CONUNDRUM

One of ways to resolve debates around validity and subjectivity is the four-point criterion proposed by Egon, Lincoln and Guba (1985), in which they suggest that credibility should replace truth and the technique for establishing this should be "member checks"[6]. Transferability should replace applicability; dependability should replace consistency and auditing, a means of methodological reflexivity, should replace neutrality. Acknowledging that research accounts

> do no more than represent a sophisticated but temporary consensus of views about what is to be considered true (Seale, 1999, p. 3).

Egon, Guba and Lincoln (1985) offer a fifth criterion: "authenticity", demonstrated by the ability of researchers to show that they have represented a range of different realities. They propose a more sophisticated understanding of the phenomenon being studied (ontological authenticity); evidence of admitting multiple perspectives (educative authenticity); demonstration of some form of resultant action (catalytic authenticity) and some evidence of empowerment of participants (tactical authenticity).

In my attempt at infusing "authenticity" and representing a range of different realities in the ELET study, I made extensive use of member checks in the process of data production. This approach yielded some unanticipated consequences, raising doubts about my relative "power" as researcher and what degree of latitude I possessed in theorising the lives of participants. The dilemma arose when I asked one of the research participants, Rene, to peruse a paper I had written which had been accepted for publication by an accredited journal of education. The paper explored the relationship between the NGO sector, the corporate sector and the state. Based on selected vignettes from interviews, the paper proposed a theory of isomorphism[7] to exemplify the relationship between the triad, arguing that Rene in her dual roles of chair of the ELET board and as development consultant to the core funder was the source of isomorphic pressures that had a significant impact on the organisation's changing identity. As part of the member checking exercise, I requested Rene's response to the paper, advising that I had edited out all references to her identity in order to protect her professional interests. Further, I indicated that I would be happy to edit any part of the paper she found unacceptable. I did this out of my conviction that the integrity of the research process should take precedence over my academic interests, and that I had an obligation to represent my research subjects as authentically and accurately as possible.

However, I had not bargained for the response I received: Rene suggested that my analysis was inaccurate and flawed. She objected to being cited as the source of isomorphic pressures that shaped the strategic direction of ELET. In response to her protests, I edited the paper further, and in the process, eliminated what I thought were crucial analytical insights, which in my view, diluted its theoretical rigour. In the interests of preserving the congenial relationship I had established with her, I desisted from challenging her further, compromising academic interests. While I rationalised my reticence then as a necessary precondition for, and one of the methodological hazards in narrative research, I now have to accept responsibility for the burden of partial and fractional authorship.

This prompts a range of questions around ethics and representation:
- In researching organisations that have a public profile, should research participants have control over a researcher's access to information about their lives and practices, and should they determine the conditions governing the release of this information for academic purposes?
- Do practitioners and administrators with a public profile have an inalienable right to ownership of "facts" about their lives?
- As a counterpoint, do researchers, by virtue of the "intrinsic" value of what they do, have a right to know about the lives of their participants?
- And, do practitioners, by virtue of this intrinsic value of the research act, have an obligation to disclosure?

I am fully cognisant of the position that, on one hand, the right to know the "truth" and to proclaim it in the public domain seems quite defensible if there is a clear association between the right and the pursuit of disinterested enquiry. I am also mindful, on the other hand, that such a connection cannot always be assumed to exist independently of the agendas, interests, prejudices, and even political ends that researchers might possess. For this reason, a framework of broad principles, that balances rights and obligations, needs to be negotiated. This ethical obligation is particularly important in developing-world contexts where ethics is an integral component in consolidating democracies, defining national identities and reclaiming lost cultures. In this regard, the ethical framework would also need to clarify the kinds of knowledge the researcher seeks and to make available the data and research papers to the research participant. Should there be any dissonance between the researcher and researched, the researched should (wherever possible) enjoy a right to a published rejoinder while issues of trust and confidentiality should take precedence over all other concerns. These mechanisms are supplementary to the rights of research participants which are already guaranteed under the principles of "informed consent" and further enshrined in the constitution and common law, which in the South African context is considered to be among the most sophisticated statutes in the world.

But what of the rights of the researcher? Are the rights accorded to research subjects disproportionate to those accorded to the researcher, constraining her analytical voice at the risk of diluting it, muting it, or at worst, repressing it?

Contemporary literature on the power relations between the researcher and research subjects/participants seems to be premised on a notion that researchers are intrinsically dishonest and patently unscrupulous, and that research subjects are helpless, vulnerable victims of predatory researchers. That these are indeed the tendencies of some researchers is undeniable. But what are the implications for academic freedom of researchers who do subscribe to ethical practices? Denying researchers **their** ethical rights induces a sense of pseudo-democracy where an inordinate proportion of rights are guaranteed for research subjects, and too few are allowed for researchers. Such ethical concerns are quite independent from methodological ones, and must not be confused with considerations in which ethics are inextricably bound up with methodology:

> It is one thing to negotiate what the publicly accessible facts of a social situation are, and quite another to negotiate whether or not they ought to remain hidden (Elliot,1993 p. 24).

This confusion in the minds of many researchers has resulted in the sacrifice of the ethics of truth for the ethics of release.

CONCLUDING COMMENTS

This chapter has pursued two reciprocal outcomes. First, it attempted method-ological elaboration. In advocating transdisciplinary research, it borrowed from the established traditions of empowerment and illuminative evaluation, appropriating their key tenets in informing an organisational ethnography. In the process of constructing organisational narratives, the approach provided opportunities for members to engage in self-reflexive interrogation of their praxis. Second, it attempted theoretical elaboration. It challenged classical organisational theory as inadequate in understanding the organisational culture of an NGO. As an alternative empirical lens, it proposed a post-structuralist mode of discourse analysis as complementary to classical management approaches in organisational analysis.

The narrative approach to understanding a non governmental organisation did yield rich insights and was able to excavate data not easily accessible to empiricist methods alone. The use of discourse analysis to make sense of the multiple worldviews that constituted the organisation proved equally useful in theorising organisational behaviour. Two notable threads stand out in the analysis. First, the morality discourse held by development professionals are rendered profane as the neo-liberal corporate narratives constitute the new discursive cultural field (Bourdieu, 1990), in which the neo-liberal speak is authorised and legitimised. Second, although corporate discourses appear immutable, the scope for agency does exist. However, the scope for agency is now defined by and mediated through the corporatist discourse where the exercise of power takes place within the new defining parameters that legitimate or silence voices.

In so far as having achieved its espoused emancipatory intent, it would be premature to make any definitive judgements at the organisational level. Such judgements are more likely to emerge from subsequent longitudinal assessments.

At the individual level, it does seem as though an organisational ethnography is undermined by the very element that is intended to ensure its legitimacy – member checking. Perhaps this is relates more to particular conceptions of the practice of member checking rather than the integrity of the practice itself. Egon, Guba and Lincoln (1985) present member checks as a means of verifying the accuracy of the data, to correct, or to amend it. I concur with Elizabeth St Pierre (1999) that this conception reflects a misplaced realist notion of member checking, one which suggests that there **is** some unequivocal interpretation the researcher is obliged to ferret out and, further, that participants have an incontrovertible capacity to certify it as true and correct – rather than use member checks as an attempt to expand existing data to enrich it.

Notwithstanding this epistemological blindspot, if we think of ethnography as both a site of failure and a site of reinscription, then different kinds of ethnography can be envisioned (St Pierre, 1999). This ontology of becoming is enriched by transdisciplinary approaches, as a way of crossing paradigmatic borders, not merely as an academic indulgence, but to bring together different disciplines and theoretical–analytical frameworks into dialogue with each other in the hope of producing richer insights into epistemology and ideology. However, as researchers, we need an acute awareness of our inherent vulnerability and fallibility, and that of the tools with which we undertake our intellectual labour.

NOTES

[1]   The notion of lay ontologies is derived from Henri Bergson's (1983) "ontology of creative evolution". According to the concept of creative dialectical evolution, the development of an organisation is grounded in organisational capabilities, which originate in the following lay ontology of its members:
(1) They have the intuition of duration, seeing time as a continuous flow that allows the preservation of the past and creation in the present.
(2) A holistic conception of space, its unity and its multiplicity.
(3) A historical and prospective view of being, as a 'being made'.
(4) The intuition of deterministic influences from the past and from the system in which beings evolve, the virtues of intents, the limits of planning and the driving force of their vital impetus, imagination and will.
(5) The intuition and the respect of individuality (their own individuality, the individuality of their group, their organisation) and integration with others, as necessary to creation and progress.
(6) The intuition of a hyperdialectical movement driving development.

[2]   Assumptions about the ontological nature of phenomena have to do with the essential character of the phenomena under investigation; in particular whether such phenomena have an independent existence, or whether they are simply constructions of our minds. It asks whether objects exist independently of our perception of them. Most organisational theorists, particularly those from the structuralist- functionalist school argue that it does, but a growing number of organisational theorists contest this naive realist position.

[3]   Lather's notion of postpositivism embraces the whole range of philosophical and methodological movements since positivism, including poststructuralism and postmodernism.

[4]   Empowerment Evaluation (EE) as an approach has been institutionalized within the American Evaluation Association since its introduction in 1993 and is consistent with the standards for Educational Evaluation (see also, Reflections on Empowerment Evaluation by David M. Fetterman, 1999 for an appraisal of EE).

5   PHASE an acronym for ELET's Project for Health and Sanitation Education: A literacy programme based on the participatory action framework to address water and sanitation problems in rural areas.
6   Lincoln and Guba (1985, p. 236) suggest the use of member checks to obtain "information that the report has constructed by the informants, or to correct and extend it". However, Seale (1993, p.274) argues that this description of member checking reflects the realist notion that there is some true interpretation the researcher is obliged to ferret out and which the participants are able to certify as correct. He believes that member checking is more about collecting additional data than about verifying the truth.
7   see Dhunpath, R. (2003). *The corporatisation and professionalisation of NGOs in South Africa.*

REFERENCES

Ackroyd, S. (1994). Recreating common ground: Elements of post-paradigmatic organisation studies. In J. Hassard & M. Parker (Eds.), *Towards a new theory of organisations.* New York: Routledge.

Bergson, H. (1983). *Creative evolution.* University Press of America.

Bhaktin, M. M. (1981). *The dialogic imagination.* Austin, TX: University of Texas.

Blumenthal, D. (1999). Representing the divided self. *Qualitative Enquiry, 5*(3), 377–392.

Bourdieu, P. (1990). *The logic of practice.* Cambridge: Polity Press.

Calori, R. (2002). Organisational development, and the ontology of creative dialectical evolution. *Organisation, 9*(1), 127–150.

Cortazzi, M. (1993) *Narrative Analysis.* London: The Falmer Press.

Cherryholmes, C. (1993). Reading research. *Journal of Curriculum Studies, 25*(1), 1–32.

Chia, R. (2000). Discourse analysis as organisational analysis. *Organisation, 7*(3), 513–518.

Cohen L., & Musson, G. (2000). Entrepreneurial identities: Reflections from two case studies. *Organisation, 7*(1), 31–48.

Eade, D., Hewitt, T., & Johnson, H. (2002). Development and management: Experiences in value based conflict. *Development in Practice.* Retrieved from http://www.developmentinpractice.org/abstracts/abstracts.htm

Egon G., Guba, E.G. & Lincoln, Y.S. (1985). *Naturalistic enquiry.* USA: Sage Publications.

Elliot, J. (1993) *Reconstructing Teacher Education.* London: The Falmer Press.

Fairclough, N. (1992). *Discourse and social change.* Oxford: Blackwell.

Fetterman, D. M. (1999). Reflections on empowerment evaluation: Learning from experience. *Canadian Journal of Programme Evaluation, Special Issue*, 5–37.

Freire, P. (1972). *Pedagogy of the oppressed.* Penguin Books.

Giroux, H. (2004). The terror of neoliberalism: Rethinking the significance of cultural politics. *College Literature, 32*(1) [Winter 2005].

Gough, N. (2001). *Occasional paper series.* University of KwaZulu-Natal, South Africa.

Hardy, C., Palmer, I., & Phillips, N. (2000) Discourse as a strategic resource. *Human Relations, Organisation, 53*(9), 1227–1248. 013430, London, Thousand Oaks, CA, New Delhi: SAGE Publications.

Hassard, J., & Parker, M. (Eds.). (1994). *Towards a new theory of organisations.* New York: Routledge.

Hassard, J., & Parker, M. (Eds.). (1993). *Postmodernism and organisations.* New Delhi: Sage.

Jansen, J. D. (1996). *Does teacher development work? True confessions of a hardened evaluator.* Paper presented at the University of KwaZulu-Natal (UDW) Research Seminar Series, UDW, South Africa.

Lather, P. (1991). *Getting smart: Feminist research and pedagogy with/in the postmodern.* New York: Routledge.

Lather, P. (2001). *The possibilities for paradigm proliferation.* Doctoral Seminar Series, University of KwaZulu-Natal, South Africa, November 2001.

Muchinsky, P. M. (2000). Emotions in the workplace: The neglect of organisational behaviour. *Journal of Organisational Behaviour, 21*, 801–805.

Oliver, C. (1991). Strategic responses to institutional processes. *Academy of Management Review*, *16*(1), 145–179.

Parlett, M., & Hamilton, D. (1976). Evaluation as illumination. In *Curriculum evaluation today*. London: McMillan.

Powell, M., & Seddon, D. (1997, March). NGOs & the Development Industry. *Review of African Political Economy*, *24*(71), 3–10.

Rhodes, C. (2000). Reading and writing organisational lives. *Organisation*, *7*(1), 7–29.

Rustin, M. (1999). *From individual life histories to sociological understanding: A preliminary report from the SOSTRIS Research Project*. UK: University of East London.

Seale, C. (1999). Quality in qualitative research. *Qualitative Enquiry*, *5*(4), 465–478.

St Pierre, E.A. (1999). The work of response in ethnography. *Journal of Contemporary Ethnography*, *28*(3), 266–287.

Stern, R. N., & Barley, R. S. (1996). Organisations and social systems: Organisation theory's neglected mandate. *Administrative Science Quarterly*, *41*(1), 146–162.

Tsoukas, H. (2000). False dilemmas in organisation theory: Realism or social constructivism? *ALBA*, *7*(3), 531–535.

Tsoukas, H., & Cummings, S. (1997). Marginalization and recovery: The emergence of Aristotelian themes in organization studies. *Organization Studies*, *18*(4), 655.

PART FOUR: A SELECTED BIBLIOGRAPHY OF LIFE HISTORY RESEARCH

THENGANI NGWENYA, MICHAEL SAMUEL AND RUBBY
DHUNPATH

A SELECTED BIBLIOGRAPHY OF LIFE HISTORY RESEARCH

This bibliography does not intend to be exhaustive of the literature available related to life history research. Instead, it represents the kinds of texts and references that informed the development of the authors thinking and writing about the fields they have engaged with during the production of their research. In sharing this literature, we have grouped the references into appropriate clusters to guide the reading in semantic units, to facilitate dialogues across different texts in this emerging field of research.

GENERAL THEORY: AUTO/BIOGRAPHY AND LIFE HISTORIES

Archer, M. S. (2000). *Being human: The problem of agency*. Cambridge: Cambridge University Press.

Atkinson, R. N. (1998). *The life story interview*. Thousand Oaks, CA: Sage.

Baron, S. H., & Plestch, C. (1985). *Introspection in biography: The biographer's quest for self-awareness*. Analytic Press.

Batchelor, J. (Ed.). (1995). *The art of literary biography*. Oxford: Clarendon Press.

Bateson, M. C. (1989). *Composing a life*. New York: The Atlantic Monthly Press.

Bertaux, D. (Ed.). (1981). *Biography and society: The life history approach in the social sciences*. Beverly Hills, CA: Sage Publications.

Bertaux, D., & Kohli, M. (1984). The life history approach: A continental view. *Annual Review of Sociology, 10*, 215–237.

Bogdan, R., & Taylor, S. (1975). *Introduction to qualitative research methods: A phenomenological approach to the social sciences*. New York: John Wiley.

Bruner, J., & Weisser, S. (1991). The invention of the self: Autobiography and its forms. In D. R. Olson & N. Toirance (Eds.), *Literacy and orality*. Cambridge: Cambridge University Press.

*R. Dhunpath and M. Samuel (eds.), Life History Research: Epistemology, Methodology
and Representation, 201–227*

Bruner, J. (1987). Life as narrative. *Social research, 54*(1), 11–32.

Bruner, E. M. (Ed.). (1986). *Text, play, and story: The construction of self and reconstruction of self and society.* Washington, DC: American Ethnographical Society.

Buss, H. M. (1993). *Mapping ourselves.* Montreal: McGill-Queen's University Press.

Castells, M. (1997). *The power of identity.* Oxford: Blackwell.

Charme, S. L. (1984). *Meaning and myth in the study of lives: A sartean perspective.* Philadelphia: University of Pennsylvania Press.

Clifford, J. L. (1970). *From puzzles to portraits: Problems of a literary biographer.* Chapel Hill, NC: University of North Carolina Press.

Cortazzi, M. (1993). *Narrative analysis.* London: Falmer.

Denzin, N. K. (1989). *Interpretive biography.* Beverly Hills, CA: Sage.

Dolby-Stahl, S. K. (1985). A literary folkloristic methodology for the study of meaning in personal narrative. *Journal of Folklore Research, 22,* 45–70.

Edel, L. (1959). *Writing lives: Principia biographica.* New York: W.W. Norton.

Eakin, J. P. (1985). *Fictions in autobiography: Studies in the art of self-invention.* Princeton, NJ: Princeton Univ Press.

Eakin, J. P. (1992). *Touching the world: Reference in autobiography.* Princeton, NJ: Princeton University Press.

Egan, S. (1999). *Mirror talk: Genres of crisis in contemporary autobiography.* Chapel Hill, NC: University of North Carolina Press.

Ermath, M. (1975). *Wilhelm Dilthey: The critique of historical reason.* Chicago: University of Chicago Press.

Epstein, W. (Ed.). (1991). *Contesting the subject.* West Lafayette, IN: Purdue University Press.

Erikson, E. (1975). *Life history and the historical moment.* New York: Norton.

Friedson, A. M. (Ed.). (1981). *New directions in biography.* Biographical Research Centre, University of Hawaii Press.

Garfinkel, H.. (1984). *Studies in ethnomethodology.* Cambridge: Polity Press.

Garraty, J. (1957). *The nature of biography*. New York: Knopf.

Geiger, S. N. G. (1986). Women's life histories: Method and content. *Signs, 11*(2), 334–351.

Giddens, A. (1991). *Modernity and self-identity: Self and society in the late modern age*. Cambridge: Polity Press.

Giele, J. Z. (Ed.). (1998). *Methods of life course research: Qualitative and quantitative approaches*. Thousand Oaks, CA: Sage.

Glass, J. M. (1993). *Shattered selves: Multiple personality in a postmodern world*. Ithaca, NY: Cornell University Press.

Gottschalk, L., et al. (1945). *The use of personal documents in history, anthropology and sociology*. New York: Social Science Research Council.

Hatch, J. A., & Wisniewski, R. (Eds.). (1995). *Life history and narrative*. London: Falmer Press.

Honan, P. (1979). The theory of biography. *Novel, 13*(1), 109–120.

Kendall, P. (1965). *The art of biography*. New York: W.W. Norton.

Linde, C. (1993). *Life stories: The creation of coherence*. New York & Oxford: Oxford Univ Press.

Lyons, J. O. (1978). *The invention of the self*. Carbondale, IL: Southern Illinois University Press.

McCntrye, A. (1981). *After virtue*. London: Duckworth.

Mandelbaum, D. G. (1982). The study of life history. In R. G. Burgess (Ed.), *Field research: A sourcebook and field manual*. London: Allen and Unwin.

Mandell, G. P. (Ed.). (1991). *Life into art*. Fayetteville, AR: University of Arkansas Press.

Mann, S. J. (1992). Telling a life story: Issues for research. *Management, Education and Development, 23*(3), 171–280.

Neisser, U., & Fivush, R. (Eds.). (1994). *The remembering self: Construction and accuracy in the self-narrative*. Cambridge: Cambridge University Press.
Oats, S. B. (Ed.). (1986). *Biography as high adventure*. Amherst, MA: University of Massachusetts Press.

Patcher, M. (Ed.). (1979). *Telling lives: The biographer's art.* Washington, DC: New Republic Books.

Personal Narratives Group. (Eds.). (1989). *Interpreting women's lives: Feminist theory and personal narratives.* Bloomington, IN: Indiana University Press.

Polkinghorne, D. E. (1988). *Narrative knowing and the human sciences.* Albany, NY: State University of New York Press.

Plummer, K. (1983). *Documents of life: An introduction to the problems and literature of a humanistic method.* London: George, Allen and Unwin.

Rabinow, P., & Sullivan, W. M. (Eds.). (1979). *Interpretive social science: A reader.* Berkeley, CA: University of Carlifornia Press.

Reissman, K. (1993). *Narrative analysis.* Chichester: Sage.

Rubin, D. (Ed.). (1986). *Autobiographical memory.* Cambridge: Cambridge University Press.

Taylor, C. (1989). *Sources of the self: The making of the modern identity.* Cambridge, MA: Cambridge University Press.

Taylor, C. (1985). *Human agency and language: Philosophical papers I.* Cambridge: Cambridge University Press.

Veniga, J. F. (Ed.). (1983). *The biographer's gift: Life histories and humanism.* College Station, TX: Texas A and M University Press.

Winkler, K. J. (1985). Questioning the science in social science, scholars signal a "Turn to Interpretation." *The Chronicle of Higher Education, 30*(17), 5–6.

Young, R. M. (1987). Darwin and the genre of biography. In G. Levine (Ed.), *One culture.* Madison, WI: University of Winsconsin Press.

Young, R. M. (1988). Biography: The basic discipline for human science. *Free Associations, 11*, 108–130.

LIFE HISTORY IN EDUCATIONAL RESEARCH

Abbs, P. (1974). *Autobiography and education.* London: Heinemann.

Altrichter, H., Posch, P., & Somekh, B. (1993). *Teachers investigate their work: An introduction to the methods of action research.* London: Routledge.

Alvesson, M., & Skoldberg, K. (2000). *Reflexive methodology: New vistas for qualitative research*. London: Sage.

Atkinson, P., & Delamont, S. (1980). The two traditions of educational ethnography: Sociology and anthropology compared. *British Journal of Sociology of Education, 1*, 139–152.

Barasa, F. S., & Mattson, E. (1998). The roles, regulation and professional development of educators in South Africa: A critical analysis of four policy documents. *Journal of Education, 23*, 40–72.

Barone, T. E. (1997). Among the chosen: A collaborative educational (auto)biography. *Qualitative Inquiry, 2*(3), 222–236.

Beecham, R., & Clark, L. (2004). *Averting the professional gaze from science: 'Connecting with Care' as a model of educational development*. 26th World Congress of the International Association of Logopedics and Phoniatrics, Conference Proceedings, Sydney, August 29–2 September.

Beecham, R. (2000). God's child. *Teaching in Higher Education, 5*(1), 127–130.

Beecham, R., & Dunley, D. (2004). *Clients as teachers: Innovations within the speech therapy curriculum at Charles Sturt University*. SARRAH National Conference Proceedings, Alice Springs, August 26–28.

Bell, S. G., & Yalom, M. (1990). *Revealing lives: Autobiography, biography, and gender*. Albany, NY: State University of New York Press.

Bowe, R., Ball, S., & Gold, A. (1992). *Reforming education and changing schools: Case studies in policy sociology*. London and New York: Routledge.

Coffey, A. (1996). The power of accounts: Authority and authorship in ethnography. *Qualitative Studies in Education, 9*(1), 61–74.

Connelly, F. M., & Clandinin, D. J. (1990). Stories of experience and narrative inquiry. *Educational Researcher, 19*(5), 2–14.

Department of Health. (1999). *Summary report: 1998 National HIV sero-prevalence survey of women attending public antenatal clinics in South Africa*. Health Systems Research and Epidemiology.

Eisner, E. (1998). *The enlightened eye: Qualitative inquiry and the enhancement of education practice*. New Jersey, NJ: Prentice-Hall.

Elbaz-Luwisch, F. (2004). Immigrant teachers: Stories of self and place. *International Journal of Qualitative Studies in Education, 17*(3), 387–414.

Elbaz-Luwisch, F., Moen, T., Gudmundsdottir, S. (2002). The multivoicedness of classrooms: Bakhtin and narratives of teaching. In H. Heikekinen, R. Huttunen, & L. Syrjala (Eds.), *Biographical research and narrativity: Voices of teachers and philosophers*. University of Jyvaskyla: SoPhi Press.

Ellis, C. (2004). *The ethnographic I: A methodological novel about ethnography*. PLACE: Rowman & Littlefield Publishers Inc.

Ensor, P. (2000). *How do we grasp mathematics teacher educators' and teachers' tacit knowledge, in research design and curriculum practice?* In SAARMSTE Conference Proceedings, Port Elizabeth, January.

Eraut, M. (1996). *Professional knowledge in teacher education.* Paper presented at Finnish conference of Teacher Education, Salonlinna, 26 June.

Erben, M. (Ed.). (1998). *Biography and education: A reader*. London: Falmer Press.

Erben, M. (1996). The purposes and processes of the biographical method. In D. Scott & R. Usher (Eds.), *Understanding Educational Research.*

Flinders, D., & Mills, G. (Eds.). (1993). *Theory and concepts in qualitative research: Perspectives from the field*. New York: Teachers College Press.

Freire, P. (1972). *Pedagogy of the oppressed*. London: Penguin Books.

Fullan, M. (2003). *Change forces with a vengeance*. London: Routledge Falmer.

Gitlin, A. (1990). Understanding teaching dialogically. *Teachers College Record, 91*(4), 537.

Goodson, I. F. (Ed.). (1992). *Studying teachers' lives*. London: Routledge.

Goodson, I. F., & Walker, R. (1991). *Biography, identity and schooling*. London: Falmer Press.

Goodson, I. F. (1992). Studying teachers' lives: An emergent field of inquiry. In I. F. Goodson (Ed.), *Studying teachers' lives*. London: Routledge.

Grumet, M. (1990). Retrospective: Autobiography and the analysis of educational experience. *Cambridge Journal of Education, 20*(3), 277–282.

Hargreaves, A. (1994). *Changing teachers, changing times: Teachers' work and culture in the postmodern age*. London: Cassell.

Harris, B., & Furlong, L. D. (1997). *Using autobiography to teach teachers: A resource for teacher educators*. Paper presented at American Educational Research Association (AERA) annual meeting, Chicago, Illinois, 28 March.

Hatch, J., & Wisniewski, R. (Eds.). (1995). *Life history and narrative*. London: Falmer.

Huberman, M. (1993). *The lives of teachers*. London: Cassell.

Jalongo, M. R., & Isenberg, J. P. (1995). *Teacher's stories: From personal narrative to professional insight*. San Francisco: Jossey- Bass Publishers.

Jansen, J. D. (1996). *Does teacher development work? True confessions of a hardened evaluator*. Paper presented at the University of KwaZulu-Natal (UDW) Research Seminar Series, UDW, South Africa.

Kamler, B. (2000). *Critical discourse in educational inquiry*. Material prepared for a Masters module, Deakin University, Australia.

Kridel, C. (Ed.). (1998). *Writing educational biography: Explorations in educational research*. New York and London: Garland Publishing.

Melnick, C. (1997). *Autobiography: Discovering self in a teacher education program*. Paper presented at American Educational Research Association (AERA) Annual Meeting, Chicago, Illinois, 28 March.

Mpumlwana, N., & Beecham, R. (2000). The monster of professional power. *Teaching in Higher Education, 5*(4), 535–540.

Pinar, W. F. (1980). Life history and educational experience. *The Journal of Curriculum Theorizing, 2*, 159–212.

Pinar, W. F. (1981). Life history and educational experience, Part Two. *The Journal of Curriculum Theorizing, 3*, 259–286.

SADTU National Education Policy Conference. (2001, April 17–21). *Education transformation: From policy to practice*. Resource documents: A decade of struggle for quality public education and job security. Gallagher Estate, Midrand, Gauteng.

Samuel, M. (1999). Exploring voice in educational research. *Perspectives in Education, 18*(2).

Schon, D. (1987). *Educating the reflective practitioner.* San Franscisco: Jossey Bass.

Schubert, W., & Ayers, W. (Eds.). (1992). *Teachers lore: Learning from our own experience.* New York: Longman.

Sherman, R., & Rodman, B. W. (Eds.). (2005). *Qualitative research in education: Focus on methods.* London, New York & Philadelphia: The Falmer Press.

Smith, L. G., & Smith, J. K. (1994). *Lives in education.* New York: St. Martin's Press.

Sparkes, A. (1994). Self, silence and invisibility as a beginning teacher: A life history of lesbian experience. *British Journal of Sociology of Education, 15*(1), 93–118.

Tatto, M. T. (1999). *Education for the rural poor in the context of educational reform: The case of Mexico.* Paper delivered at The Oxford International Conference for Education and Development, 9–13 September 1999; Oxford University, United Kingdom.

Van Manen, M. (1994). Pedagogy, virtue, and narrative identity in teaching. *Curriculum Inquiry, 24*(2), 135–170.

Volmink, J. (1998). Who shapes the discourse on science and technology education? In P. Naidoo & M. Savage (Eds.), *African science and technology education into the new millenium: Practice, policy and priorities.* Kenwyn: Juta & Co. Ltd.

Winter, R. (1989). *Learning from experience.* London: Falmer Press.

ANTHROPOLOGY AND LIFE HISTORY RESEARCH

Agar, M.. H. (1980). Stories, background knowledge, and themes: Problems in the analysis of life history narrative. *American Ethnologist, 7,* 223–239.

Angrosino, M. V. (1976). The use of autobiography as life history. *Ethos, 4*(1), 133–154.

Atkinson, P. (2000). *Handbook of ethnography.* London, Thousand Oaks and New Delhi: Sage Publications.

Atkinson, P. (1990). *The ethnographic imagination: Textual constructions of reality.* London: Routledge.

Atkinson, R. (1998). *The life story interview.* Thousand Oaks, CA: Sage.

Benson, P. (Ed.). (1993). *Anthropology and literature*. Chicago: University of Illinois Press.

Caplan, P. (1988). Engendering knowledge: The politics of ethnography. *Anthropology Today*, *4*, 8–12; *5*, 14–17.

Dollard, J. (1935). *Criteria for the life history*. New York: Peter Smith.

Frank, G. (1979). Finding the common denominator: A phenomenological critique of life history method. *Ethos*, *7*, 68–94.

Goldmann, A. E. (1993). Is that what she said? The politics of collaborative autobiography. *Cultural Critique*, *23*, 177–204.

Harris, G. G. (1989). Concepts of individual, self, and person in description and analysis. *American Anthropologist*, *91*(3), 599–612.

Hoffman, E. (1989). *Lost in translation: A life in a new language*. London: Heinemann.

Josselon, R., et al. (Eds.). (1993). *The narrative study of lives*. London: Sage.

Langness, L. L. (1965). *The life history in anthropological science*. New York: Holt, Rinehart and Winston.

Langness, L. L., & Frank, G. (1981). *Lives: An anthropological approach to biography*. Monato, CA: Chandler and Sharp.

Chambon, A. S. (1995). Life history as dialogical activity: If you ask me the right questions, I could tell you. *Current Sociology*, *43*(2/3), 125–135.

Clifford, J. (1988). *Predicament of culture: Twentieth-century ethnography, literature and art*. Cambridge, MA and London: Harvard University Press.

Clifford, J., & Marcus, G. E. (Eds.). (1986). *Writing culture: The poetics and politics of ethnography*. Berkeley, CA, Los Angeles and London: University of California Press.
Crapanzano, V. (1984). Life histories. *American Anthropologist*, *86*, 953–959.

Crapanzano, V. (1977). The writing of ethnography. *Dialectical anthropology*, *2*(1), 69–73.

Crapanzano, V. (1977). The life history in anthropological fieldwork. *Anthropology and Humanism Quarterly*, *2&3*, 3–7.

Little, K. (1980). Explanation and individual lives: A reconsideration of life writing in anthropology. *Dialectical Anthropology, 5*, 215–226.

Mandelbaum, D. (1973). The study of life history: Ghandi. *Current Anthropology, 14*(3).

Marcus, G., & Cushman, D. (1982). Ethnographies as texts. *Annual Review of Anthropology, 11*, 25–69.

Rabinow, P. (1977). *Reflections on fieldwork in Morocco.* Berkeley, CA: University of California Press.

Radin, P. (1933). *Method and theory of ethnology: An essay in criticism.* New York: McGraw Hill.

Stahl, S. (1977). The personal narrative as folkore. *Journal of the Folklore Institute, 14*, 9–30.

Thornton, R. (1983). Narrative ethnography in Africa, 1850–1920. *Man, 18*, 502–520.

Titon, J. T. (1980). The life story. *Journal of American Folklore, 93*, 276–292.

Turner, V. W., & Bruner, E. (Eds.). (1986). *The anthropology of experience.* Urbana, IL: University of Illinois Press.

Vidich, A. J., & Lyman, S. M. (1998). Qualitative methods: Their history in sociology and anthropology. In N. K. Denzin & Y. S. Lincoln (Eds.), *The landscape of qualitative research: Theories and issues.* Thousand Oaks, CA: Sage.

Watson, L. C., & Watson-Franke, M. B. (1985). *Interpreting life histories.* New Brunswick, NJ: Rutgers University Press.

Watson, L. C. (1976). Understanding life history as a subjective document: Hermeneutical and phenomenological perspectives. *Ethos, 4*, 95–131.

Watson, L. C. (1978). The study of personality and the study of individuals: Two approaches, two types of explanation. *Ethos, 6*, 3–21.
Watson, L. C. (1983). Second thoughts on Oscar Lewis's family autobiography. *Anthropology and Humanism Quarterly, 8*(1), 2–7.

White, R. W. (1973). *Lives in progress* (3rd ed.). New York: Holt, Rheinhart and Winston.

Zimmerman, A. (2001). Looking beyond history: The optics of German anthropology and the critique of humanism. *Studies in History and Philosophy of Biological and Biomedical Sciences, 32*(3), 385–411.

SOCIOLOGY AND LIFE HISTORY RESEARCH

Ackroyd, S. (1994). Recreating common ground: Elements of post-paradigmatic organisation studies. In J. Hassard & M. Parker (Eds.), *Towards a new theory of organisations.* New York: Routledge.

Bennell, P., Hyde, K., & Swainson, N. (2002). *The impact of the HIV and AIDS epidemic on the education sector in Sub-Saharan Africa.* Centre for International Education, University of Sussex, Institute of Education, UK.

Bergson, H. (1983). *Creative evolution.* University Press of America.

Bourdieu, P. (1990). *The logic of practice.* Cambridge: Polity Press.

Bourdieu, P. (Ed.). (1999). *The weight of the world. Social suffering in contemporary society.* London: Polity Press.

Calori, R. (2002). Organisational development, and the ontology of creative dialectical evolution. *Organisation, 9*(1), 127–150.

Cawthra, H. C., Helman-Smith, A., & Moloi, D. (2001). Development update. Annual review: The voluntary sector and development in South Africa 1999/2000. *Quarterly Journal of the South African National NGO Coalition and INTERFUND, 3*(3).

Chomsky, N. (2003). *Hegemony or survival.* New York: Metropolitan Books.

Cohen, L., & Musson, G. (2000). Entrepreneurial identities: Reflections from two case studies. *Organisation, 7*(1), 31–48.

Denzin, N. K. (1989). *The research act: A theoretical introduction to sociological methods* (3rd ed.). New Jersey, NJ: Prentice Hall.

Denzin, N. (1989). *Interpretive biography.* Thousand Oaks, CA: Sage Publications.

Denzin, N. K., & Lincoln, Y. S. (Eds.). (1994). *Handbook of qualitative research.* Thousand Oaks, CA: Sage Publications.

Eade, D., Hewitt, T., & Johnson, H. (2002). *Development and management: Experiences in value based conflict. Development in practice.* Retrieved from http://www.developmentinpractice.org/abstracts/abstracts.htm

Fairclough, N. (1992). *Discourse and social change*. Oxford: Blackwell.

Faraday, A., & Plummer, K. (1979). Doing life stories. *The Sociological Review*, *27*(4).

Fetterman, D. M. (1999). Reflections on empowerment evaluation: Learning from experience. *Canadian Journal of Programme Evaluation, Special Issue*, 5–37.

Giroux, H. (2004). The terror of neoliberalism: Rethinking the significance of cultural politics. *College Literature*, *32*(1). [Winter 2005]

Giroux, H. A. (1994). *Disturbing pleasures: Learning popular culture*. London: Routledge.

Goldthorpe, J. (1980). *Social mobility and class structure in modern Britain*. Oxford: Clarendon Press.

Grace, P. A., Hill, J. P., Johnson, W. C., & Lewis, B. J. (2004). In other words: Queer voices/dissident subjectivities impelling social change. *International Journal of Qualitative Studies in Education*, *17*(3), 301–324.

Habib, S. (2003). *Queering the middle east and the new Anti Semitism*. Retrieved December 18, 2003, from http://www.brunel.ac.uk/faculty/arts/EnterText/3_2_pdfs/habib.pdf

Hassard, J., & Parker, M. (Eds.). (1993). *Postmodernism and organisations*. New Delhi: Sage.

Hassard, J., & Parker, M. (Eds.). (1994). *Towards a new theory of organisations*. New York: Routledge.

hooks, b. (1989). *Talking back: Thinking feminist, thinking black*. London: Sheba Feminist Publishers.

Kelly, M. J. (2003). The HIV/AIDS context for the leadership response. In B. Otaala (Ed.), *Proceedings of a workshop on HIV/AIDS – Government leaders in Namibia responding to the HIV/AIDS epidemic*. Windhoek: University of Namibia Press.

Luria, A. R. (1976). *Cognitive development: Its cultural and social foundations*. Cambridge, MA: Harvard University Press.

Maclennan, B. (2000, March 19). Dissent over AIDS cause. *Sunday Tribune*, KwaZulu-Natal.

Mamaila, K., & Brand, R. (2000, September 15). State in a bid to quell AIDS row. *The Daily News*, KwaZulu-Natal.

Marx, K., & Engels, F. (1968). *The German ideology*. Chicago: University of Chicago Press.

Mills, C. W. (1959). *The sociological imagination*. New York: Oxford University Press.

Muchinsky, P. M. (2000). Emotions in the workplace: The neglect of organisational behaviour. *Journal of Organisational Behaviour, 21*, 801–805.

Oliver, C. (1991). Strategic responses to institutional processes. *Academy of Management Review, 16*(1), 145–179.

Oliver, M. (1992). Changing the social relations of research production. *Disability, Handicap & Society, 7*(2), 101114.

Parlett, M., & Hamilton, D. (1976). *Evaluation as illumination. Curriculum evaluation today*. London: McMillan.

Patai, D. (1988). *Brazilian women speak: Contemporary life stories*. New Brunswick, NJ: Rutgers University Press.

Ramose, M. (2002). *African philosophy through Ubuntu*. Harare: Mond Books.

Rustin, M. (1999). *From individual life histories to sociological understanding: A preliminary report from the SOSTRIS Research Project*. London: University of East.

Sen, A. (2001). *Development as freedom*. New York: Alfred A. Knopf.

Smith, A. (2001). *Trends in HIV and AIDS surveillance*. Paper presented at the National Teachers' Union Advocacy Conference, held at Durban College of Education, 21 June 2001.

Smyth, J., & Shacklock, G. (2004). Teachers doing their 'economic' work. In S. Ball (Ed.), *Sociology of education*. London and New York: Routledge Falmer.

Stern, R. N., & Barley, R. S. (1996). Organisations and social systems: Organisation theory's neglected mandate. *Administrative Science Quarterly, 41*(1), 146–162.

Thomas, E. A. (1978). Herbert Blummer's critique of *The Polish Peasant*: A postmortem of the life history approach in sociology. *Journal of the History of the Behavioral Sciences, 14*, 124–131.

Tsoukas, H. (2000). False dilemmas in organisation theory: Realism or social constructivism? *ALBA, 7*(3), 531–535.

Tsoukas, H., & Cummings, S. (1997). Marginalization and recovery: The emergence of Aristotelian themes in organization studies. *Organization Studies, 18*(4), 655.

PYSCHOLOGY AND LIFE HISTORY RESEARCH

Anderson, W. J. (1981). The methodology of psychological biography. *Journal of Interdisciplinary History, XI*(3), 455–475.

Bruner, J. (1987). *Actual minds, possible worlds.* Cambridge, MA: Harvard University Press.

De Wade, J. P., & Harre, R. (1979). Autobiography as a psychological method. In G. P. Ginsberg (Ed.), *Emerging strategies in psychological research.* Chichester: John Wiley.

Dilollo, A., Manning, W., & Neimeyer, R. (2002). A personal construct psychology view of relapse: Indications for a narrative component to stuttering treatment. *Journal of Fluency Disorders, 27*(1), 19–42.

Finkelstein, V. (2002). *A personal journey into disability politics.* Paper presented at Leeds University Centre for Disability Studies, Leeds, England.

Freeman, M. (1991). *Rewriting the self: History, memory, narrative.* London & New York: Routledge.

Gergen, K. J. (1991). *The saturated self: Dilemmas of identity in contemporary life.* New York: Basic Books.

Gesell, A. (1925). *The mental growth of the pre-school child: A psychological outline of normal development from birth to the sixth year, including a system of developmental diagnosis.* New York: Macmillan.

Kundera, M. (1978/1996). *The book of laughter and forgetting.* London: Faber & Faber.
Levinson, D. J., et al. (1978). *The seasons of a man's life.* New York: Alfred Knopf; London: Hans Zell Press.

Manganyi, N. C. (1991). Psychobiography and the truth of the subject. In *Treachery and innocence: Psychology and racial difference in South Africa.*

Maturana, H., & Varela, F. J. (1980). *Autopoiesis and cognition: The realization of the living.* Dordrecht/Boston: Reidel.

McAdams, D. P., & Ochberg, R. L. (Eds.). (1988). *Psychobiography and life narratives.* Durham, NC: Duke University Press.

McAdams, D. P. (1985). *Power, intimacy, and the life story: Personological inquiries into identity.* New York: The Guilford Press.

McAdams, D. P. (1993). *The stories we live by: Personal myths and the making of the self.* New York: William Morrow & Co.

Peta, B. (2005, March 11). The burning issue that needs to be addressed: Corruption. *The Independent*, UK.

Price-Williams, D. (1980). Toward the idea of cultural psychology: A superordinate theme for study. *Journal of Cross-Cultural Psychology*, 75–88.

Rabinm, A. I., et al. (Eds.). (1989). *Studying persons and lives.* New York: Springer.

Rainwater, J. (1989). *Self-therapy.* London: Crucible.

Runyan, W. M. (1982). *Life histories and psychobiography: Explorations in theory and method.* New York: Oxford University Press.

Salomon, G. (Ed.). (1993). *Distributed cognitions: Psychological and educational considerations.* Cambridge: Cambridge University Press.

Sarbin, T. R. (Ed.). (1986). *Narrative psychology: The storied nature of human conduct.* New York: Praeger Press.

Sedgewick, E. (1990). *The epistemology of the closet.* Berkeley, CA: University of California Press.

Sober, E., & Wilson, D. (1998). *Unto others: The evolution and psychology of unselfish ehaviour.* Cambridge, MA: Harvard University Press.

Steiner, C. M. (1974). *Scripts people live.* New York: Grove Press.
Tzu, S., (1998). *The art of war* (Y. Shibing, Trans.). Hertfordshire: Wordsworth Editions Limited.

Vygotsky, L. S. (1978). *Mind in society: The development of higher psychological processes.* Cambridge, MA: Harvard University Press.

Vygotsky, L. S. (1987). *Thinking and speech.* New York: Plenum.

HISTORY AND LIFE HISTORY RESEARCH

Alexander, A. (2001). The politics of identity in post-apartheid South Africa. In J. Muller (Ed.), *Challenges of globalisation: South African debates with Manuel Castells.*

Breisach, E. (1994). *Historiography: Ancient, medieval and modern.* Chicago: University of Chicago Press.

Finkelstein, V. (2002). *Whose history???* Keynote address, Disability History Week, Birmingham, England.

Goff, J. (1995). Writing historical biography today. *Current Sociology, 43*(2–3), 11–17.

Grele, R. (Ed.). (1975). *Envelopes of sound: Six practitioners discuss the method, theory and practice of oral history and oral testimony.* Chicago: Precedent Publishing.

Gupta, A. (1995). On the reliability of oral and traditional history. *American Ethnologist, 22*(2), 412–417.

Matthews, R. (1998, November). Flukes and flaws. *Prospect.*

McGill, A. (1989). Recounting the past: Description, explanation and narrative in historiography. *American Historical Review, 94*(3), 627–653.

Muller, J., Cloete, N., & Badat, S. (Eds.). (2001). *Challenges of globalisation: ... debates with Manuel Castells.* Pinelands, Cape Town: Maskew Miller Longman.

Starfield, J. (1988). Not quite history: The autobiographies of H. Selby Msimang and R. V. Selope Thema and the writing of South African history. *Social Dynamics, 14*(2), 16–35.

Thompson, P. (1978). *The voice of the past: Oral history.* Thousand Oaks, CA: Sage Publications.

Tonkin, E. (1992). *Narrating our past: The social construction of oral history.* Cambridge: Cambridge University Press.

Yow, V. R. (1994). *Recording oral history.* Thousand Oaks, CA: Sage Publications.

A SELECTION OF LIFE HISTORIES

Burgos-Debray. (1984) [1983]. *I, Rigoberta Menchu: An Indian woman in Guatemala*. London: Verso.

Caplan, P. (1997). *African voices, African lives: Personal narratives from a Swahili village*. London and New York: Routledge.

Crapanzano, V. (1980). *Tuhamini: A portrait of a Moroccan*. Chicago: Chicago University Press.

Lewis, O. (1961). *The children of Sanchez: Autobiography of a Mexican family*. New York: Random House.

Mandela, N. R. (1994). *Long walk to freedom: The autobiography of Nelson Mandela*. London: Abacus.

Shostak, M. (1983). *The life and words of a ! Kung woman*. Harmondsworth: Penguin.

White, W. F. (1994). *Participant observer: An autobiography*. New York: I LR.

REPRESENTATION AND LIFE HISTORIES

Culture Shock: Flashpoints. 'Vis…: Picasso's Les Demoiselles d'Avignon'. Retrieved January 2, 2003, from http://www.geocities.com/rr17bb/LesDemoi.html

Arnason, H. H. (1969). *A history of modern art: Painting. Sculpture. Architecture*. London: Thames and Hudson.

Arnason, H. H. (1988). *A history of modern art*. London: Thames and Hudson.

Bach, H., Kennedy, M., & Mickelson, J. R. (1997). *Bodies at work: Sensory knowing*. Paper presented at the annual meeting of the American Educational Research Association, Chicago.

Bakhtin, M. M. (1981). *The dialogical imagination*. Austin, TX: University of Texas Press.

Berger, J. (1986). *Ways of seeing*. London: Penguin.

Blumenthal, D. (1999). Representing the divided self. *Qualitative Enquiry, 5*(3), 377–392.

Branch, R. M. (2000). A taxonomy of visual literacy. *Advances in Reading/Language Research, 7*, 377–402.

Bruner, J. (1984). The opening up of anthropology. In E. M. Bruner (Ed.), *Text play and story: The construction and reconstruction of experience*. Urbana, IL: University of Illinois Press.

Cherryholmes, C. (1993). Reading research. *Journal of Curriculum Studies*, *25*(1), 1–32.

Cole, A. L., & Knowles, J. G. (2001). *Lives in context: The art of life history research*. Walnut Creek, CA: AltaMira Press, p. 262.

Day, E. (2002). September, Me, My*Self and I: Personal and professional re-constructions in ethnographic research. *Forum Qualitative Sozialforschung/Forum Qualitative Research* [On-Line Journal], *3*(3). Retrieved on June 18, 2004, from http://www.qualitative-research.net/fqs-eng.htm

Denzin, N. K. (2000). Aesthetics and the practices of qualitative inquiry. *Qualitative Inquiry*, *6*(2), 256–265.

Eisner, E. (1997, August–September). The promises and perils of alternative forms of data representation. *Educational Researcher*, pp. 4–9.

Eisner, E. W. (1998). *The enlightened eye: Qualitative enquiry and the enhancement of educational practice*. New Jersey, NJ: Prentice-Hall.

Fairclough, N. (1989). *Language and power*. London: Longman.

Freeman, M. P. (1993). *Rewriting the self: History, memory, narrative*. New York: Routledge; Cambridge: Cambridge University Press.

Geertz, C. (1983). Blurred genres: The refiguration of social thought. In C. Geertz (Ed.), *Local knowledge: Further essays in interpretive anthropology*. New York: Basic Books.

Gough, N. (1994). Plotting research: Educational inquiry's continuities with detective fiction. *Deakin Centre for Education and Change Working Paper 35*, pp. 1–35.

Gough, N. (2001). *Occasional paper series*. South Africa: University of KwaZulu-Natal.

Hanrahan, M. (2003). May, challenging the dualistic assumptions of academic writing: Representing Ph.D research as embodied practice. *Forum Qualitative Sozialforschung/Forum Qualitative Research* [On-Line Journal], *4*(2), Retrieved on June 18, 2004, from http://www.qualitative-research.net/fqs-texte/2-03/2-03hanrahan-e.htm

Heylighen, F. (2001). Memetics. In F. Heylighen, C. Joslyn, & V. Turchin (Eds.), *Principia Cybernetica Web*. Brussels: Principia Cybernetica. Retrieved April 10, 2002, from http://pespmc1.vub.ac.be/MEMES.html

Hooks, b. (1995). *Art on my mind: Visual politics*. New York: The New York Press.

Iser, W. (1974). *The implied reader*. Baltimore: John Hopkins University Press.

Kim, J. (undated). *From commodity production to sign production*. PhD candidate at The Annenberg School for Communication, University of Pennsylvania.

Krieger, S. (1991). *Social science and the self: Personal essays on an art form*. New Brunswick, NJ: Rutgers University Press.

Lawrence-Lightfoot, S., & Hoffman-Davis, J. (1997). *The art and science of portraiture*. San Francisco: Jossey-Bass.

Maranhao, T. (1991). Reflection, dialogue, and the subject. In F. Steier (Ed.), *Research and reflexivity*. London: Sage.

Morrison, T. (1970/1993). *The bluest eye*. New York: Plume.

Okri, B. (1998). *Infinite riches*. London: Phoenix.

Rhodes, C. (2000). Ghostwriting research: Positioning the researcher in the interview text. *Qualitative inquiry, 6*(4), 511–525.

Richardson, L. (1992). The consequences of poetic representation: Writing the other. Rewriting the self. In C. Ellis & M. G Flaherty (Eds.), *Investigating subjectivity. Research on lived experience*. London: Sage Publications.

Rubin, W. (1984). "Primitivism" in 20th century art: Affinity of the tribal and the modern. In H. H. A. Arnason (Eds.), *History of modern art* (1988). London: Thames & Hudson.

Shiffrin, D. (1996). Narrative as self-portrait: Sociolinguistic constructions of identity. *Language in Society, 25*(2), 167–203.

St Pierre, E. A. (1997). Methodology in the fold and the irruption of transgressive data. *Qualitative Studies in Education, 10*(2), 175–189.

St Pierre, E. A. (1999). The work of response in ethnography. *Journal of Contemporary Ethnography, 28*, 266–287.

Stankiewicz, M. A. (1996). Metaphor and meaning. *The Journal of the National Art Education Association, 49*(3), 4–5.

Stanley, L. (2001). *Mourning becomes ... the spaces between lives lived and lives written.* Texas Press. Retrieved January 29, 2002, from Liz.stanley@man.ac.uk

Van Maanen, J. (Ed.). (1995). *Representation in ethnography.* Thousand Oaks, CA: Routledge.

Widdowson. (1984). Reading and communcation. In J. C. Alderson & A. H.Urquhart (Eds.), *Reading in a foreign language.* New York: Longman.

NARRATIVE RESEARCH AND LIFE HISTORIES

Abma, T. A. (2002). Emerging narrative forms of knowledge representation in health sciences. Two texts in the postmodern context. *Qualitative Health Research, 12*(1), 5–27.

Bach, H. E. F. (1998). *A visual narrative concerning curriculum, girls, photography, etc.* Edmonton: Qual Institute Press.

Bakhtin, M. (1981). *The dialogical imagination.* Austin, TX: University of Texas Press.

Bakhtin, M. M. (1984). *Problems of Dostoyevsky's poetics.* Manchester: University Press.

Barone, T. E. (2001). Pragmatizing the imaginary: Using life narratives as fiction. *Annual meeting of the American Educational Research Association,* Sec 44.28: The Educated Imagination: Fiction and Knowledge.

Barthes, R. (1977). Introduction to the structural analysis of narratives. In R. Barthes (Eds.), *Images-music-text.* London: Macmillan.

Bloom, L. R., & Munro, P. (1995). Conflicts of selves: Nonunitary subjectivity in women administrators' life history narratives. In J. A. Hatch & R. Wisniewski (Eds.), *Life history and narrative.* London and Washington: The Falmer Press.

Blumfeld-Jones, D. (1995). Fidelity as a criterion for practising and evaluating narrative inquiry. In J. A. Hatch & R. Wisniewski (Eds.), *Life history and narrative.* London and Washington: The Falmer Press.

Chia, R. (2000). Discourse analysis as organizational analysis. *Organisation, 7*(3), 513–518.

Clandinin, D. J., & Connelly, F. M. (2000). *Narrative inquiry: Experience and story in qualitative research*. San Francisco: Jossey Bass.

Connelly, F. M., & Clandinin, D. J. (1990). Stories of experience and narrative inquiry. *Educational Researcher*, *19*(5), 2–14.

Fairclough, N., & Wodak, R. (1997). Critical discourse analysis. In T. A. van Dijk (Ed.), *Discourse as a social interaction*. London: Sage Publications.

Fairclough, N. (1989). *Language and power*. United Kingdom: Longman Group UK Limited.

Frank, A. W. (2000). The standpoint of storyteller. *Qualitative Health Researcher*, *10*(3), 354–365.

Frank, A. W. (2001). Can we research suffering. *Qualitative Health Research*, *11*(3), 353–362.

Goodson, I. F. (1995). The story so far: Personal knowledge and the political. In J. A. Hatch & R. Wisniewski (Eds.), *Life history and narrative*. London: Falmer Press.

Gough, N. (1994). Narration, reflection, diffraction: Aspects of fiction in educational inquiry. *Australian Educational Researcher*, *21*(3), 1–26.

Greenlagh, T., & Hurwitz, B. (1999). Narrative based medicine: Why study narrative? *British Medical Journal*, 318, 48–50.

Greenlagh, T. (1999). Narrative based medicine in an evidence based world. *British Medical Journal*, 318, 323–325.

Grumet, M. R. (1991). The politics of personal knowledge. In C. Witherell & N. Noddings (Eds.), *Stories, lives tell: narrative and dialogue in education*. New York: Teachers College Press.

Hatch, J. A., & Wisneiwski, R. (1995). *Life history and narrative*. London: The Falmer Press.

Janks, H. (1997). Critical discourse analysis as a research tool. *Discourse*, *18*(3), 329–342.

Josselson, R. (1995). Imagining the real: Empathy, narrative and the dialogic self. In R. Josselson (Ed.), *Interpreting experience. The narrative study of lives* (Vol. 3, pp. 27–44). Thousand Oaks, CA: Sage.

Kathard, H. (2001). Sharing stories: Life history narratives in stuttering research. *International Journal of Language and Communication Disorders*, *36*, Special Supplement, pp. 52–57.

McLaren, P. (1993). Border disputes: Multicultural narrative, identity formation, and critical pedagogy in postmodern America. In D. McLaughlin & W. G. Tierney (Eds.). *Naming silenced lives: Personal narratives and the process of educational change*. New York: Routledge.

Mishler, E. G. (1999). *Storylines. Craftartists Narratives of identity*. London: Harvard University Press.

Munro, P. (1998). *Subject to fiction: Women teachers' life history narratives and the cultural politics of resistance*. Buckingham, Philadelphia: Open University Press.

Pillay, M. (2003). *I-visibility as a theorising process*. Kenton Education Association & Southern African Comparative and History of Education Society Conference, Cape Town, South Africa, 30 October–02 November 2003.

Plummer, K. (2001). *Documents of life. 2. An invitation to critical humanism*. London: Sage Publications.

Polkinghorne, D. E. (1995). Narrative configuration in qualitative analysis. In J. A. Hatch & R. Wisniewski (Eds.), *Life history and narrative*. London and Washington, DC: The Falmer Press.

Polkinghorne, D. E. (1995). Narrative configuration in qualitative analysis. In J. A. Hatch & R. Wisniewski (Eds.), *Life history and narrative*. London: Falmer Press.

Rhodes, C. (2000). Reading and writing organizational lives. *Organisation*, *7*(1), 7–29.

Skultans, V. (1999). Narratives of the body and history: Illness in udgement on the Soviet past. *Sociology of Health & Illness*, *21*(3), 310–328.

Spence, D. P. (1986). Narrative smoothing and clinical wisdom. In T. R. Sarbin (Ed.), *Narrative psychology: The storied nature of human conduct*. New York: Praeger.

St. Pierre, E. A. (1999). The work of response in ethnography. *Journal of Contemporary Ethnography*, *28*(3), 266–287.

St. Louis, K. O. (2001). *Living with stuttering. Stories, basic resources and hope*. Morgantown, WV: Populore Publishers.

Toolan, M. (1997). What is critical discourse analysis and why are people saying such terrible things about it? *Language and Literature*, 6(2), 83–103.

Trinh Minh-Ha, T. (1989). *woman' native' other*. Bloomington, IN: Indiana University Press.

Van Maanen, J. (1988). *Tales of the field: On writing ethnography*. Chicago: University of Chicago Press.

Vanhoozer, K. J. (1991). Philosophical antecedents to Ricoeur's time and narrative. In D. Wood (Ed.), *On Paul Ricoeur: Narrative and interpretation*. London: Routledge.

Wagner, E. L. (2002). *(Inter)Connecting IS narrative research: Current status and future opportunities for process-oriented field studies*. Unpublished paper, Working Paper Series, London School of Economics.

GENERAL METHODOLOGY TEXTS

Ackroyd, S. (1994). Recreating common ground: Elements of post-paradigmatic organisation studies. In J. Hassard & M. Parker (Eds.), *Towards a new theory of organisations*. New York: Routeledge.

Anderson, K., & Jack, D. C. (1991). Learning to listen. Interview techniques and analyses. In S. B. Luck & D. Pataki (Eds.), *Women's words. The feminist practice of oral history*. New York: Routledge.

Ashcroft, B., Griffiths, G., & Tiffin, H. (1989). *The empire writes back: Theory and practice in post-colonial literatures*. London: Routledge.

Borradori, G. (2003). *Philosophy in a time of terror: Dialogues with Jurgen Habermas and Jacque Derrida*. Chicago: University of Chicago Press.

Carr, W., & Kemmis, S. (1986). *Becoming critical*. London: Falmer Press.
Chandler, D. (undated). *Semiotics for beginners*. Retrieved from http://www.aber.ac.uk/~dgc/semiotic.html

Clandinin, D. J., & Connelly, F. M. (1994). Personal experience methods. In N. K. Denzin & Y. S. Lincoln (Eds.), *Handbook of qualitative research*. Thousand Oakes, CA: Sage.

Crane, N. (2002). *Mercator: The man who mapped the planet*. Great Britain: Phoenix.

Denzin, N., & Lincoln, Y. (Eds.). (1994). *Handbook of qualitative research.* Thousand Oaks, CA: Sage.

Denzin, N. (1989). *Interpretive interactionism.* Newbury Park, CA: Sage.

Egon, G., Guba, E. G., & Lincoln, Y. (1985). *Naturalistic enquiry.* USA: Sage Publications.

Elliot, J. (1985). Educational action research. In J. Nisbet & S. Nisbet (Eds.), *Research policy and practice.* World Year Book of Education.

Engestrom, Y., & Miettinen, R. (1999). Introduction. In Y. Engestrom, R. Miettinen, & R. Punamaki (Eds.), *Perspectives on activity theory.* Cambridge: Cambridge University Press.

Etherington, K. (2004). *Becoming a reflexive researcher – Using ourselves in research.* London: Jessica Kingsley Publishers.

Fairclough, N. (1989). *Language and power.* London: Longman.

Fine, M. (1998). Working the hyphens: Reinventing self and other in qualitative research. In N. K. Denzin & Y. S. Lincoln (Eds.), *The landscape of qualitative research. Theories and issues.* London: Sage Publications.

Flick, U. (1998). *An introduction to qualitative research.* London: Sage.

Freeman, D. (1996). The "unstudied problem": Research on teacher learning in language teaching. In D. Freeman & J. Richards (Eds.), *Teacher learning in language teaching.* Cambridge: Cambridge University Press.

Giddens, A. (1987). Structuralism, post-structuralism and production of culture. In A. Giddens & J. Turner (Eds.), *Social theory today.* Stanford, CA: University Press.

Gough, N. (1998). Narrative and educational inquiry. In J. Mousley, N. Gough, M. Robinson, & D. Colquhoun (Eds.), *Horizons, images and experiences: The research stories collection.* Geelong: Deakin University.

Kennedy, M. (1991, Spring). An agenda for research on teacher learning. *National Center for Research on Teacher Learning Special Report.*

Lather, P. (2001). *The possibilities for paradigm proliferation.* Doctoral Seminar Series, University of KwaZulu-Natal, South Africa, November.

Lather, P. (1991). *Getting smart: Feminist research and pedagogy with/in the postmodern.* New York: Routledge.

MacIntyre, A. (1984). *After virtue*. Nortre Dame, IN: University of Notre Dame Press.

Miles, M., & Huberman, A. M. (1994). *Qualitative data analysis* (2nd ed.). Thousand Oaks, CA: Sage.

Miles, M. B., & Huberman, A. M. (1984). *Qualitative data analysis: A sourcebook for new methods*. Beverley Hills, CA: Sage.

Noakes, T. D., Harley, Y. X. R., Bosch, A. N., Marino, F. E., St Clair Gibson, A., & Lambert, M. I. (2004). Physiological function and neuromuscular recruitment in elite South Africa distance runners. *Equine and Comparative Exercise Physiology*, *1*(4), 261–271(11).

Orland-Barak, L. (2002). The theoretical sensitivity of the researcher: Reflections on a complex construct. *Reflective Practice*, *3*(3), 263–278.

Rabinow, P. (Ed.). (1997). *Ethics: Subjectivity and truth, selections*. New York: The New Press.

Peshkin, A. (1988). In search of one of subjectivity - one's own. *Educational Researcher*, *17*(1), 17–22.

Peshkin, A. (2001). Angles of vision: Enhancing perception in qualitative research. *Qualitative Inquiry*, *7*(2), 238–253.

Rhedding-Jones, J. (1995). What do you do after you've met poststructuralism? Research possibilities regarding feminism, ethnography and literacy. *Journal of Curriculum Studies*, *27*(5), 479–500.

Rubin, H. J., & Rubin, I. (1995). *Qualitative interviewing. The art of hearing data*. London: Sage Publications.

Sarup, M. (1993). Derida and deconstruction. In *An Introductory Guide to post-structuralism and postmodernism*. New York

Seale, C. (1999). Quality in qualitative research. *Qualitative Enquiry*, *5*(4), 465–478.

Searle, J. R. (1969). *Speech acts*. Cambridge: Cambridge University Press.

Silverman, E. (2001). *Consumer alert: Stuttering and gender research*. Paper presented at Fourth International Stuttering Awareness Day conference, October, 2001. Retrieved from, http://www.mnsu.edu/dept/comradis/isad4/papers/silverman2.html

Snyder, G. J. (2001). Exploratory research in the measurement and modification of attitudes toward stuttering. *Journal of Fluency Disorders, 26*(2), 149–160.

Spivak, G. C. (1985). The Rani of Simur. In F. Barker, et al. (Eds.), *Europe and its others* (Vol. 1). Colchester: University of Essex Press.

Spivak, G. C. (1988). Can the subaltern speak? In C. Nelson & L. Grossberg (Eds.), *Marxism and the interpretation of culture.* Chicago: University of Illinois Press.

Spivak, G. C. (1985, Winter/Spring). Can the subaltern speak? Speculations on widow sacrifice. *Wedge, 7/8.*

St. Pierre, E. A. (1999). The work of response in ethnography. *Journal of Contemporary Ethnography, 28*(3), 266–287.

Strauss, A. (1987). *Qualitative analysis for social scientists.* New York: Cambridge University Press.

United Nations Educational, Scientific and Cultural Organisation (UNESCO) Institute for Statistics. (2004). *Global education digest 2004: Comparing education statistics across the world.* Canada: Montreal.

Usher, R., & Edwards, R. (1994). *Postmodernism and education.* London and New York: Routledge.

Vernon, A. (1997). Reflexivity: The dilemmas of researching from the inside. In C. Barnes & G. Mercer (Eds.), *Doing disability research.* Leeds: The Disability Press.

Welman, J. C, & Kruger, S. J. (1999). *Research methodologies for the business and administrative sciences.* Oxford: Oxford University Press.

Winter, R. (1989). *Learning from experience: Principles and practice in action research.* London: Falmer Press.

A SELECTION OF DISSERTATIONS AND THESES UPON WHICH THIS BOOK DRAWS

Beecham, R. (2002). *A failure of care: A story of a South African speech & hearing therapy student.* Unpublished DEd Thesis, Faculty of Education, University of KwaZulu-Natal, Durban, South Africa.

Dhunpath, R. (2002). *Archaeology of a language development NGO: Excavating the identity of the English language education trust.* Unpublished D.Ed Thesis, Faculty of Education, University of KwaZulu-Natal, South Africa.

Kathard, H. (2003). *Life histories of people who stutter. On becoming someone.* Unpublished DEd thesis, Faculty of Education, University of KwaZulu-Natal, South Africa.

Pillay, G. (2003). *Successful teachers: A cubist narrative of lives, practices and the evaded.* Unpublished D.Ed Thesis, Faculty of Education, University of KwaZulu-Natal, South Africa.

Pillay, M. (1992). *Zulu communication disorders: Beliefs and perceptions.* Undergraduate Research Study, University of KwaZulu-Natal, South Africa.

Pillay, M. (1997). *Speech-language therapy & audiology: Practice with a Black African first language clientele.* Unpublished M.Ed Dissertation. Faculty of Education, University of KwaZulu-Natal, Durban, South Africa.

Pillay, M. (2003). *(Re)Positioning the powerful expert and the sick person: The case of communication pathology.* Unpublished D.Ed Thesis. Faculty of Education, University of KwaZulu-Natal, South Africa.

Ramrathan, P. (2002). *Teacher attrition and demand within KwaZulu-Natal in the context of HIV/AIDS.* Unpublished D.Ed Thesis, Faculty of Education, University of KwaZulu-Natal, South Africa.

Reddy, V. (2000). *Lifehistories of Black South African scientists: Academic success in an unequal society.* Unpublished D.Ed, Faculty of Education, University of KwaZulu-Natal, Durban, South Africa.

Samuel, M. (1998). *Words, lives and music: On becoming a teacher of English.* Unpublished D.Ed thesis, Faculty of Education, University of KwaZulu-Natal, Durban, South Africa.

Singh, S. K. (2001). *Teacher resignations: Perceptions of teaching as a career.* MA Thesis, Faculty of Education, University of KwaZulu-Natal, South Africa.

Lightning Source UK Ltd.
Milton Keynes UK
31 October 2010

162190UK00003B/6/P